WE
DISSENT

WE DISSENT

DISSENT

JUSTICES BREYER,
SOTOMAYOR, AND KAGAN
ON *DOBBS V. JACKSON*,
THE SUPREME COURT'S
DECISION BANNING
ABORTION

MELVILLE HOUSE
BROOKLYN • LONDON

**United States Supreme Court decision on
Thomas E. Dobbs, State Health Officer of The Mississippi
Department of Health, et al., Petitioners v. Jackson
Women's Health Organization, et al.**

First Melville House printing: July 2022

Melville House Publishing
46 John Street
Brooklyn, NY 11201

and

Melville House UK
Suite 2000
16/18 Woodford Road
London E7 0HA

mhpbooks.com
@melvillehouse

ISBN: 978-1-68589-051-3

Printed in the United States of America
10 9 8 7 6 5 4 3 2 1

A catalog record for this book is available from the Library of Congress

CONTENTS

WE
DISSENT

SUPREME COURT OF THE UNITED STATES

No. 19–1392

THOMAS E. DOBBS, STATE HEALTH OFFICER OF THE MISSISSIPPI DEPARTMENT OF HEALTH, ET AL., PETITIONERS *v.* JACKSON WOMEN'S HEALTH ORGANIZATION, ET AL.

ON WRIT OF CERTIORARI TO THE UNITED STATES COURT OF APPEALS FOR THE FIFTH CIRCUIT

[June 24, 2022]

JUSTICE BREYER, JUSTICE SOTOMAYOR, and JUSTICE KAGAN, dissenting.

For half a century, *Roe* v. *Wade*, 410 U. S. 113 (1973), and *Planned Parenthood of Southeastern Pa.* v. *Casey*, 505 U. S. 833 (1992), have protected the liberty and equality of women. *Roe* held, and *Casey* reaffirmed, that the Constitution safeguards a woman's right to decide for herself whether to bear a child. *Roe* held, and *Casey* reaffirmed, that in the first stages of pregnancy, the government could not make that choice for women. The government could not control a woman's body or the course of a woman's life: It could not determine what the woman's future would be. See *Casey*, 505 U. S., at 853; *Gonzales* v. *Carhart*, 550 U. S. 124, 171–172 (2007) (Ginsburg, J., dissenting). Respecting a woman as an autonomous being, and granting her full equality, meant giving her substantial choice over this most personal and most consequential of all life decisions.

Roe and *Casey* well understood the difficulty and divisiveness of the abortion issue. The Court knew that Americans hold profoundly different views about the "moral[ity]" of "terminating a pregnancy, even in its earliest stage." *Casey*, 505 U. S., at 850. And the Court recognized that "the

State has legitimate interests from the outset of the pregnancy in protecting" the "life of the fetus that may become a child." *Id.*, at 846. So the Court struck a balance, as it often does when values and goals compete. It held that the State could prohibit abortions after fetal viability, so long as the ban contained exceptions to safeguard a woman's life or health. It held that even before viability, the State could regulate the abortion procedure in multiple and meaningful ways. But until the viability line was crossed, the Court held, a State could not impose a "substantial obstacle" on a woman's "right to elect the procedure" as she (not the government) thought proper, in light of all the circumstances and complexities of her own life. *Ibid.*

Today, the Court discards that balance. It says that from the very moment of fertilization, a woman has no rights to speak of. A State can force her to bring a pregnancy to term, even at the steepest personal and familial costs. An abortion restriction, the majority holds, is permissible whenever rational, the lowest level of scrutiny known to the law. And because, as the Court has often stated, protecting fetal life is rational, States will feel free to enact all manner of restrictions. The Mississippi law at issue here bars abortions after the 15th week of pregnancy. Under the majority's ruling, though, another State's law could do so after ten weeks, or five or three or one—or, again, from the moment of fertilization. States have already passed such laws, in anticipation of today's ruling. More will follow. Some States have enacted laws extending to all forms of abortion procedure, including taking medication in one's own home. They have passed laws without any exceptions for when the woman is the victim of rape or incest. Under those laws, a woman will have to bear her rapist's child or a young girl her father's—no matter if doing so will destroy her life. So too, after today's ruling, some States may compel women to carry to term a fetus with severe physical anomalies—for example, one afflicted with Tay-Sachs disease, sure to die within a few years of birth. States may even argue that a prohibition on abortion need make no provision for protecting a woman from risk of death or physical harm. Across a vast array of circumstances, a State will be able to impose its moral choice on a woman and coerce her to give birth to a child.

Enforcement of all these draconian restrictions will also be left largely to the States' devices. A State can of course impose criminal penalties on abortion providers, including lengthy prison sentences. But some States will not stop there. Perhaps, in the wake of today's decision, a state law will criminalize the woman's conduct too, incarcerating or fining her for daring to seek or obtain an abortion. And as Texas has recently shown, a State can turn neighbor against neighbor, enlisting fellow citizens in the effort to root out anyone who tries to get an abortion, or to assist another in doing so.

The majority tries to hide the geographically expansive effects of its holding. Today's decision, the majority says, permits "each State" to address abortion as it pleases. *Ante*, at 79. That is cold comfort, of course, for the poor woman who cannot get the money to fly to a distant State for a procedure. Above all others, women lacking financial resources will suffer from today's decision. In any event, interstate restrictions will also soon be in the offing. After this decision, some States may block women from traveling out of State to obtain abortions, or even from receiving abortion medications from out of State. Some may criminalize efforts, including the provision of information or funding, to help women gain access to other States' abortion services. Most threatening of all, no language in today's decision stops the Federal Government from prohibiting abortions nationwide, once again from the moment of conception and without exceptions for rape or incest. If that happens, "the views of [an individual State's] citizens" will not matter. *Ante*, at 1. The challenge for a woman will be to finance a trip not to "New York [or] California" but to Toronto. *Ante,* at 4 (KAVANAUGH, J., concurring).

Whatever the exact scope of the coming laws, one result of today's decision is certain: the curtailment of women's rights, and of their status as free and equal citizens. Yesterday, the Constitution guaranteed that a woman confronted with an unplanned pregnancy could (within reasonable limits) make her own decision about whether to bear a child, with all the life-transforming consequences that act involves. And in thus safeguarding each woman's reproductive freedom, the Constitution also protected "[t]he ability of women to participate equally in [this Nation's] economic and social life." *Casey,* 505 U. S., at 856. But no longer. As of today, this Court holds, a State can always force a woman to give birth, prohibiting even the earliest abortions. A State can thus transform what, when freely undertaken, is a wonder into what, when forced, may be a nightmare. Some women, especially women of means, will find ways around the State's assertion of power. Others—those without money or childcare or the ability to take time off from work—will not be so fortunate. Maybe they will try an unsafe method of abortion, and come to physical harm, or even die. Maybe they will undergo pregnancy and have a child, but at significant personal or familial cost. At the least, they will incur the cost of losing control of their lives. The Constitution will, today's majority holds, provide no shield, despite its guarantees of liberty and equality for all.

And no one should be confident that this majority is done with its work. The right *Roe* and *Casey* recognized does not stand alone. To the contrary, the Court has linked it for decades to other settled freedoms involving bodily integrity, familial relationships, and procreation. Most obviously, the right to terminate a pregnancy arose straight out of the right to purchase and use contraception. See *Griswold* v. *Connecticut,* 381 U. S. 479 (1965); *Eisenstadt* v. *Baird,* 405 U. S. 438 (1972). In turn, those rights led, more recently,

to rights of same-sex intimacy and marriage. See *Lawrence*
v. *Texas*, 539 U. S. 558 (2003); *Obergefell* v. *Hodges*, 576
U. S. 644 (2015). They are all part of the same constitutional fabric, protecting autonomous decisionmaking over
the most personal of life decisions. The majority (or to be
more accurate, most of it) is eager to tell us today that nothing it does "cast[s] doubt on precedents that do not concern
abortion." *Ante*, at 66; cf. *ante*, at 3 (THOMAS, J., concurring)
(advocating the overruling of *Griswold*, *Lawrence*, and
Obergefell). But how could that be? The lone rationale for
what the majority does today is that the right to elect an
abortion is not "deeply rooted in history": Not until *Roe*, the
majority argues, did people think abortion fell within the
Constitution's guarantee of liberty. *Ante*, at 32. The same
could be said, though, of most of the rights the majority
claims it is not tampering with. The majority could write
just as long an opinion showing, for example, that until the
mid-20th century, "there was no support in American law
for a constitutional right to obtain [contraceptives]." *Ante*,
at 15. So one of two things must be true. Either the majority does not really believe in its own reasoning. Or if it does,
all rights that have no history stretching back to the mid-
19th century are insecure. Either the mass of the majority's
opinion is hypocrisy, or additional constitutional rights are
under threat. It is one or the other.

One piece of evidence on that score seems especially sa-
lient: The majority's cavalier approach to overturning this
Court's precedents. *Stare decisis* is the Latin phrase for a
foundation stone of the rule of law: that things decided
should stay decided unless there is a very good reason for
change. It is a doctrine of judicial modesty and humility.
Those qualities are not evident in today's opinion. The majority has no good reason for the upheaval in law and society
it sets off. *Roe* and *Casey* have been the law of the land for
decades, shaping women's expectations of their choices
when an unplanned pregnancy occurs. Women have relied

on the availability of abortion both in structuring their relationships and in planning their lives. The legal framework *Roe* and *Casey* developed to balance the competing interests in this sphere has proved workable in courts across the country. No recent developments, in either law or fact, have eroded or cast doubt on those precedents. Nothing, in short, has changed. Indeed, the Court in *Casey* already found all of that to be true. *Casey* is a precedent about precedent. It reviewed the same arguments made here in support of overruling *Roe*, and it found that doing so was not warranted. The Court reverses course today for one reason and one reason only: because the composition of this Court has changed. *Stare decisis*, this Court has often said, "contributes to the actual and perceived integrity of the judicial process" by ensuring that decisions are "founded in the law rather than in the proclivities of individuals." *Payne* v. *Tennessee*, 501 U. S. 808, 827 (1991); *Vasquez* v. *Hillery*, 474 U. S. 254, 265 (1986). Today, the proclivities of individuals rule. The Court departs from its obligation to faithfully and impartially apply the law. We dissent.

I

We start with *Roe* and *Casey*, and with their deep connections to a broad swath of this Court's precedents. To hear the majority tell the tale, *Roe* and *Casey* are aberrations: They came from nowhere, went nowhere—and so are easy to excise from this Nation's constitutional law. That is not true. After describing the decisions themselves, we explain how they are rooted in—and themselves led to—other rights giving individuals control over their bodies and their most personal and intimate associations. The majority does not wish to talk about these matters for obvious reasons; to do so would both ground *Roe* and *Casey* in this Court's precedents and reveal the broad implications of today's decision. But the facts will not so handily disappear. *Roe* and *Casey* were from the beginning, and are even more now, embedded in core constitutional concepts of individual freedom, and of the equal rights of citizens to decide on the shape of their lives. Those legal concepts, one might even say, have gone far toward defining what it means to be an American. For in this Nation, we do not believe that a government controlling all private choices is compatible with a free people. So we do not (as the majority insists today) place everything within "the reach of majorities and [government] officials." *West Virginia Bd. of Ed.* v. *Barnette*, 319 U. S. 624, 638 (1943). We believe in a Constitution that puts some issues off limits to majority rule. Even in the face of public opposition, we uphold the right of individuals—yes, including women—to make their own choices and chart their own futures. Or at least, we did once.

A

Some half-century ago, *Roe* struck down a state law making it a crime to perform an abortion unless its purpose was to save a woman's life. The *Roe* Court knew it was treading on difficult and disputed ground. It understood that different people's "experiences," "values," and "religious training" and beliefs led to "opposing views" about abortion. 410 U. S., at 116. But by a 7-to-2 vote, the Court held that in the earlier stages of pregnancy, that contested and contestable choice must belong to a woman, in consultation with her family and doctor. The Court explained that a long line of precedents, "founded in the Fourteenth Amendment's concept of personal liberty," protected individual decisionmaking related to "marriage, procreation, contraception, family relationships, and child rearing and education." *Id.*, at 152–153 (citations omitted). For the same reasons, the Court held, the Constitution must protect "a woman's decision whether or not to terminate her pregnancy." *Id.*, at 153. The Court recognized the myriad ways bearing a child can alter the "life and future" of a woman and other members of her family. *Ibid.* A State could not, "by adopting one theory of life," override all "rights of the pregnant woman." *Id.*, at 162.

At the same time, though, the Court recognized "valid interest[s]" of the State "in regulating the abortion decision." *Id.*, at 153. The Court noted in particular "important interests" in "protecting potential life," "maintaining medical standards," and "safeguarding [the] health" of the woman. *Id.*, at 154. No "absolut[ist]" account of the woman's right could wipe away those significant state claims. *Ibid.*

The Court therefore struck a balance, turning on the stage of the pregnancy at which the abortion would occur. The Court explained that early on, a woman's choice must prevail, but that "at some point the state interests" become "dominant." *Id.*, at 155. It then set some guideposts. In the first trimester of pregnancy, the State could not interfere at all with the decision to terminate a pregnancy. At any time after that point, the State could regulate to protect the pregnant woman's health, such as by insisting that abortion providers and facilities meet safety requirements. And after the fetus's viability—the point when the fetus "has the capability of meaningful life outside the mother's womb"—the State could ban abortions, except when necessary to preserve the woman's life or health. *Id.*, at 163–164.

In the 20 years between *Roe* and *Casey*, the Court expressly reaffirmed *Roe* on two occasions, and applied it on many more. Recognizing that "arguments [against *Roe*] continue to be made," we responded that the doctrine of *stare decisis* "demands respect in a society governed by the rule of law." *Akron* v. *Akron Center for Reproductive Health, Inc.*, 462 U. S. 416, 419–420 (1983). And we avowed that the "vitality" of "constitutional principles cannot be allowed to yield simply because of disagreement with them." *Thornburgh* v. *American College of Obstetricians and Gynecologists*, 476 U. S. 747, 759 (1986). So the Court, over and over, enforced the constitutional principles *Roe* had declared. See, *e.g.*, *Ohio* v. *Akron Center for Reproductive Health*, 497 U. S. 502 (1990); *Hodgson* v. *Minnesota*, 497 U. S. 417 (1990); *Simopoulos* v. *Virginia*, 462 U. S. 506 (1983); *Planned Parenthood Assn. of Kansas City, Mo., Inc.* v. *Ashcroft*, 462 U. S. 476 (1983); *H. L.* v. *Matheson*, 450 U. S. 398 (1981); *Bellotti* v. *Baird*, 443 U. S. 622 (1979); *Planned Parenthood of Central Mo.* v. *Danforth*, 428 U. S. 52 (1976).

Then, in *Casey*, the Court considered the matter anew, and again upheld *Roe*'s core precepts. *Casey* is in significant measure a precedent about the doctrine of precedent—until today, one of the Court's most important. But we leave for later that aspect of the Court's decision. The key thing now is the substantive aspect of the Court's considered conclusion that "the essential holding of *Roe* v. *Wade* should be retained and once again reaffirmed." 505 U. S., at 846.

Central to that conclusion was a full-throated restatement of a woman's right to choose. Like *Roe*, *Casey* grounded that right in the Fourteenth Amendment's guarantee of "liberty." That guarantee encompasses realms of conduct not specifically referenced in the Constitution: "Marriage is mentioned nowhere" in that document, yet the Court was "no doubt correct" to protect the freedom to marry "against state interference." 505 U. S., at 847–848. And the guarantee of liberty encompasses conduct today that was not protected at the time of the Fourteenth Amendment. See *id.*, at 848. "It is settled now," the Court said—though it was not always so—that "the Constitution places limits on a State's right to interfere with a person's most basic decisions about family and parenthood, as well as bodily integrity." *Id.*, at 849 (citations omitted); see *id.*, at 851 (similarly describing the constitutional protection given to "personal decisions relating to marriage, procreation, contraception, [and] family relationships"). Especially important in this web of precedents protecting an individual's most "personal choices" were those guaranteeing the right to contraception. *Ibid.*; see *id.*, at 852–853. In those cases, the Court had recognized "the right of the individual" to make the vastly consequential "decision whether to bear" a child. *Id.*, at 851 (emphasis deleted). So too, *Casey* reasoned, the liberty clause protects the decision of a woman confronting an unplanned pregnancy. Her decision about abortion was central, in the same way, to her capacity to chart her life's course. See *id.*, at 853.

In reaffirming the right *Roe* recognized, the Court took full account of the diversity of views on abortion, and the importance of various competing state interests. Some Americans, the Court stated, "deem [abortion] nothing short of an act of violence against innocent human life." 505 U. S., at 852. And each State has an interest in "the protection of potential life"—as *Roe* itself had recognized. 505 U. S., at 871 (plurality opinion). On the one hand, that interest was not conclusive. The State could not "resolve" the "moral and spiritual" questions raised by abortion in "such a definitive way that a woman lacks all choice in the matter." *Id.*, at 850 (majority opinion). It could not force her to bear the "pain" and "physical constraints" of "carr[ying] a child to full term" when she would have chosen an early abortion. *Id.*, at 852. But on the other hand, the State had, as *Roe* had held, an exceptionally significant interest in disallowing abortions in the later phase of a pregnancy. And it had an ever-present interest in "ensur[ing] that the woman's choice is informed" and in presenting the case for "choos[ing] childbirth over abortion." 505 U. S., at 878 (plurality opinion).

So *Casey* again struck a balance, differing from *Roe*'s in only incremental ways. It retained *Roe*'s "central holding" that the State could bar abortion only after viability. 505 U. S., at 860 (majority opinion). The viability line, *Casey* thought, was "more workable" than any other in marking the place where the woman's liberty interest gave way to a State's efforts to preserve potential life. *Id.*, at 870 (plurality opinion). At that point, a "second life" was capable of "independent existence." *Ibid.* If the woman even by then had not acted, she lacked adequate grounds to object to "the State's intervention on [the developing child's] behalf." *Ibid.* At the same time, *Casey* decided, based on two decades of experience, that the *Roe* framework did not give States sufficient ability to regulate abortion prior to viability. In that period, *Casey* now made clear, the State could regulate not only to protect the woman's health but also to "promot[e] prenatal life." 505 U. S., at 873 (plurality opinion). In particular, the State could ensure informed choice and could try to promote childbirth. See *id.*, at 877–878. But the State still could not place an "undue burden"—or "substantial obstacle"—"in the path of a woman seeking an abortion." *Id.*, at 878. Prior to viability, the woman, consistent with the constitutional "meaning of liberty," must "retain the ultimate control over her destiny and her body." *Id.*, at 869.

We make one initial point about this analysis in light of the majority's insistence that *Roe* and *Casey*, and we in defending them, are dismissive of a "State's interest in protecting prenatal life." *Ante*, at 38. Nothing could get those decisions more wrong. As just described, *Roe* and *Casey* invoked powerful state interests in that protection, operative at every stage of the pregnancy and overriding the woman's liberty after viability. The strength of those state interests is exactly why the Court allowed greater restrictions on the abortion right than on other rights deriving from the Fourteenth Amendment.[1] But what *Roe* and *Casey* also recognized—which today's majority does not—is that a woman's

---

[1] For this reason, we do not understand the majority's view that our analogy between the right to an abortion and the rights to contraception and same-sex marriage shows that we think "[t]he Constitution does not permit the States to regard the destruction of a 'potential life' as a matter

freedom and equality are likewise involved. That fact—the presence of countervailing interests—is what made the abortion question hard, and what necessitated balancing. The majority scoffs at that idea, castigating us for "repeatedly prais[ing] the 'balance'" the two cases arrived at (with the word "balance" in scare quotes). *Ante,* at 38. To the majority "balance" is a dirty word, as moderation is a foreign concept. The majority would allow States to ban abortion from conception onward because it does not think forced childbirth at all implicates a woman's rights to equality and freedom. Today's Court, that is, does not think there is anything of constitutional significance attached to a woman's control of her body and the path of her life. *Roe* and *Casey* thought that one-sided view misguided. In some sense, that is the difference in a nutshell between our precedents and the majority opinion. The constitutional regime we have lived in for the last 50 years recognized competing interests, and sought a balance between them. The constitutional regime we enter today erases the woman's interest and recognizes only the State's (or the Federal Government's).

B

The majority makes this change based on a single question: Did the reproductive right recognized in *Roe* and *Casey*

---

of any significance." *Ante,* at 38. To the contrary. The liberty interests underlying those rights are, as we will describe, quite similar. See *infra,* at 22–24. But only in the sphere of abortion is the state interest in protecting potential life involved. So only in that sphere, as both *Roe* and *Casey* recognized, may a State impinge so far on the liberty interest (barring abortion after viability and discouraging it before). The majority's failure to understand this fairly obvious point stems from its rejection of the idea of balancing interests in this (or maybe in any) constitutional context. Cf. *New York State Rifle & Pistol Assn., Inc.* v. *Bruen,* 597 U. S. ___, ___, ___–___ (2022) (slip op., at 8, 15–17). The majority thinks that a woman has *no* liberty or equality interest in the decision to bear a child, so a State's interest in protecting fetal life necessarily prevails.

exist in "1868, the year when the Fourteenth Amendment was ratified"? *Ante*, at 23. The majority says (and with this much we agree) that the answer to this question is no: In 1868, there was no nationwide right to end a pregnancy, and no thought that the Fourteenth Amendment provided one.

Of course, the majority opinion refers as well to some later and earlier history. On the one side of 1868, it goes back as far as the 13th (the 13th!) century. See *ante*, at 17. But that turns out to be wheel-spinning. First, it is not clear what relevance such early history should have, even to the majority. See *New York State Rifle & Pistol Assn., Inc.* v. *Bruen*, 597 U. S. ___, ___ (2022) (slip op., at 26) ("Historical evidence that long predates [ratification] may not illuminate the scope of the right"). If the early history obviously supported abortion rights, the majority would no doubt say that only the views of the Fourteenth Amendment's ratifiers are germane. See *ibid.* (It is "better not to go too far back into antiquity," except if olden "law survived to become our Founders' law"). Second—and embarrassingly for the majority—early law in fact does provide some support for abortion rights. Common-law authorities did not treat abortion as a crime before "quickening"—the point when the fetus moved in the womb.[2] And early American law followed the common-law rule.[3] So the criminal law of that early time might be taken as roughly consonant with

---

[2] See, *e.g.*, 1 W. Blackstone, Commentaries on the Laws of England 129–130 (7th ed. 1775) (Blackstone); E. Coke, Institutes of the Laws of England 50 (1644).

[3] See J. Mohr, Abortion in America: The Origins and Evolution of National Policy, 1800–1900, pp. 3–4 (1978). The majority offers no evidence to the contrary—no example of a founding-era law making pre-quickening abortion a crime (except when a woman died). See *ante*, at 20–21. And even in the mid-19th century, more than 10 States continued to allow pre-quickening abortions. See Brief for American Historical Association et al. as *Amici Curiae* 27, and n. 14.

Roe's and *Casey*'s different treatment of early and late abortions. Better, then, to move forward in time. On the other side of 1868, the majority occasionally notes that many States barred abortion up to the time of *Roe.* See *ante,* at 24, 36. That is convenient for the majority, but it is window dressing. As the same majority (plus one) just informed us, "post-ratification adoption or acceptance of laws that are *inconsistent* with the original meaning of the constitutional text obviously cannot overcome or alter that text." *New York State Rifle & Pistol Assn., Inc.,* 597 U. S., at ___–___ (slip op., at 27–28). Had the pre-*Roe* liberalization of abortion laws occurred more quickly and more widely in the 20th century, the majority would say (once again) that only the ratifiers' views are germane.

The majority's core legal postulate, then, is that we in the 21st century must read the Fourteenth Amendment just as its ratifiers did. And that is indeed what the majority emphasizes over and over again. See *ante,* at 47 ("[T]he most important historical fact [is] how the States regulated abortion when the Fourteenth Amendment was adopted"); see also *ante,* at 5, 16, and n. 24, 23, 25, 28. If the ratifiers did not understand something as central to freedom, then neither can we. Or said more particularly: If those people did not understand reproductive rights as part of the guarantee of liberty conferred in the Fourteenth Amendment, then those rights do not exist.

As an initial matter, note a mistake in the just preceding sentence. We referred there to the "people" who ratified the Fourteenth Amendment: What rights did those "people" have in their heads at the time? But, of course, "people" did not ratify the Fourteenth Amendment. Men did. So it is perhaps not so surprising that the ratifiers were not perfectly attuned to the importance of reproductive rights for women's liberty, or for their capacity to participate as equal members of our Nation. Indeed, the ratifiers—both in 1868 and when the original Constitution was approved in 1788—

did not understand women as full members of the community embraced by the phrase "We the People." In 1868, the first wave of American feminists were explicitly told—of course by men—that it was not their time to seek constitutional protections. (Women would not get even the vote for another half-century.) To be sure, most women in 1868 also had a foreshortened view of their rights: If most men could not then imagine giving women control over their bodies, most women could not imagine having that kind of autonomy. But that takes away nothing from the core point. Those responsible for the original Constitution, including the Fourteenth Amendment, did not perceive women as equals, and did not recognize women's rights. When the majority says that we must read our foundational charter as viewed at the time of ratification (except that we may also check it against the Dark Ages), it consigns women to second-class citizenship.

Casey itself understood this point, as will become clear. See *infra*, at 23–24. It recollected with dismay a decision this Court issued just five years after the Fourteenth Amendment's ratification, approving a State's decision to deny a law license to a woman and suggesting as well that a woman had no legal status apart from her husband. See 505 U. S., at 896–897 (majority opinion) (citing *Bradwell* v. *State*, 16 Wall. 130 (1873)). "There was a time," *Casey* explained, when the Constitution did not protect "men and women alike." 505 U. S., at 896. But times had changed. A woman's place in society had changed, and constitutional law had changed along with it. The relegation of women to inferior status in either the public sphere or the family was "no longer consistent with our understanding" of the Constitution. *Id.*, at 897. Now, "[t]he Constitution protects all individuals, male or female," from "the abuse of governmental power" or "unjustified state interference." *Id.*, at 896, 898.

So how is it that, as *Casey* said, our Constitution, read

now, grants rights to women, though it did not in 1868? How is it that our Constitution subjects discrimination against them to heightened judicial scrutiny? How is it that our Constitution, through the Fourteenth Amendment's liberty clause, guarantees access to contraception (also not legally protected in 1868) so that women can decide for themselves whether and when to bear a child? How is it that until today, that same constitutional clause protected a woman's right, in the event contraception failed, to end a pregnancy in its earlier stages?

The answer is that this Court has rejected the majority's pinched view of how to read our Constitution. "The Founders," we recently wrote, "knew they were writing a document designed to apply to ever-changing circumstances over centuries." *NLRB* v. *Noel Canning*, 573 U. S. 513, 533–534 (2014). Or in the words of the great Chief Justice John Marshall, our Constitution is "intended to endure for ages to come," and must adapt itself to a future "seen dimly," if at all. *McCulloch* v. *Maryland*, 4 Wheat. 316, 415 (1819). That is indeed why our Constitution is written as it is. The Framers (both in 1788 and 1868) understood that the world changes. So they did not define rights by reference to the specific practices existing at the time. Instead, the Framers defined rights in general terms, to permit future evolution in their scope and meaning. And over the course of our history, this Court has taken up the Framers' invitation. It has kept true to the Framers' principles by applying them in new ways, responsive to new societal understandings and conditions.

Nowhere has that approach been more prevalent than in construing the majestic but open-ended words of the Fourteenth Amendment—the guarantees of "liberty" and "equality" for all. And nowhere has that approach produced prouder moments, for this country and the Court. Consider an example *Obergefell* used a few years ago. The Court there confronted a claim, based on *Washington* v. *Glucksberg*, 521 U. S. 702 (1997), that the Fourteenth Amendment "must be defined in a most circumscribed manner, with central reference to specific historical practices"—exactly the view today's majority follows. *Obergefell*, 576 U. S., at 671. And the Court specifically rejected that view.[4] In doing so, the Court reflected on what the proposed, historically circumscribed approach would have meant for interracial marriage. See *ibid.* The Fourteenth Amendment's ratifiers did not think it gave black and white people a right to marry each other. To the contrary, contemporaneous practice deemed that act quite as unprotected as abortion. Yet the Court in *Loving* v. *Virginia*, 388 U. S. 1 (1967), read the Fourteenth Amendment to embrace the Lovings' union. If, *Obergefell* explained, "rights were defined by who exercised them in the past, then received practices could serve as their own continued justification"—even when they conflict with "liberty" and "equality" as later and more broadly understood. 576 U. S., at 671. The Constitution does not freeze for all time the original view of what those rights guarantee, or how they apply.

That does not mean anything goes. The majority wishes people to think there are but two alternatives: (1) accept the original applications of the Fourteenth Amendment and no others, or (2) surrender to judges' "own ardent views," ungrounded in law, about the "liberty that Americans should enjoy." *Ante*, at 14. At least, that idea is what the majority *sometimes* tries to convey. At other times, the majority (or, rather, most of it) tries to assure the public that it has no designs on rights (for example, to contraception) that arose only in the back half of the 20th century—in other words,

---

[4] The majority ignores that rejection. See *ante*, at 5, 13, 36. But it is unequivocal: The *Glucksberg* test, *Obergefell* said, "may have been appropriate" in considering physician-assisted suicide, but "is inconsistent with the approach this Court has used in discussing other fundamental rights, including marriage and intimacy." 576 U. S., at 671.

that it is happy to pick and choose, in accord with individual preferences. See *ante*, at 32, 66, 71–72; *ante*, at 10 (KAVANAUGH, J., concurring); but see *ante*, at 3 (THOMAS, J., concurring). But that is a matter we discuss later. See *infra*, at 24–29. For now, our point is different: It is that applications of liberty and equality can evolve while remaining grounded in constitutional principles, constitutional history, and constitutional precedents. The second Justice Harlan discussed how to strike the right balance when he explained why he would have invalidated a State's ban on contraceptive use. Judges, he said, are not "free to roam where unguided speculation might take them." *Poe* v. *Ullman*, 367 U. S. 497, 542 (1961) (dissenting opinion). Yet they also must recognize that the constitutional "tradition" of this country is not captured whole at a single moment. *Ibid.* Rather, its meaning gains content from the long sweep of our history and from successive judicial precedents—each looking to the last and each seeking to apply the Constitution's most fundamental commitments to new conditions. That is why Americans, to go back to *Obergefell*'s example, have a right to marry across racial lines. And it is why, to go back to Justice Harlan's case, Americans have a right to use contraceptives so they can choose for themselves whether to have children.

All that is what *Casey* understood. *Casey* explicitly rejected the present majority's method. "[T]he specific practices of States at the time of the adoption of the Fourteenth Amendment," *Casey* stated, do not "mark[ ] the outer limits of the substantive sphere of liberty which the Fourteenth Amendment protects." 505 U. S., at 848.[5] To hold otherwise—as the majority does today—"would be inconsistent

---

[5] In a perplexing paragraph in its opinion, the majority declares that it need not say whether that statement from *Casey* is true. See *ante*, at 32–33. But how could that be? Has not the majority insisted for the prior 30 or so pages that the "specific practice[]" respecting abortion at the

with our law." *Id.*, at 847. Why? Because the Court has "vindicated [the] principle" over and over that (no matter the sentiment in 1868) "there is a realm of personal liberty which the government may not enter"—especially relating to "bodily integrity" and "family life." *Id.*, at 847, 849, 851. *Casey* described in detail the Court's contraception cases. See *id.*, at 848–849, 851–853. It noted decisions protecting the right to marry, including to someone of another race. See *id.*, at 847–848 ("[I]nterracial marriage was illegal in most States in the 19th century, but the Court was no doubt correct in finding it to be an aspect of liberty protected against state interference"). In reviewing decades and decades of constitutional law, *Casey* could draw but one conclusion: Whatever was true in 1868, "[i]t is settled now, as it was when the Court heard arguments in *Roe* v. *Wade*, that the Constitution places limits on a State's right to interfere with a person's most basic decisions about family and parenthood." *Id.*, at 849.

And that conclusion still held good, until the Court's intervention here. It was settled at the time of *Roe*, settled at the time of *Casey*, and settled yesterday that the Constitution places limits on a State's power to assert control over an individual's body and most personal decisionmaking. A multitude of decisions supporting that principle led to *Roe*'s recognition and *Casey*'s reaffirmation of the right to choose; and *Roe* and *Casey* in turn supported additional protections for intimate and familial relations. The majority has em-

---

time of the Fourteenth Amendment precludes its recognition as a constitutional right? *Ante*, at 33. It has. And indeed, it has given no other reason for overruling *Roe* and *Casey*. *Ante*, at 15–16. We are not mindreaders, but here is our best guess as to what the majority means. It says next that "[a]bortion is nothing new." *Ante*, at 33. So apparently, the Fourteenth Amendment might provide protection for things wholly unknown in the 19th century; maybe one day there could be constitutional protection for, oh, time travel. But as to anything that was known back then (such as abortion or contraception), no such luck.

barrassingly little to say about those precedents. It (literally) rattles them off in a single paragraph; and it implies that they have nothing to do with each other, or with the right to terminate an early pregnancy. See *ante*, at 31–32 (asserting that recognizing a relationship among them, as addressing aspects of personal autonomy, would ineluctably "license fundamental rights" to illegal "drug use [and] prostitution"). But that is flat wrong. The Court's precedents about bodily autonomy, sexual and familial relations, and procreation are all interwoven—all part of the fabric of our constitutional law, and because that is so, of our lives. Especially women's lives, where they safeguard a right to self-determination.

And eliminating that right, we need to say before further describing our precedents, is not taking a "neutral" position, as JUSTICE KAVANAUGH tries to argue. *Ante*, at 2–3, 5, 7, 11–12 (concurring opinion). His idea is that neutrality lies in giving the abortion issue to the States, where some can go one way and some another. But would he say that the Court is being "scrupulously neutral" if it allowed New York and California to ban all the guns they want? *Ante*, at 3. If the Court allowed some States to use unanimous juries and others not? If the Court told the States: Decide for yourselves whether to put restrictions on church attendance? We could go on—and in fact we will. Suppose JUSTICE KAVANAUGH were to say (in line with the majority opinion) that the rights we just listed are more textually or historically grounded than the right to choose. What, then, of the right to contraception or same-sex marriage? Would it be "scrupulously neutral" for the Court to eliminate those rights too? The point of all these examples is that when it comes to rights, the Court does not act "neutrally" when it leaves everything up to the States. Rather, the Court acts neutrally when it protects the right against all comers. And to apply that point to the case here: When the Court decimates a right women have held for 50 years, the Court is not being "scrupulously neutral." It is instead taking sides: against women who wish to exercise the right, and for States (like Mississippi) that want to bar them from doing so. JUSTICE KAVANAUGH cannot obscure that point by appropriating the rhetoric of even-handedness. His position just is what it is: A brook-no-compromise refusal to recognize a woman's right to choose, from the first day of a pregnancy. And that position, as we will now show, cannot be squared with this Court's longstanding view that women indeed have rights (whatever the state of the world in 1868) to make the most personal and consequential decisions about their bodies and their lives.

Consider first, then, the line of this Court's cases protecting "bodily integrity." *Casey*, 505 U. S., at 849. "No right," in this Court's time-honored view, "is held more sacred, or is more carefully guarded," than "the right of every individual to the possession and control of his own person." *Union Pacific R. Co.* v. *Botsford*, 141 U. S. 250, 251 (1891); see *Cruzan* v. *Director, Mo. Dept. of Health*, 497 U. S. 261, 269 (1990) (Every adult "has a right to determine what shall be done with his own body"). Or to put it more simply: Everyone, including women, owns their own bodies. So the Court has restricted the power of government to interfere with a person's medical decisions or compel her to undergo medical procedures or treatments. See, *e.g.*, *Winston* v. *Lee*, 470 U. S. 753, 766–767 (1985) (forced surgery); *Rochin* v. *California*, 342 U. S. 165, 166, 173–174 (1952) (forced stomach pumping); *Washington* v. *Harper*, 494 U. S. 210, 229, 236 (1990) (forced administration of antipsychotic drugs).

Casey recognized the "doctrinal affinity" between those precedents and *Roe*. 505 U. S., at 857. And that doctrinal affinity is born of a factual likeness. There are few greater incursions on a body than forcing a woman to complete a pregnancy and give birth. For every woman, those experiences involve all manner of physical changes, medical treatments (including the possibility of a cesarean section), and medical risk. Just as one example, an American woman is 14 times more likely to die by carrying a pregnancy to term than by having an abortion. See *Whole Woman's Health* v. *Hellerstedt*, 579 U. S. 582, 618 (2016). That women happily undergo those burdens and hazards of their own accord does not lessen how far a State impinges on a woman's body when it compels her to bring a pregnancy to term. And for some women, as *Roe* recognized, abortions are medically necessary to prevent harm. See 410 U. S., at 153. The majority does not say—which is itself ominous—whether a State may prevent a woman from obtaining an abortion when she and her doctor have determined it is a needed medical treatment.

So too, *Roe* and *Casey* fit neatly into a long line of decisions protecting from government intrusion a wealth of private choices about family matters, child rearing, intimate relationships, and procreation. See *Casey*, 505 U. S., at 851, 857; *Roe*, 410 U. S., at 152–153; see also *ante*, at 31–32 (listing the myriad decisions of this kind that *Casey* relied on). Those cases safeguard particular choices about whom to marry; whom to have sex with; what family members to live with; how to raise children—and crucially, whether and when to have children. In varied cases, the Court explained that those choices—"the most intimate and personal" a person can make—reflect fundamental aspects of personal identity; they define the very "attributes of personhood." *Casey*, 505 U. S., at 851. And they inevitably shape the nature and future course of a person's life (and often the lives of those closest to her). So, the Court held, those choices belong to the individual, and not the government. That is the essence of what liberty requires.

And liberty may require it, this Court has repeatedly said, even when those living in 1868 would not have recognized the claim—because they would not have seen the person making it as a full-fledged member of the community. Throughout our history, the sphere of protected liberty has expanded, bringing in individuals formerly excluded. In that way, the constitutional values of liberty and equality go hand in hand; they do not inhabit the hermetically sealed containers the majority portrays. Compare *Obergefell*, 576 U. S., at 672–675, with *ante*, at 10–11. So before *Roe* and *Casey*, the Court expanded in successive cases those who could claim the right to marry—though their relationships would have been outside the law's protection in the mid-19th century. See, *e.g.*, *Loving*, 388 U. S. 1 (interracial couples); *Turner* v. *Safley*, 482 U. S. 78 (1987) (prisoners); see also, *e.g.*, *Stanley* v. *Illinois*, 405 U. S. 645, 651–652 (1972) (offering constitutional protection to untraditional "family unit[s]"). And after *Roe* and *Casey*, of course, the Court continued in that vein. With a critical stop to hold that the Fourteenth Amendment protected same-sex intimacy, the Court resolved that the Amendment also conferred on same-sex couples the right to marry. See *Lawrence*, 539 U. S. 558; *Obergefell*, 576 U. S. 644. In considering that question, the Court held, "[h]istory and tradition," especially as reflected in the course of our precedent, "guide and discipline [the] inquiry." *Id.*, at 664. But the sentiments of 1868 alone do not and cannot "rule the present." *Ibid.*

Casey similarly recognized the need to extend the constitutional sphere of liberty to a previously excluded group. The Court then understood, as the majority today does not, that the men who ratified the Fourteenth Amendment and wrote the state laws of the time did not view women as full and equal citizens. See *supra*, at 15. A woman then, *Casey* wrote, "had no legal existence separate from her husband." 505 U. S., at 897. Women were seen only "as the center of home and family life," without "full and independent legal status under the Constitution." *Ibid.* But that could not be true any longer: The State could not now insist on the historically dominant "vision of the woman's role." *Id.*, at 852. And equal citizenship, *Casey* realized, was inescapably connected to reproductive rights. "The ability of women to participate equally" in the "life of the Nation"—in all its economic, social, political, and legal aspects—"has been facilitated by their ability to control their reproductive lives." *Id.*, at 856. Without the ability to decide whether and when to have children, women could not—in the way men took for granted—determine how they would live their lives, and how they would contribute to the society around them.

For much that reason, *Casey* made clear that the precedents *Roe* most closely tracked were those involving contraception. Over the course of three cases, the Court had held that a right to use and gain access to contraception was part of the Fourteenth Amendment's guarantee of liberty. See *Griswold*, 381 U. S. 479; *Eisenstadt*, 405 U. S. 438; *Carey* v. *Population Services Int'l*, 431 U. S. 678 (1977). That clause, we explained, necessarily conferred a right "to be free from unwarranted governmental intrusion into matters so fundamentally affecting a person as the decision whether to bear or beget a child." *Eisenstadt*, 405 U. S., at 453; see *Carey*, 431 U. S., at 684–685. *Casey* saw *Roe* as of a piece: In "critical respects the abortion decision is of the same character." 505 U. S., at 852. "[R]easonable people," the Court noted, could also oppose contraception; and indeed, they could believe that "some forms of contraception" similarly implicate a concern with "potential life." *Id.*, at 853, 859. Yet the views of others could not automatically prevail against a woman's right to control her own body and make her own choice about whether to bear, and probably to raise, a child. When an unplanned pregnancy is involved—because either contraception or abortion is outlawed—"the liberty of the woman is at stake in a sense unique to the human condition." *Id.*, at 852. No State could undertake to resolve the moral questions raised "in such a definitive way" as to deprive a woman of all choice. *Id.*, at 850.

Faced with all these connections between *Roe/Casey* and judicial decisions recognizing other constitutional rights, the majority tells everyone not to worry. It can (so it says) neatly extract the right to choose from the constitutional edifice without affecting any associated rights. (Think of someone telling you that the Jenga tower simply will not collapse.) Today's decision, the majority first says, "does not undermine" the decisions cited by *Roe* and *Casey*—the ones involving "marriage, procreation, contraception, [and] family relationships"—"in any way." *Ante*, at 32; *Casey*, 505 U. S., at 851. Note that this first assurance does not extend to rights recognized after *Roe* and *Casey*, and partly based on them—in particular, rights to same-sex intimacy and marriage. See *supra*, at 23.[6] On its later tries, though, the majority includes those too: "Nothing in this opinion should be understood to cast doubt on precedents that do not concern abortion." *Ante*, at 66; see *ante*, at 71–72. That right is unique, the majority asserts, "because [abortion] terminates life or potential life." *Ante*, at 66 (internal quotation marks omitted); see *ante*, at 32, 71–72. So the majority depicts today's decision as "a restricted railroad ticket, good for this day and train only." *Smith* v. *Allwright*, 321 U. S. 649, 669 (1944) (Roberts, J., dissenting). Should the audience for these too-much-repeated protestations be duly satisfied? We think not.

The first problem with the majority's account comes from JUSTICE THOMAS's concurrence—which makes clear he is not with the program. In saying that nothing in today's opinion casts doubt on non-abortion precedents, JUSTICE THOMAS explains, he means only that they are not at issue

---

[6]And note, too, that the author of the majority opinion recently joined a statement, written by another member of the majority, lamenting that *Obergefell* deprived States of the ability "to resolve th[e] question [of same-sex marriage] through legislation." *Davis* v. *Ermold*, 592 U. S. __, ___ (2020) (statement of THOMAS, J.) (slip op., at 1). That might sound familiar. Cf. *ante*, at 44 (lamenting that *Roe* "short-circuited the democratic process"). And those two Justices hardly seemed content to let the matter rest: The Court, they said, had "created a problem that only it can fix." *Davis*, 592 U. S., at ___ (slip op., at 4).

in this very case. See *ante*, at 7 ("[T]his case does not present the opportunity to reject" those precedents). But he lets us know what he wants to do when they are. "[I]n future cases," he says, "we should reconsider all of this Court's substantive due process precedents, including *Griswold*, *Lawrence*, and *Obergefell*." *Ante*, at 3; see also *supra*, at 25, and n. 6. And when we reconsider them? Then "we have a duty" to "overrul[e]" these demonstrably erroneous decisions." *Ante*, at 3. So at least one Justice is planning to use the ticket of today's decision again and again and again.

Even placing the concurrence to the side, the assurance in today's opinion still does not work. Or at least that is so if the majority is serious about its sole reason for overturning *Roe* and *Casey*: the legal status of abortion in the 19th century. Except in the places quoted above, the state interest in protecting fetal life plays no part in the majority's analysis. To the contrary, the majority takes pride in not expressing a view "about the status of the fetus." *Ante*, at 65; see *ante*, at 32 (aligning itself with *Roe*'s and *Casey*'s stance of not deciding whether life or potential life is involved); *ante*, at 38–39 (similar). The majority's departure from *Roe* and *Casey* rests instead—and only—on whether a woman's decision to end a pregnancy involves any Fourteenth Amendment liberty interest (against which *Roe* and *Casey* balanced the state interest in preserving fetal life).[7]

---

[7] Indulge a few more words about this point. The majority had a choice of two different ways to overrule *Roe* and *Casey*. It could claim that those cases underrated the State's interest in fetal life. Or it could claim that they overrated a woman's constitutional liberty interest in choosing an abortion. (Or both.) The majority here rejects the first path, and we can see why. Taking that route would have prevented the majority from claiming that it means only to leave this issue to the democratic process—that it does not have a dog in the fight. See *ante*, at 38–39, 65. And indeed, doing so might have suggested a revolutionary proposition: that the fetus is itself a constitutionally protected "person," such that an abortion ban is constitutionally *mandated*. The majority therefore chooses the second path, arguing that the Fourteenth Amendment does

According to the majority, no liberty interest is present—because (and only because) the law offered no protection to the woman's choice in the 19th century. But here is the rub. The law also did not then (and would not for ages) protect a wealth of other things. It did not protect the rights recognized in *Lawrence* and *Obergefell* to same-sex intimacy and marriage. It did not protect the right recognized in *Loving* to marry across racial lines. It did not protect the right recognized in *Griswold* to contraceptive use. For that matter, it did not protect the right recognized in *Skinner* v. *Oklahoma ex rel. Williamson*, 316 U. S. 535 (1942), not to be sterilized without consent. So if the majority is right in its legal analysis, all those decisions were wrong, and all those matters properly belong to the States too—whatever the particular state interests involved. And if that is true, it is impossible to understand (as a matter of logic and principle) how the majority can say that its opinion today does not threaten—does not even "undermine"—any number of other constitutional rights. *Ante*, at 32.[8]

Nor does it even help just to take the majority at its word. Assume the majority is sincere in saying, for whatever reason, that it will go so far and no further. Scout's honor. Still, the future significance of today's opinion will be decided in the future. And law often has a way of evolving

---

not conceive of the abortion decision as implicating liberty, because the law in the 19th century gave that choice no protection. The trouble is that the chosen path—which is, again, the solitary rationale for the Court's decision—provides no way to distinguish between the right to choose an abortion and a range of other rights, including contraception.

[8]The majority briefly (very briefly) gestures at the idea that some *stare decisis* factors might play out differently with respect to these other constitutional rights. But the majority gives no hint as to why. And the majority's (mis)treatment of *stare decisis* in this case provides little reason to think that the doctrine would stand as a barrier to the majority's redoing any other decision it considered egregiously wrong. See *infra*, at 30–57.

without regard to original intentions—a way of actually following where logic leads, rather than tolerating hard-to-explain lines. Rights can expand in that way. Dissenting in *Lawrence*, Justice Scalia explained why he took no comfort in the Court's statement that a decision recognizing the right to same-sex intimacy did "not involve" same-sex marriage. 539 U. S., at 604. That could be true, he wrote, "only if one entertains the belief that principle and logic have nothing to do with the decisions of this Court." *Id.*, at 605. Score one for the dissent, as a matter of prophecy. And logic and principle are not one-way ratchets. Rights can contract in the same way and for the same reason—because whatever today's majority might say, one thing really does lead to another. We fervently hope that does not happen because of today's decision. We hope that we will not join Justice Scalia in the book of prophets. But we cannot understand how anyone can be confident that today's opinion will be the last of its kind.

Consider, as our last word on this issue, contraception. The Constitution, of course, does not mention that word. And there is no historical right to contraception, of the kind the majority insists on. To the contrary, the American legal landscape in the decades after the Civil War was littered with bans on the sale of contraceptive devices. So again, there seem to be two choices. See *supra*, at 5, 26–27. If the majority is serious about its historical approach, then *Griswold* and its progeny are in the line of fire too. Or if it is not serious, then . . . what *is* the basis of today's decision? If we had to guess, we suspect the prospects of this Court approving bans on contraception are low. But once again, the future significance of today's opinion will be decided in the future. At the least, today's opinion will fuel the fight to get contraception, and any other issues with a moral dimension, out of the Fourteenth Amendment and into state legislatures.[9]

Anyway, today's decision, taken on its own, is catastrophic enough. As a matter of constitutional method, the majority's commitment to replicate in 2022 every view about the meaning of liberty held in 1868 has precious little to recommend it. Our law in this constitutional sphere, as in most, has for decades upon decades proceeded differently. It has considered fundamental constitutional principles, the whole course of the Nation's history and traditions, and the step-by-step evolution of the Court's precedents. It is disciplined but not static. It relies on accumulated judgments, not just the sentiments of one long-ago generation of men (who themselves believed, and drafted the Constitution to reflect, that the world progresses). And by doing so, it includes those excluded from that olden conversation, rather than perpetuating its bounds.

As a matter of constitutional substance, the majority's opinion has all the flaws its method would suggest. Because laws in 1868 deprived women of any control over their bodies, the majority approves States doing so today. Because those laws prevented women from charting the course of their own lives, the majority says States can do the same again. Because in 1868, the government could tell a pregnant woman—even in the first days of her pregnancy—that she could do nothing but bear a child, it can once more impose that command. Today's decision strips women of agency over what even the majority agrees is a

---

[9] As this Court has considered this case, some state legislators have begun to call for restrictions on certain forms of contraception. See I. Stevenson, After *Roe* Decision, Idaho Lawmakers May Consider Restricting Some Contraception, Idaho Statesman (May 10, 2022), https://www.idahostatesman.com/news/politics-government/state-politics/article261207007.html; T. Weinberg, "Anything's on the Table": Missouri Legislature May Revisit Contraceptive Limits Post-*Roe*, Missouri Independent (May 20, 2022), https://www.missouriindependent.com/2022/05/20/anythings-on-the-table-missouri-legislature-may-revisit-contraceptive-limits-post-roe/.

contested and contestable moral issue. It forces her to carry out the State's will, whatever the circumstances and whatever the harm it will wreak on her and her family. In the Fourteenth Amendment's terms, it takes away her liberty. Even before we get to *stare decisis*, we dissent.

II

By overruling *Roe*, *Casey*, and more than 20 cases reaffirming or applying the constitutional right to abortion, the majority abandons *stare decisis*, a principle central to the rule of law. *"Stare decisis"* means "to stand by things decided." Black's Law Dictionary 1696 (11th ed. 2019). Blackstone called it the "established rule to abide by former precedents." 1 Blackstone 69. *Stare decisis* "promotes the evenhanded, predictable, and consistent development of legal principles." *Payne*, 501 U. S., at 827. It maintains a stability that allows people to order their lives under the law. See H. Hart & A. Sacks, The Legal Process: Basic Problems in the Making and Application of Law 568–569 (1994).

Stare decisis also "contributes to the integrity of our constitutional system of government" by ensuring that decisions "are founded in the law rather than in the proclivities of individuals." *Vasquez*, 474 U. S., at 265. As Hamilton wrote: It "avoid[s] an arbitrary discretion in the courts." The Federalist No. 78, p. 529 (J. Cooke ed. 1961) (A. Hamilton). And as Blackstone said before him: It "keep[s] the scale of justice even and steady, and not liable to waver with every new judge's opinion." 1 Blackstone 69. The "glory" of our legal system is that it "gives preference to precedent rather than . . . jurists." H. Humble, Departure From Precedent, 19 Mich. L. Rev. 608, 614 (1921). That is why, the story goes, Chief Justice John Marshall donned a plain black robe when he swore the oath of office. That act personified an American tradition. Judges' personal preferences do not make law; rather, the law speaks through them.

That means the Court may not overrule a decision, even a constitutional one, without a "special justification." *Gamble* v. *United States*, 587 U. S. ___, ___ (2019) (slip op., at 11). *Stare decisis* is, of course, not an "inexorable command"; it is sometimes appropriate to overrule an earlier decision. *Pearson* v. *Callahan*, 555 U. S. 223, 233 (2009). But the Court must have a good reason to do so over and above the belief "that the precedent was wrongly decided." *Halliburton Co.* v. *Erica P. John Fund, Inc.*, 573 U. S. 258, 266 (2014). "[I]t is not alone sufficient that we would decide a case differently now than we did then." *Kimble* v. *Marvel Entertainment, LLC*, 576 U. S. 446, 455 (2015).

The majority today lists some 30 of our cases as overruling precedent, and argues that they support overruling *Roe* and *Casey*. But none does, as further described below and in the Appendix. See *infra*, at 61–66. In some, the Court only partially modified or clarified a precedent. And in the rest, the Court relied on one or more of the traditional *stare decisis* factors in reaching its conclusion. The Court found, for example, (1) a change in legal doctrine that undermined or made obsolete the earlier decision; (2) a factual change that had the same effect; or (3) an absence of reliance because the earlier decision was less than a decade old. (The majority is wrong when it says that we insist on a test of changed law or fact alone, although that is present in most of the cases. See *ante*, at 69.) None of those factors apply here: Nothing—and in particular, no significant legal or factual change—supports overturning a half-century of settled law giving women control over their reproductive lives.

First, for all the reasons we have given, *Roe* and *Casey* were correct. In holding that a State could not "resolve" the debate about abortion "in such a definitive way that a woman lacks all choice in the matter," the Court protected women's liberty and women's equality in a way comporting with our Fourteenth Amendment precedents. *Casey*, 505

U. S., at 850. Contrary to the majority's view, the legal status of abortion in the 19th century does not weaken those decisions. And the majority's repeated refrain about "usurp[ing]" state legislatures' "power to address" a publicly contested question does not help it on the key issue here. *Ante,* at 44; see *ante,* at 1. To repeat: The point of a right is to shield individual actions and decisions "from the vicissitudes of political controversy, to place them beyond the reach of majorities and officials and to establish them as legal principles to be applied by the courts." *Barnette,* 319 U. S., at 638; *supra,* at 7. However divisive, a right is not at the people's mercy.

In any event "[w]hether or not we . . . agree" with a prior precedent is the beginning, not the end, of our analysis—and the remaining "principles of *stare decisis* weigh heavily against overruling" *Roe* and *Casey. Dickerson* v. *United States,* 530 U. S. 428, 443 (2000). *Casey* itself applied those principles, in one of this Court's most important precedents about precedent. After assessing the traditional *stare decisis* factors, *Casey* reached the only conclusion possible—that *stare decisis* operates powerfully here. It still does. The standards *Roe* and *Casey* set out are perfectly workable. No changes in either law or fact have eroded the two decisions. And tens of millions of American women have relied, and continue to rely, on the right to choose. So under traditional *stare decisis* principles, the majority has no special justification for the harm it causes.

And indeed, the majority comes close to conceding that point. The majority barely mentions any legal or factual changes that have occurred since *Roe* and *Casey.* It suggests that the two decisions are hard for courts to implement, but cannot prove its case. In the end, the majority says, all it must say to override *stare decisis* is one thing: that it believes *Roe* and *Casey* "egregiously wrong." *Ante,* at 70. That rule could equally spell the end of any precedent with which a bare majority of the present Court disagrees.

So how does that approach prevent the "scale of justice" from "waver[ing] with every new judge's opinion"? 1 Blackstone 69. It does not. It makes radical change too easy and too fast, based on nothing more than the new views of new judges. The majority has overruled *Roe* and *Casey* for one and only one reason: because it has always despised them, and now it has the votes to discard them. The majority thereby substitutes a rule by judges for the rule of law.

A

Contrary to the majority's view, there is nothing unworkable about *Casey*'s "undue burden" standard. Its primary focus on whether a State has placed a "substantial obstacle" on a woman seeking an abortion is "the sort of inquiry familiar to judges across a variety of contexts." *June Medical Services L. L. C.* v. *Russo*, 591 U. S. ___, ___ (2020) (slip op., at 6) (ROBERTS, C. J., concurring in judgment). And it has given rise to no more conflict in application than many standards this Court and others unhesitatingly apply every day.

General standards, like the undue burden standard, are ubiquitous in the law, and particularly in constitutional adjudication. When called on to give effect to the Constitution's broad principles, this Court often crafts flexible standards that can be applied case-by-case to a myriad of unforeseeable circumstances. See *Dickerson*, 530 U. S., at 441 ("No court laying down a general rule can possibly foresee the various circumstances" in which it must apply). So, for example, the Court asks about undue or substantial burdens on speech, on voting, and on interstate commerce. See, *e.g.*, *Arizona Free Enterprise Club's Freedom Club PAC* v. *Bennett*, 564 U. S. 721, 748 (2011); *Burdick* v. *Takushi*, 504 U. S. 428, 433–434 (1992); *Pike* v. *Bruce Church, Inc.*, 397 U. S. 137, 142 (1970). The *Casey* undue burden standard is the same. It also resembles general standards that courts work with daily in other legal spheres—like the "rule of reason" in antitrust law or the "arbitrary and capricious" standard for agency decisionmaking. See *Standard Oil Co. of N. J. v. United States*, 221 U. S. 1, 62 (1911); *Motor Vehicle Mfrs. Assn. of United States, Inc. v. State Farm Mut. Automobile Ins. Co.*, 463 U. S. 29, 42–43 (1983). Applying general standards to particular cases is, in many contexts, just what it means to do law.

And the undue burden standard has given rise to no unusual difficulties. Of course, it has provoked some disagreement among judges. *Casey* knew it would: That much "is to be expected in the application of any legal standard which must accommodate life's complexity." 505 U. S., at 878 (plurality opinion). Which is to say: That much is to be expected in the application of any legal standard. But the majority vastly overstates the divisions among judges applying the standard. We count essentially two. THE CHIEF JUSTICE disagreed with other Justices in the *June Medical* majority about whether *Casey* called for weighing the benefits of an abortion regulation against its burdens. See 591 U. S., at ___–___ (slip op., at 6–7); *ante*, at 59, 60, and n. 53.[10] We agree that the *June Medical* difference is a difference—but not one that would actually make a difference in the result of most cases (it did not in *June Medical*), and not one incapable of resolution were it ever to matter. As for lower courts, there is now a one-year-old, one-to-one Circuit split about how the undue burden standard applies to state laws that ban abortions for certain reasons, like fetal abnormality. See *ante*, at 61, and n. 57. That is about it, as far as we can see.[11] And that is not much. This Court

---

[10] Some lower courts then differed over which opinion in *June Medical* was controlling—but that is a dispute not about the undue burden standard, but about the "*Marks* rule," which tells courts how to determine the precedential effects of a divided decision.

[11] The rest of the majority's supposed splits are, shall we say, unim-

mostly does not even grant certiorari on one-year-old, one-to-one Circuit splits, because we know that a bit of disagreement is an inevitable part of our legal system. To borrow an old saying that might apply here: Not one or even a couple of swallows can make the majority's summer.

Anyone concerned about workability should consider the majority's substitute standard. The majority says a law regulating or banning abortion "must be sustained if there is a rational basis on which the legislature could have thought that it would serve legitimate state interests." *Ante*, at 77. And the majority lists interests like "respect for and preservation of prenatal life," "protection of maternal health," elimination of certain "medical procedures," "mitigation of fetal pain," and others. *Ante*, at 78. This Court will surely face critical questions about how that test applies. Must a state law allow abortions when necessary to protect a woman's life and health? And if so, exactly when? How much risk to a woman's life can a State force

---

pressive. The majority says that lower courts have split over how to apply the undue burden standard to parental notification laws. See *ante*, at 60, and n. 54. But that is not so. The state law upheld had an exemption for minors demonstrating adequate maturity, whereas the ones struck down did not. Compare *Planned Parenthood of Blue Ridge* v. *Camblos*, 155 F. 3d 352, 383–384 (CA4 1998), with *Planned Parenthood of Ind. & Ky., Inc.* v. *Adams*, 937 F. 3d 973, 981 (CA7 2019), cert. granted, judgment vacated, 591 U. S. ___ (2020), and *Planned Parenthood, Sioux Falls Clinic* v. *Miller*, 63 F. 3d 1452, 1460 (CA8 1995). The majority says there is a split about bans on certain types of abortion procedures. See *ante*, at 61, and n. 55. But the one court to have separated itself on that issue did so based on a set of factual findings significantly different from those in other cases. Compare *Whole Woman's Health* v. *Paxton*, 10 F. 4th 430, 447–453 (CA5 2021), with *EMW Women's Surgical Center, P.S.C.* v. *Friedlander*, 960 F. 3d 785, 798–806 (CA6 2020), and *West Ala. Women's Center* v. *Williamson*, 900 F. 3d 1310, 1322–1324 (CA11 2018). Finally, the majority says there is a split about whether an increase in travel time to reach a clinic is an undue burden. See *ante*, at 61, and n. 56. But the cases to which the majority refers predate this Court's decision in *Whole Woman's Health* v. *Hellerstedt*, 579 U. S. 582 (2016), which clarified how to apply the undue burden standard to that context.

her to incur, before the Fourteenth Amendment's protection of life kicks in? Suppose a patient with pulmonary hypertension has a 30-to-50 percent risk of dying with ongoing pregnancy; is that enough? And short of death, how much illness or injury can the State require her to accept, consistent with the Amendment's protection of liberty and equality? Further, the Court may face questions about the application of abortion regulations to medical care most people view as quite different from abortion. What about the morning-after pill? IUDs? In vitro fertilization? And how about the use of dilation and evacuation or medication for miscarriage management? See generally L. Harris, Navigating Loss of Abortion Services—A Large Academic Medical Center Prepares for the Overturn of *Roe* v. *Wade*, 386 New England J. Med. 2061 (2022).[12]

Finally, the majority's ruling today invites a host of questions about interstate conflicts. See *supra*, at 3; see generally D. Cohen, G. Donley, & R. Rebouché, The New Abortion Battleground, 123 Colum. L. Rev. (forthcoming 2023), https://ssrn.com/abstract=4032931. Can a State bar women from traveling to another State to obtain an abortion? Can a State prohibit advertising out-of-state abortions or helping women get to out-of-state providers? Can a State inter-

---

[12] To take just the last, most medical treatments for miscarriage are identical to those used in abortions. See Kaiser Family Foundation (Kaiser), G. Weigel, L. Sobel, & A. Salganicoff, Understanding Pregnancy Loss in the Context of Abortion Restrictions and Fetal Harm Laws (Dec. 4, 2019), https://www.kff.org/womens-health-policy/issue-brief/understanding-pregnancy-loss-in-the-context-of-abortion-restrictions-and-fetal-harm-laws/. Blanket restrictions on "abortion" procedures and medications therefore may be understood to deprive women of effective treatment for miscarriages, which occur in about 10 to 30 percent of pregnancies. See Health Affairs, J. Strasser, C. Chen, S. Rosenbaum, E. Schenk, & E. Dewhurst, Penalizing Abortion Providers Will Have Ripple Effects Across Pregnancy Care (May 3, 2022), https://www.healthaffairs.org/do/10.1377/forefront.20220503.129912/.

fere with the mailing of drugs used for medication abortions? The Constitution protects travel and speech and interstate commerce, so today's ruling will give rise to a host of new constitutional questions. Far from removing the Court from the abortion issue, the majority puts the Court at the center of the coming "interjurisdictional abortion wars." *Id.*, at ___ (draft, at 1).

In short, the majority does not save judges from unwieldy tests or extricate them from the sphere of controversy. To the contrary, it discards a known, workable, and predictable standard in favor of something novel and probably far more complicated. It forces the Court to wade further into hotly contested issues, including moral and philosophical ones, that the majority criticizes *Roe* and *Casey* for addressing.

B

When overruling constitutional precedent, the Court has almost always pointed to major legal or factual changes undermining a decision's original basis. A review of the Appendix to this dissent proves the point. See *infra*, at 61–66. Most "successful proponent[s] of overruling precedent," this Court once said, have carried "the heavy burden of persuading the Court that changes in society or in the law dictate that the values served by *stare decisis* yield in favor of a greater objective." *Vasquez*, 474 U. S., at 266. Certainly, that was so of the main examples the majority cites: *Brown* v. *Board of Education*, 347 U. S. 483 (1954), and *West Coast Hotel Co.* v. *Parrish*, 300 U. S. 379 (1937). But it is not so today. Although nodding to some arguments others have made about "modern developments," the majority does not really rely on them, no doubt seeing their slimness. *Ante*, at 33; see *ante*, at 34. The majority briefly invokes the current controversy over abortion. See *ante*, at 70–71. But it has to acknowledge that the same dispute has existed for decades: Conflict over abortion is not a change but a constant. (And as we will later discuss, the presence of that continuing division provides more of a reason to stick with, than to jettison, existing precedent. See *infra*, at 55–57.) In the end, the majority throws longstanding precedent to the winds without showing that anything significant has changed to justify its radical reshaping of the law. See *ante*, at 43.

1

Subsequent legal developments have only reinforced *Roe* and *Casey*. The Court has continued to embrace all the decisions *Roe* and *Casey* cited, decisions which recognize a constitutional right for an individual to make her own choices about "intimate relationships, the family," and contraception. *Casey*, 505 U. S., at 857. *Roe* and *Casey* have themselves formed the legal foundation for subsequent decisions protecting these profoundly personal choices. As discussed earlier, the Court relied on *Casey* to hold that the Fourteenth Amendment protects same-sex intimate relationships. See *Lawrence*, 539 U. S., at 578; *supra*, at 23. The Court later invoked the same set of precedents to accord constitutional recognition to same-sex marriage. See *Obergefell*, 576 U. S., at 665–666; *supra*, at 23. In sum, *Roe* and *Casey* are inextricably interwoven with decades of precedent about the meaning of the Fourteenth Amendment. See *supra*, at 21–24. While the majority might wish it otherwise, *Roe* and *Casey* are the very opposite of "'obsolete constitutional thinking.'" *Agostini* v. *Felton*, 521 U. S. 203, 236 (1997) (quoting *Casey*, 505 U. S., at 857).

Moreover, no subsequent factual developments have undermined *Roe* and *Casey*. Women continue to experience unplanned pregnancies and unexpected developments in pregnancies. Pregnancies continue to have enormous physical, social, and economic consequences. Even an uncomplicated pregnancy imposes significant strain on the body, unavoidably involving significant physiological change and excruciating pain. For some women, pregnancy and childbirth can mean life-altering physical ailments or even death. Today, as noted earlier, the risks of carrying a pregnancy to term dwarf those of having an abortion. See *supra*, at 22. Experts estimate that a ban on abortions increases maternal mortality by 21 percent, with white women facing a 13 percent increase in maternal mortality while black women face a 33 percent increase.[13] Pregnancy and childbirth may also impose large-scale financial costs. The majority briefly refers to arguments about changes in laws relating to healthcare coverage, pregnancy discrimination, and family leave. See *ante*, at 33–34. Many women, however, still do not have adequate healthcare coverage before and after pregnancy; and, even when insurance coverage is available, healthcare services may be far away.[14] Women also continue to face pregnancy discrimination that interferes with their ability to earn a living. Paid family leave remains inaccessible to many who need it most. Only 20 percent of private-sector workers have access to paid family leave, including a mere 8 percent of workers in the bottom

_____

[13] See L. Harris, Navigating Loss of Abortion Services—A Large Academic Medical Center Prepares for the Overturn of *Roe* v. *Wade*, 386 New England J. Med. 2061, 2063 (2022). This projected racial disparity reflects existing differences in maternal mortality rates for black and white women. Black women are now three to four times more likely to die during or after childbirth than white women, often from preventable causes. See Brief for Howard University School of Law Human and Civil Rights Clinic as *Amicus Curiae* 18.

[14] See Centers for Medicare and Medicaid Services, Issue Brief: Improving Access to Maternal Health Care in Rural Communities 4, 8, 11 (Sept. 2019), https://www.cms.gov/About-CMS/Agency-Information/OMH/equity-initiatives/rural-health/09032019-Maternal-Health-Care-in-Rural-Communities.pdf. In Mississippi, for instance, 19 percent of women of reproductive age are uninsured and 60 percent of counties lack a single obstetrician-gynecologist. Brief for Lawyers' Committee for Civil Rights Under Law et al. as *Amici Curiae* 12–13.

quartile of wage earners.[15]

The majority briefly notes the growing prevalence of safe haven laws and demand for adoption, see *ante*, at 34, and nn. 45–46, but, to the degree that these are changes at all, they too are irrelevant.[16] Neither reduces the health risks or financial costs of going through pregnancy and childbirth. Moreover, the choice to give up parental rights after giving birth is altogether different from the choice not to carry a pregnancy to term. The reality is that few women denied an abortion will choose adoption.[17] The vast majority will continue, just as in *Roe* and *Casey*'s time, to shoulder the costs of childrearing. Whether or not they choose to parent, they will experience the profound loss of autonomy and dignity that coerced pregnancy and birth always impose.[18]

---

[15] Dept. of Labor, National Compensation Survey: Employee Benefits in the United States, Table 31 (Sept. 2020), https://www.bls.gov/ncs/ebs/benefits/2020/employee-benefits-in-the-united-states-march-2020.pdf#page=299.

[16] Safe haven laws, which allow parents to leave newborn babies in designated safe spaces without threat of prosecution, were not enacted as an alternative to abortion, but in response to rare situations in which birthing mothers in crisis would kill their newborns or leave them to die. See Centers for Disease Control and Prevention (CDC), R. Wilson, J. Klevens, D. Williams, & L. Xu, Infant Homicides Within the Context of Safe Haven Laws—United States, 2008–2017, 69 Morbidity and Mortality Weekly Report 1385 (2020).

[17] A study of women who sought an abortion but were denied one because of gestational limits found that only 9 percent put the child up for adoption, rather than parenting themselves. See G. Sisson, L. Ralph, H. Gould, & D. Foster, Adoption Decision Making Among Women Seeking Abortion, 27 Women's Health Issues 136, 139 (2017).

[18] The majority finally notes the claim that "people now have a new appreciation of fetal life," partly because of viewing sonogram images. *Ante*, at 34. It is hard to know how anyone would evaluate such a claim and as we have described above, the majority's reasoning does not rely on any reevaluation of the interest in protecting fetal life. See *supra*, at 26, and n. 7. It is worth noting that sonograms became widely used in

Mississippi's own record illustrates how little facts on the ground have changed since *Roe* and *Casey*, notwithstanding the majority's supposed "modern developments." *Ante*, at 33. Sixty-two percent of pregnancies in Mississippi are un-planned, yet Mississippi does not require insurance to cover contraceptives and prohibits educators from demonstrating proper contraceptive use.[19] The State neither bans preg-nancy discrimination nor requires provision of paid paren-tal leave. Brief for Yale Law School Information Society Project as *Amicus Curiae* 13 (Brief for Yale Law School); Brief for National Women's Law Center et al. as *Amici Cu-riae* 32. It has strict eligibility requirements for Medicaid and nutrition assistance, leaving many women and families without basic medical care or enough food. See Brief for 547 Deans, Chairs, Scholars and Public Health Professionals et al. as *Amici Curiae* 32–34 (Brief for 547 Deans). Alt-hough 86 percent of pregnancy-related deaths in the State are due to postpartum complications, Mississippi rejected federal funding to provide a year's worth of Medicaid cover-age to women after giving birth. See Brief for Yale Law School 12–13. Perhaps unsurprisingly, health outcomes in Mississippi are abysmal for both women and children. Mis-sissippi has the highest infant mortality rate in the country,

---

the 1970s, long before *Casey*. Today, 60 percent of women seeking abor-tions have at least one child, and one-third have two or more. See CDC, K. Kortsmit et al., Abortion Surveillance—United States, 2019, 70 Mor-bidity and Mortality Weekly Report 6 (2021). These women know, even as they choose to have an abortion, what it is to look at a sonogram image and to value a fetal life.

[19] Guttmacher Institute, K. Kost, Unintended Pregnancy Rates at the State Level: Estimates for 2010 and Trends Since 2002, Table 1 (2015), https://www.guttmacher.org/sites/default/files/report_pdf/stateup10.pdf; Kaiser, State Requirements for Insurance Coverage of Contraceptives (May 1, 2022), https://www.kff.org/state-category/womens-health/family-planning; Miss. Code Ann. §37–13–171(2)(d) (Cum. Supp. 2021) ("In no case shall the instruction or program include any demonstration of how condoms or other contraceptives are applied").

and some of the highest rates for preterm birth, low birth-weight, cesarean section, and maternal death.[20] It is approximately 75 times more dangerous for a woman in the State to carry a pregnancy to term than to have an abortion. See Brief for 547 Deans 9–10. We do not say that every State is Mississippi, and we are sure some have made gains since *Roe* and *Casey* in providing support for women and children. But a state-by-state analysis by public health professionals shows that States with the most restrictive abortion policies also continue to invest the least in women's and children's health. See Brief for 547 Deans 23–34.

The only notable change we can see since *Roe* and *Casey* cuts in favor of adhering to precedent: It is that American abortion law has become more and more aligned with other nations. The majority, like the Mississippi Legislature, claims that the United States is an extreme outlier when it comes to abortion regulation. See *ante*, at 6, and n. 15. The global trend, however, has been toward increased provision of legal and safe abortion care. A number of countries, including New Zealand, the Netherlands, and Iceland, permit abortions up to a roughly similar time as *Roe* and *Casey* set. See Brief for International and Comparative Legal Scholars as *Amici Curiae* 18–22. Canada has decriminalized abortion at any point in a pregnancy. See *id.*, at 13–15. Most Western European countries impose restrictions on abor-

---

[20] See CDC, Infant Mortality Rates by State (Mar. 3, 2022), https://www.cdc.gov/nchs/pressroom/sosmap/infant_mortality_rates/infant_mortality.htm; Mississippi State Dept. of Health, Infant Mortality Report 2019 & 2020, pp. 18–19 (2021), https://www.msdh.ms.gov/msdhsite/_static/resources/18752.pdf; CDC, Percentage of Babies Born Low Birthweight by State (Feb. 25, 2022), https://www.cdc.gov/nchs/pressroom/sosmap/lbw_births/lbw.htm; CDC, Cesarean Delivery Rate by State (Feb. 25, 2022), https://www.cdc.gov/nchs/pressroom/sosmap/cesarean_births/cesareans.htm; Mississippi State Dept. of Health, Mississippi Maternal Mortality Report 2013–2016, pp. 5, 25 (Mar. 2021), https://www.msdh.ms.gov/msdhsite/_static/resources/8127.pdf.

tion after 12 to 14 weeks, but they often have liberal exceptions to those time limits, including to prevent harm to a woman's physical or mental health. See *id.*, at 24–27; Brief for European Law Professors as *Amici Curiae* 16–17, Appendix. They also typically make access to early abortion easier, for example, by helping cover its cost.[21] Perhaps most notable, more than 50 countries around the world—in Asia, Latin America, Africa, and Europe—have expanded access to abortion in the past 25 years. See Brief for International and Comparative Legal Scholars as *Amici Curiae* 28–29. In light of that worldwide liberalization of abortion laws, it is American States that will become international outliers after today.

In sum, the majority can point to neither legal nor factual developments in support of its decision. Nothing that has happened in this country or the world in recent decades undermines the core insight of *Roe* and *Casey*. It continues to be true that, within the constraints those decisions established, a woman, not the government, should choose whether she will bear the burdens of pregnancy, childbirth, and parenting.

2

In support of its holding, see *ante*, at 40, the majority invokes two watershed cases overruling prior constitutional precedents: *West Coast Hotel Co.* v. *Parrish* and *Brown* v. *Board of Education*. But those decisions, unlike today's, responded to changed law and to changed facts and attitudes that had taken hold throughout society. As *Casey* recognized, the two cases are relevant only to show—by stark contrast—how unjustified overturning the right to choose is. See 505 U. S., at 861–864.

West Coast Hotel overruled *Adkins* v. *Children's Hospital*

---

[21] See D. Grossman, K. Grindlay, & B. Burns, Public Funding for Abortion Where Broadly Legal, 94 Contraception 451, 458 (2016) (discussing funding of abortion in European countries).

of D. C., 261 U. S. 525 (1923), and a whole line of cases beginning with *Lochner* v. *New York*, 198 U. S. 45 (1905). *Adkins* had found a state minimum-wage law unconstitutional because, in the Court's view, the law interfered with a constitutional right to contract. 261 U. S., at 554–555. But then the Great Depression hit, bringing with it unparalleled economic despair. The experience undermined—in fact, it disproved—*Adkins*'s assumption that a wholly unregulated market could meet basic human needs. As Justice Jackson (before becoming a Justice) wrote of that time: "The older world of *laissez faire* was recognized everywhere outside the Court to be dead." The Struggle for Judicial Supremacy 85 (1941). In *West Coast Hotel*, the Court caught up, recognizing through the lens of experience the flaws of existing legal doctrine. See also *ante*, at 11 (ROBERTS, C. J., concurring in judgment). The havoc the Depression had worked on ordinary Americans, the Court noted, was "common knowledge through the length and breadth of the land." 300 U. S., at 399. The *laissez-faire* approach had led to "the exploiting of workers at wages so low as to be insufficient to meet the bare cost of living." *Ibid.* And since *Adkins* was decided, the law had also changed. In several decisions, the Court had started to recognize the power of States to implement economic policies designed to enhance their citizens' economic well-being. See, *e.g.*, *Nebbia* v. *New York*, 291 U. S. 502 (1934); *O'Gorman & Young, Inc.* v. *Hartford Fire Ins. Co.*, 282 U. S. 251 (1931). The statements in those decisions, *West Coast Hotel* explained, were "impossible to reconcile" with *Adkins*. 300 U. S., at 398. There was no escaping the need for *Adkins* to go.

Brown v. *Board of Education* overruled *Plessy* v. *Ferguson*, 163 U. S. 537 (1896), along with its doctrine of "separate but equal." By 1954, decades of Jim Crow had made clear what *Plessy*'s turn of phrase actually meant: "inherent[ ] [in]equal[ity]." *Brown*, 347 U. S., at 495. Segregation was not, and could not ever be, consistent with the Reconstruction Amendments, ratified to give the former slaves full citizenship. Whatever might have been thought in *Plessy*'s time, the *Brown* Court explained, both experience and "modern authority" showed the "detrimental effect[s]" of state-sanctioned segregation: It "affect[ed] [children's] hearts and minds in a way unlikely ever to be undone." 347 U. S., at 494. By that point, too, the law had begun to reflect that understanding. In a series of decisions, the Court had held unconstitutional public graduate schools' exclusion of black students. See, *e.g.*, *Sweatt* v. *Painter*, 339 U. S. 629 (1950); *Sipuel* v. *Board of Regents of Univ. of Okla.*, 332 U. S. 631 (1948) (*per curiam*); *Missouri ex rel. Gaines* v. *Canada*, 305 U. S. 337 (1938). The logic of those cases, *Brown* held, "appl[ied] with added force to children in grade and high schools." 347 U. S., at 494. Changed facts and changed law required *Plessy*'s end.

The majority says that in recognizing those changes, we are implicitly supporting the half-century interlude between *Plessy* and *Brown*. See *ante*, at 70. That is not so. First, if the *Brown* Court had used the majority's method of constitutional construction, it might not ever have overruled *Plessy*, whether 5 or 50 or 500 years later. *Brown* thought that whether the ratification-era history supported desegregation was "[a]t best . . . inconclusive." 347 U. S., at 489. But even setting that aside, we are not saying that a decision can *never* be overruled just because it is terribly wrong. Take *West Virginia Bd. of Ed.* v. *Barnette*, 319 U. S. 624, which the majority also relies on. See *ante*, at 40–41, 70. That overruling took place just three years after the initial decision, before any notable reliance interests had developed. It happened as well because individual Justices changed their minds, not because a new majority wanted to undo the decisions of their predecessors. Both *Barnette* and *Brown*, moreover, share another feature setting them apart from the Court's ruling today. They protected individual

rights with a strong basis in the Constitution's most fundamental commitments; they did not, as the majority does
here, take away a right that individuals have held, and relied on, for 50 years. To take *that* action based on a new
and bare majority's declaration that two Courts got the result egregiously wrong? And to justify that action by reference to *Barnette*? Or to *Brown*—a case in which the Chief
Justice also wrote an (11-page) opinion in which the entire
Court could speak with one voice? These questions answer
themselves.

   Casey itself addressed both *West Coast Hotel* and *Brown*,
and found that neither supported *Roe*'s overruling. In *West
Coast Hotel*, *Casey* explained, "the facts of economic life"
had proved "different from those previously assumed." 505
U. S., at 862. And even though "*Plessy* was wrong the day
it was decided," the passage of time had made that ever
more clear to ever more citizens: "Society's understanding
of the facts" in 1954 was "fundamentally different" than in
1896. *Id.*, at 863. So the Court needed to reverse course.
"In constitutional adjudication as elsewhere in life, changed
circumstances may impose new obligations." *Id.*, at 864.
And because such dramatic change had occurred, the public
could understand why the Court was acting. "[T]he Nation
could accept each decision" as a "response to the Court's
constitutional duty." *Ibid.* But that would not be true of a
reversal of *Roe*—"[b]ecause neither the factual underpinnings of *Roe*'s central holding nor our understanding of it
has changed." 505 U. S., at 864.

   That is just as much so today, because *Roe* and *Casey* continue to reflect, not diverge from, broad trends in American
society. It is, of course, true that many Americans, including many women, opposed those decisions when issued and
do so now as well. Yet the fact remains: *Roe* and *Casey* were
the product of a profound and ongoing change in women's
roles in the latter part of the 20th century. Only a dozen
years before *Roe*, the Court described women as "the center

of home and family life," with "special responsibilities" that precluded their full legal status under the Constitution. *Hoyt* v. *Florida*, 368 U. S. 57, 62 (1961). By 1973, when the Court decided *Roe*, fundamental social change was underway regarding the place of women—and the law had begun to follow. See *Reed* v. *Reed*, 404 U. S. 71, 76 (1971) (recognizing that the Equal Protection Clause prohibits sex-based discrimination). By 1992, when the Court decided *Casey*, the traditional view of a woman's role as only a wife and mother was "no longer consistent with our understanding of the family, the individual, or the Constitution." 505 U. S., at 897; see *supra*, at 15, 23–24. Under that charter, *Casey* understood, women must take their place as full and equal citizens. And for that to happen, women must have control over their reproductive decisions. Nothing since *Casey*—no changed law, no changed fact—has undermined that promise.

C

The reasons for retaining *Roe* and *Casey* gain further strength from the overwhelming reliance interests those decisions have created. The Court adheres to precedent not just for institutional reasons, but because it recognizes that stability in the law is "an essential thread in the mantle of protection that the law affords the individual." *Florida Dept. of Health and Rehabilitative Servs.* v. *Florida Nursing Home Assn.*, 450 U. S. 147, 154 (1981) (Stevens, J., concurring). So when overruling precedent "would dislodge [individuals'] settled rights and expectations," *stare decisis* has "added force." *Hilton* v. *South Carolina Public Railways Comm'n*, 502 U. S. 197, 202 (1991). *Casey* understood that to deny individuals' reliance on *Roe* was to "refuse to face the fact[s]." 505 U. S., at 856. Today the majority refuses to face the facts. "The most striking feature of the [majority] is the absence of any serious discussion" of how its ruling will affect women. *Ante,* at 37. By characterizing *Casey*'s reliance arguments as "generalized assertions about the national psyche," *ante,* at 64, it reveals how little it knows or cares about women's lives or about the suffering its decision will cause.

In *Casey,* the Court observed that for two decades individuals "have organized intimate relationships and made" significant life choices "in reliance on the availability of abortion in the event that contraception should fail." 505 U. S., at 856. Over another 30 years, that reliance has solidified. For half a century now, in *Casey*'s words, "[t]he ability of women to participate equally in the economic and social life of the Nation has been facilitated by their ability to control their reproductive lives." *Ibid.*; see *supra,* at 23–24. Indeed, all women now of childbearing age have grown up expecting that they would be able to avail themselves of *Roe*'s and *Casey*'s protections.

The disruption of overturning *Roe* and *Casey* will therefore be profound. Abortion is a common medical procedure and a familiar experience in women's lives. About 18 percent of pregnancies in this country end in abortion, and about one quarter of American women will have an abortion before the age of 45.[22] Those numbers reflect the predictable and life-changing effects of carrying a pregnancy, giving birth, and becoming a parent. As *Casey* understood, people today rely on their ability to control and time pregnancies when making countless life decisions: where to live, whether and how to invest in education or careers, how to allocate financial resources, and how to approach intimate and family relationships. Women may count on abortion access for when contraception fails. They may count on abortion access for when contraception cannot be used, for

---

[22] See CDC, K. Kortsmit et al., Abortion Surveillance—United States, 2019, 70 Morbidity and Mortality Weekly Report 7 (2021); Brief for American College of Obstetricians and Gynecologists et al. as *Amici Curiae* 9.

example, if they were raped. They may count on abortion
for when something changes in the midst of a pregnancy,
whether it involves family or financial circumstances, un-
anticipated medical complications, or heartbreaking fetal
diagnoses. Taking away the right to abortion, as the majority does today, destroys all those individual plans and expectations. In so doing, it diminishes women's opportuni-
ties to participate fully and equally in the Nation's political,
social, and economic life. See Brief for Economists as *Amici
Curiae* 13 (showing that abortion availability has "large effects on women's education, labor force participation, occu-
pations, and earnings" (footnotes omitted)).

The majority's response to these obvious points exists far
from the reality American women actually live. The majority proclaims that "'reproductive planning could take virtually immediate account of any sudden restoration of state
authority to ban abortions.'" *Ante*, at 64 (quoting *Casey*,
505 U. S., at 856).[23] The facts are: 45 percent of pregnancies
in the United States are unplanned. See Brief for 547
Deans 5. Even the most effective contraceptives fail, and
effective contraceptives are not universally accessible.[24]
Not all sexual activity is consensual and not all contraceptive choices are made by the party who risks pregnancy.
See Brief for Legal Voice et al. as *Amici Curiae* 18–19. The
Mississippi law at issue here, for example, has no exception
for rape or incest, even for underage women. Finally, the

_____

[23] Astoundingly, the majority casts this statement as a "conce[ssion]"
from *Casey* with which it "agree[s]." *Ante*, at 64. In fact, *Casey* used this
language as part of describing an argument that it *rejected*. See 505
U. S., at 856. It is only today's Court that endorses this profoundly mistaken view.

[24] See Brief for 547 Deans 6–7 (noting that 51 percent of women who
terminated their pregnancies reported using contraceptives during the
month in which they conceived); Brief for Lawyers' Committee for Civil
Rights Under Law et al. as *Amici Curiae* 12–14 (explaining financial and
geographic barriers to access to effective contraceptives).

majority ignores, as explained above, that some women decide to have an abortion because their circumstances change during a pregnancy. See *supra*, at 49. Human bodies care little for hopes and plans. Events can occur after conception, from unexpected medical risks to changes in family circumstances, which profoundly alter what it means to carry a pregnancy to term. In all these situations, women have expected that they will get to decide, perhaps in consultation with their families or doctors but free from state interference, whether to continue a pregnancy. For those who will now have to undergo that pregnancy, the loss of *Roe* and *Casey* could be disastrous.

That is especially so for women without money. When we "count[] the cost of [*Roe*'s] repudiation" on women who once relied on that decision, it is not hard to see where the greatest burden will fall. *Casey*, 505 U. S., at 855. In States that bar abortion, women of means will still be able to travel to obtain the services they need.[25] It is women who cannot afford to do so who will suffer most. These are the women most likely to seek abortion care in the first place. Women living below the federal poverty line experience unintended pregnancies at rates five times higher than higher income women do, and nearly half of women who seek abortion care live in households below the poverty line. See Brief for 547 Deans 7; Brief for Abortion Funds and Practical Support Organizations as *Amici Curiae* 8 (Brief for Abortion Funds).

---

[25] This statement of course assumes that States are not successful in preventing interstate travel to obtain an abortion. See *supra*, at 3, 36–37. Even assuming that is so, increased out-of-state demand will lead to longer wait times and decreased availability of service in States still providing abortions. See Brief for State of California et al. as *Amici Curiae* 25–27. This is what happened in Oklahoma, Kansas, Colorado, New Mexico, and Nevada last fall after Texas effectively banned abortions past six weeks of gestation. See *United States* v. *Texas*, 595 U. S. ___, ___ (2021) (SOTOMAYOR, J., concurring in part and dissenting in part) (slip op., at 6).

Even with *Roe*'s protection, these women face immense obstacles to raising the money needed to obtain abortion care early in their pregnancy. See Brief for Abortion Funds 7–12.[26] After today, in States where legal abortions are not available, they will lose any ability to obtain safe, legal abortion care. They will not have the money to make the trip necessary; or to obtain childcare for that time; or to take time off work. Many will endure the costs and risks of pregnancy and giving birth against their wishes. Others will turn in desperation to illegal and unsafe abortions. They may lose not just their freedom, but their lives.[27]

Finally, the expectation of reproductive control is integral to many women's identity and their place in the Nation. See *Casey*, 505 U. S., at 856. That expectation helps define

---

[26] The average cost of a first-trimester abortion is about $500. See Brief for Abortion Funds 7. Federal insurance generally does not cover the cost of abortion, and 35 percent of American adults do not have cash on hand to cover an unexpected expense that high. Guttmacher Institute, M. Donovan, In Real Life: Federal Restrictions on Abortion Coverage and the Women They Impact (Jan. 5, 2017), https://www.guttmacher.org/gpr/2017/01/real-life-federal-restrictions-abortion-coverage-and-women-they-impact#:~:text=Although%20the%20Hyde%20Amendment%20bars,provide%20abortion%20coverage%20to%20enrollees; Brief for Abortion Funds 11.

[27] Mississippi is likely to be one of the States where these costs are highest, though history shows that it will have company. As described above, Mississippi provides only the barest financial support to pregnant women. See *supra*, at 41–42. The State will greatly restrict abortion care without addressing any of the financial, health, and family needs that motivate many women to seek it. The effects will be felt most severely, as they always have been, on the bodies of the poor. The history of state abortion restrictions is a history of heavy costs exacted from the most vulnerable women. It is a history of women seeking illegal abortions in hotel rooms and home kitchens; of women trying to self-induce abortions by douching with bleach, injecting lye, and penetrating themselves with knitting needles, scissors, and coat hangers. See L. Reagan, When Abortion Was a Crime 42–43, 198–199, 208–209 (1997). It is a history of women dying.

a woman as an "equal citizen[]," with all the rights, privileges, and obligations that status entails. *Gonzales*, 550 U. S., at 172 (Ginsburg, J., dissenting); see *supra*, at 23–24. It reflects that she is an autonomous person, and that society and the law recognize her as such. Like many constitutional rights, the right to choose situates a woman in relationship to others and to the government. It helps define a sphere of freedom, in which a person has the capacity to make choices free of government control. As *Casey* recognized, the right "order[s]" her "thinking" as well as her "living." 505 U. S., at 856. Beyond any individual choice about residence, or education, or career, her whole life reflects the control and authority that the right grants.

Withdrawing a woman's right to choose whether to continue a pregnancy does not mean that no choice is being made. It means that a majority of today's Court has wrenched this choice from women and given it to the States. To allow a State to exert control over one of "the most intimate and personal choices" a woman may make is not only to affect the course of her life, monumental as those effects might be. *Id.*, at 851. It is to alter her "views of [herself]" and her understanding of her "place[] in society" as someone with the recognized dignity and authority to make these choices. *Id.*, at 856. Women have relied on *Roe* and *Casey* in this way for 50 years. Many have never known anything else. When *Roe* and *Casey* disappear, the loss of power, control, and dignity will be immense.

The Court's failure to perceive the whole swath of expectations *Roe* and *Casey* created reflects an impoverished view of reliance. According to the majority, a reliance interest must be "very concrete," like those involving "property" or "contract." *Ante*, at 64. While many of this Court's cases addressing reliance have been in the "commercial context," *Casey*, 505 U. S., at 855, none holds that interests must be analogous to commercial ones to warrant *stare de-*

cisis protection.[28] This unprecedented assertion is, at bottom, a radical claim to power. By disclaiming any need to consider broad swaths of individuals' interests, the Court arrogates to itself the authority to overrule established legal principles without even acknowledging the costs of its decisions for the individuals who live under the law, costs that this Court's *stare decisis* doctrine instructs us to privilege when deciding whether to change course.

The majority claims that the reliance interests women have in *Roe* and *Casey* are too "intangible" for the Court to consider, even if it were inclined to do so. *Ante*, at 65. This is to ignore as judges what we know as men and women. The interests women have in *Roe* and *Casey* are perfectly, viscerally concrete. Countless women will now make different decisions about careers, education, relationships, and whether to try to become pregnant than they would have when *Roe* served as a backstop. Other women will carry pregnancies to term, with all the costs and risk of harm that involves, when they would previously have chosen to obtain an abortion. For millions of women, *Roe* and *Casey* have been critical in giving them control of their bodies and their lives. Closing our eyes to the suffering today's decision will impose will not make that suffering disappear. The majority cannot escape its obligation to "count[] the cost[s]" of its decision by invoking the "conflicting arguments" of "contending sides." *Casey*, 505 U. S., at 855; *ante*, at 65. *Stare decisis* requires that the Court calculate the costs of a decision's repudiation on those who have relied on the decision,

---

[28]The majority's sole citation for its "concreteness" requirement is *Payne* v. *Tennessee*, 501 U. S. 808 (1991). But *Payne* merely discounted reliance interests in cases involving "procedural and evidentiary rules." *Id.*, at 828. Unlike the individual right at stake here, those rules do "not alter primary conduct." *Hohn* v. *United States*, 524 U. S. 236, 252 (1998). Accordingly, they generally "do not implicate the reliance interests of private parties" at all. *Alleyne* v. *United States*, 570 U. S. 99, 119 (2013) (SOTOMAYOR, J., concurring).

not on those who have disavowed it. See *Casey*, 505 U. S., at 855.

More broadly, the majority's approach to reliance cannot be reconciled with our Nation's understanding of constitutional rights. The majority's insistence on a "concrete," economic showing would preclude a finding of reliance on a wide variety of decisions recognizing constitutional rights— such as the right to express opinions, or choose whom to marry, or decide how to educate children. The Court, on the majority's logic, could transfer those choices to the State without having to consider a person's settled understanding that the law makes them hers. That must be wrong. All those rights, like the right to obtain an abortion, profoundly affect and, indeed, anchor individual lives. To recognize that people have relied on these rights is not to dabble in abstractions, but to acknowledge some of the most "concrete" and familiar aspects of human life and liberty. *Ante*, at 64.

All those rights, like the one here, also have a societal dimension, because of the role constitutional liberties play in our structure of government. See, *e.g.*, *Dickerson*, 530 U. S., at 443 (recognizing that *Miranda* "warnings have become part of our national culture" in declining to overrule *Miranda* v. *Arizona*, 384 U. S. 436 (1966)). Rescinding an individual right in its entirety and conferring it on the State, an action the Court takes today for the first time in history, affects all who have relied on our constitutional system of government and its structure of individual liberties protected from state oversight. *Roe* and *Casey* have of course aroused controversy and provoked disagreement. But the right those decisions conferred and reaffirmed is part of society's understanding of constitutional law and of how the Court has defined the liberty and equality that women are entitled to claim.

After today, young women will come of age with fewer

rights than their mothers and grandmothers had. The majority accomplishes that result without so much as considering how women have relied on the right to choose or what it means to take that right away. The majority's refusal even to consider the life-altering consequences of reversing *Roe* and *Casey* is a stunning indictment of its decision.

D

One last consideration counsels against the majority's ruling: the very controversy surrounding *Roe* and *Casey*. The majority accuses *Casey* of acting outside the bounds of the law to quell the conflict over abortion—of imposing an unprincipled "settlement" of the issue in an effort to end "national division." *Ante*, at 67. But that is not what *Casey* did. As shown above, *Casey* applied traditional principles of *stare decisis*—which the majority today ignores—in reaffirming *Roe*. *Casey* carefully assessed changed circumstances (none) and reliance interests (profound). It considered every aspect of how *Roe*'s framework operated. It adhered to the law in its analysis, and it reached the conclusion that the law required. True enough that *Casey* took notice of the "national controversy" about abortion: The Court knew in 1992, as it did in 1973, that abortion was a "divisive issue." *Casey*, 505 U. S., at 867–868; see *Roe*, 410 U. S., at 116. But *Casey*'s reason for acknowledging public conflict was the exact opposite of what the majority insinuates. *Casey* addressed the national controversy in order to emphasize how important it was, in that case of all cases, for the Court to stick to the law. Would that today's majority had done likewise.

Consider how the majority itself summarizes this aspect of *Casey*:

> "The American people's belief in the rule of law would be shaken if they lost respect for this Court as an institution that decides important cases based on principle, not 'social and political pressures.' There is a special

danger that the public will perceive a decision as having been made for unprincipled reasons when the Court overrules a controversial 'watershed' decision, such as *Roe.* A decision overruling *Roe* would be perceived as having been made 'under fire' and as a 'surrender to political pressure.'" *Ante,* at 66–67 (citations omitted). That seems to us a good description. And it seems to us right. The majority responds (if we understand it correctly): well, yes, but we have to apply the law. See *ante,* at 67. To which *Casey* would have said: That is exactly the point. Here, more than anywhere, the Court needs to apply the law—particularly the law of *stare decisis.* Here, we know that citizens will continue to contest the Court's decision, because "[m]en and women of good conscience" deeply disagree about abortion. *Casey,* 505 U. S., at 850. When that contestation takes place—but when there is no legal basis for reversing course—the Court needs to be steadfast, to stand its ground. That is what the rule of law requires. And that is what respect for this Court depends on.

"The promise of constancy, once given" in so charged an environment, *Casey* explained, "binds its maker for as long as" the "understanding of the issue has not changed so fundamentally as to render the commitment obsolete." *Id.,* at 868. A breach of that promise is "nothing less than a breach of faith." *Ibid.* "[A]nd no Court that broke its faith with the people could sensibly expect credit for principle." *Ibid.* No Court breaking its faith in that way would *deserve* credit for principle. As one of *Casey*'s authors wrote in another case, "Our legitimacy requires, above all, that we adhere to *stare decisis*" in "sensitive political contexts" where "partisan controversy abounds." *Bush* v. *Vera,* 517 U. S. 952, 985 (1996) (opinion of O'Connor, J.).

Justice Jackson once called a decision he dissented from a "loaded weapon," ready to hand for improper uses. *Korematsu* v. *United States,* 323 U. S. 214, 246 (1944). We fear that today's decision, departing from *stare decisis* for no legitimate reason, is its own loaded weapon. Weakening *stare decisis* threatens to upend bedrock legal doctrines, far beyond any single decision. Weakening *stare decisis* creates profound legal instability. And as *Casey* recognized, weakening *stare decisis* in a hotly contested case like this one calls into question this Court's commitment to legal principle. It makes the Court appear not restrained but aggressive, not modest but grasping. In all those ways, today's decision takes aim, we fear, at the rule of law.

III

"Power, not reason, is the new currency of this Court's decisionmaking." *Payne*, 501 U. S., at 844 (Marshall, J., dissenting). *Roe* has stood for fifty years. *Casey*, a precedent about precedent specifically confirming *Roe*, has stood for thirty. And the doctrine of *stare decisis*—a critical element of the rule of law—stands foursquare behind their continued existence. The right those decisions established and preserved is embedded in our constitutional law, both originating in and leading to other rights protecting bodily integrity, personal autonomy, and family relationships. The abortion right is also embedded in the lives of women— shaping their expectations, influencing their choices about relationships and work, supporting (as all reproductive rights do) their social and economic equality. Since the right's recognition (and affirmation), nothing has changed to support what the majority does today. Neither law nor facts nor attitudes have provided any new reasons to reach a different result than *Roe* and *Casey* did. All that has changed is this Court.

Mississippi—and other States too—knew exactly what they were doing in ginning up new legal challenges to *Roe* and *Casey*. The 15-week ban at issue here was enacted in 2018. Other States quickly followed: Between 2019 and 2021, eight States banned abortion procedures after six to eight weeks of pregnancy, and three States enacted all-out bans.[29] Mississippi itself decided in 2019 that it had not gone far enough: The year after enacting the law under review, the State passed a 6-week restriction. A state senator who championed both Mississippi laws said the obvious out loud. "[A] lot of people thought," he explained, that "finally, we have" a conservative Court "and so now would be a good time to start testing the limits of *Roe*."[30] In its petition for certiorari, the State had exercised a smidgen of restraint. It had urged the Court merely to roll back *Roe* and *Casey*, specifically assuring the Court that "the questions presented in this petition do not require the Court to overturn" those precedents.   Pet. for Cert. 5; see *ante*, at 5–6 (ROBERTS, C. J., concurring in judgment).   But as Mississippi grew ever more confident in its prospects, it resolved to go all in. It urged the Court to overrule *Roe* and *Casey*. Nothing but everything would be enough.

Earlier this Term, this Court signaled that Mississippi's stratagem would succeed.   Texas was one of the fistful of States to have recently banned abortions after six weeks of pregnancy.   It added to that "flagrantly unconstitutional" restriction an unprecedented scheme to "evade judicial

---

[29] Guttmacher Institute, E. Nash, State Policy Trends 2021: The Worst Year for Abortion Rights in Almost Half a Century (Dec. 16, 2021), https://www.guttmacher.org/article/2021/12/state-policy-trends-2021-worst-year-abortion-rights-almost-half-century; Guttmacher Institute, E. Nash, L. Mohammed, O. Cappello, & S. Naide, State Policy Trends 2020: Reproductive Health and Rights in a Year Like No Other (Dec. 15, 2020), https://www.guttmacher.org/article/2020/12/state-policy-trends-2020-reproductive-health-and-rights-year-no-other; Guttmacher Institute, E. Nash, L. Mohammed, O. Cappello, & S. Naide, State Policy Trends 2019: A Wave of Abortion Bans, But Some States Are Fighting Back (Dec. 10, 2019), https://www.guttmacher.org/article/2019/12/state-policy-trends-2019-wave-abortion-bans-some-states-are-fighting-back.

[30] A. Pittman, Mississippi's Six-Week Abortion Ban at 5th Circuit Appeals Court Today, Jackson Free Press (Oct. 7, 2019), https://www.jacksonfreepress.com/news/2019/oct/07/mississippis-six-week-abortion-ban-5th-circuit-app/.

scrutiny." *Whole Woman's Health* v. *Jackson*, 594 U. S. ___,
___ (2021) (SOTOMAYOR, J., dissenting) (slip op., at 1). And
five Justices acceded to that cynical maneuver. They let
Texas defy this Court's constitutional rulings, nullifying
Roe and *Casey* ahead of schedule in the Nation's second
largest State.

And now the other shoe drops, courtesy of that same five-
person majority. (We believe that THE CHIEF JUSTICE's
opinion is wrong too, but no one should think that there is
not a large difference between upholding a 15-week ban on
the grounds he does and allowing States to prohibit abortion from the time of conception.) Now a new and bare majority of this Court—acting at practically the first moment
possible—overrules *Roe* and *Casey*. It converts a series of
dissenting opinions expressing antipathy toward *Roe* and
Casey into a decision greenlighting even total abortion
bans. See *ante*, at 57, 59, 63, and nn. 61–64 (relying on former dissents). It eliminates a 50-year-old constitutional
right that safeguards women's freedom and equal station.
It breaches a core rule-of-law principle, designed to promote
constancy in the law. In doing all of that, it places in jeopardy other rights, from contraception to same-sex intimacy
and marriage. And finally, it undermines the Court's legitimacy.

Casey itself made the last point in explaining why it
would not overrule *Roe*—though some members of its majority might not have joined *Roe* in the first instance. Just
as we did here, *Casey* explained the importance of *stare decisis*; the inappositeness of *West Coast Hotel* and *Brown*; the
absence of any "changed circumstances" (or other reason)
justifying the reversal of precedent. 505 U. S., at 864; see
supra, at 30–33, 37–47. "[T]he Court," *Casey* explained,
"could not pretend" that overruling *Roe* had any "justification beyond a present doctrinal disposition to come out differently from the Court of 1973." 505 U. S., at 864. And to
overrule for that reason? Quoting Justice Stewart, *Casey*

explained that to do so—to reverse prior law "upon a ground no firmer than a change in [the Court's] membership"— would invite the view that "this institution is little different from the two political branches of the Government." *Ibid.* No view, *Casey* thought, could do "more lasting injury to this Court and to the system of law which it is our abiding mission to serve." *Ibid.* For overruling *Roe*, *Casey* concluded, the Court would pay a "terrible price." 505 U. S., at 864.

The Justices who wrote those words—O'Connor, Kennedy, and Souter—they were judges of wisdom. They would not have won any contests for the kind of ideological purity some court watchers want Justices to deliver. But if there were awards for Justices who left this Court better than they found it? And who for that reason left this country better? And the rule of law stronger? Sign those Justices up.

They knew that "the legitimacy of the Court [is] earned over time." *Id.*, at 868. They also would have recognized that it can be destroyed much more quickly. They worked hard to avert that outcome in *Casey*. The American public, they thought, should never conclude that its constitutional protections hung by a thread—that a new majority, adhering to a new "doctrinal school," could "by dint of numbers" alone expunge their rights. *Id.*, at 864. It is hard—no, it is impossible—to conclude that anything else has happened here. One of us once said that "[i]t is not often in the law that so few have so quickly changed so much." S. Breyer, Breaking the Promise of *Brown*: The Resegregation of America's Schools 30 (2022). For all of us, in our time on this Court, that has never been more true than today. In overruling *Roe* and *Casey*, this Court betrays its guiding principles.

With sorrow—for this Court, but more, for the many millions of American women who have today lost a fundamental constitutional protection—we dissent.

APPENDIX

This Appendix analyzes in full each of the 28 cases the majority says support today's decision to overrule *Roe* v. *Wade*, 410 U. S. 113 (1973), and *Planned Parenthood of Southeastern Pa.* v. *Casey*, 505 U. S. 833 (1992). As explained herein, the Court in each case relied on traditional *stare decisis* factors in overruling.

A great many of the overrulings the majority cites involve a prior precedent that had been rendered out of step with or effectively abrogated by contemporary case law in light of intervening developments in the broader doctrine. See *Ramos* v. *Louisiana*, 590 U. S. ___, ___ (2020) (slip op., at 22) (holding the Sixth Amendment requires a unanimous jury verdict in state prosecutions for serious offenses, and overruling *Apodaca* v. *Oregon*, 406 U. S. 404 (1972), because "in the years since *Apodaca*, this Court ha[d] spoken inconsistently about its meaning" and had undercut its validity "on at least eight occasions"); *Ring* v. *Arizona*, 536 U. S. 584, 608–609 (2002) (recognizing a Sixth Amendment right to have a jury find the aggravating factors necessary to impose a death sentence and, in so doing, rejecting *Walton* v. *Arizona*, 497 U. S. 639 (1990), as overtaken by and irreconcilable with *Apprendi* v. *New Jersey*, 530 U. S. 466 (2000)); *Agostini* v. *Felton*, 521 U. S. 203, 235–236 (1997) (considering the Establishment Clause's constraint on government aid to religious instruction, and overruling *Aguilar* v. *Felton*, 473 U. S. 402 (1985), in light of several related doctrinal developments that had so undermined *Aguilar* and the assumption on which it rested as to render it no longer good law); *Batson* v. *Kentucky*, 476 U. S. 79, 93–96 (1986) (recognizing that a defendant may make a prima facie showing of purposeful racial discrimination in selection of a jury venire by relying solely on the facts in his case, and, based on subsequent developments in equal protection law, rejecting part of *Swain* v. *Alabama*, 380 U. S. 202 (1965), which had imposed a more demanding evidentiary burden); *Brandenburg* v. *Ohio*, 395 U. S. 444, 447–448 (1969) (*per curiam*) (holding that mere advocacy of violence is protected by the First Amendment, unless intended to incite it or produce imminent lawlessness, and rejecting the contrary rule in *Whitney* v. *California*, 274 U. S. 357 (1927), as having been "thoroughly discredited by later decisions"); *Katz* v. *United States*, 389 U. S. 347, 351, 353 (1967) (recognizing that the Fourth Amendment extends to material and communications that a person "seeks to preserve as private," and rejecting the more limited construction articulated in *Olmstead* v. *United States*, 277 U. S. 438 (1928), because "we have since departed from the narrow view on which that decision rested," and "the underpinnings of *Olmstead* . . . have been so eroded by our subsequent decisions that the 'trespass' doctrine there enunciated can no longer be regarded as controlling"); *Miranda* v. *Arizona*, 384 U. S. 436, 463–467, 479, n. 48 (1966) (recognizing that the Fifth Amendment requires certain procedural safeguards for custodial interrogation, and rejecting *Crooker* v. *California*, 357 U. S. 433 (1958), and *Cicenia* v. *Lagay*, 357 U. S. 504 (1958), which had already been undermined by *Escobedo* v. *Illinois*, 378 U. S. 478 (1964)); *Malloy* v. *Hogan*, 378 U. S. 1, 6–9 (1964) (explaining that the Fifth Amendment privilege against "self-incrimination is also protected by the Fourteenth Amendment against abridgment by the States," and rejecting *Twining* v. *New Jersey*, 211 U. S. 78 (1908), in light of a "marked shift" in Fifth Amendment precedents that had "necessarily repudiated" the prior decision); *Gideon* v. *Wainwright*, 372 U. S. 335, 343–345 (1963) (acknowledging a right to counsel for indigent criminal defendants in state court under the Sixth and Fourteenth Amendments, and overruling the earlier precedent failing to recognize such a right, *Betts* v. *Brady*, 316 U. S.

455 (1942));[31] *Smith* v. *Allwright*, 321 U. S. 649, 659–662 (1944) (recognizing all-white primaries are unconstitutional after reconsidering in light of "the unitary character of the electoral process" recognized in *United States* v. *Classic*, 313 U. S. 299 (1941), and overruling *Grovey* v. *Townsend*, 295 U. S. 45 (1935)); *United States* v. *Darby*, 312 U. S. 100, 115–117 (1941) (recognizing Congress's Commerce Clause power to regulate employment conditions and explaining as "inescapable" the "conclusion . . . that *Hammer* v. *Dagenhart*, [247 U. S. 251 (1918)]," and its contrary rule had "long since been" overtaken by precedent construing the Commerce Clause power more broadly); *Erie R. Co.* v. *Tompkins*, 304 U. S. 64, 78–80 (1938) (applying state substantive law in diversity actions in federal courts and overruling *Swift* v. *Tyson*, 16 Pet. 1 (1842), because an intervening decision had "made clear" the "fallacy underlying the rule").

Additional cases the majority cites involved fundamental factual changes that had undermined the basic premise of the prior precedent. See *Citizens United* v. *Federal Election Comm'n*, 558 U. S. 310, 364 (2010) (expanding First Amendment protections for campaign-related speech and citing technological changes that undermined the distinctions of the earlier regime and made workarounds easy, and overruling *Austin* v. *Michigan Chamber of Commerce*, 494 U. S. 652 (1990), and partially overruling *McConnell* v. *Federal Election Comm'n*, 540 U. S. 93 (2003)); *Crawford* v. *Washington*, 541 U. S. 36, 62–65 (2004) (expounding on the Sixth Amendment right to confront witnesses and rejecting the prior framework, based on its practical failing to keep

[31] We have since come to understand *Gideon* as part of a larger doctrinal shift—already underway at the time of *Gideon*—where "the Court began to hold that the Due Process Clause fully incorporates particular rights contained in the first eight Amendments." *McDonald* v. *Chicago*, 561 U. S. 742, 763 (2010); see also *id.*, at 766.

out core testimonial evidence, and overruling *Ohio* v. *Roberts*, 448 U. S. 56 (1980)); *Mapp* v. *Ohio*, 367 U. S. 643, 651–652 (1961) (holding that the exclusionary rule under the Fourth Amendment applies to the States, and overruling the contrary rule of *Wolf* v. *Colorado*, 338 U. S. 25 (1949), after considering and rejecting "the current validity of the factual grounds upon which *Wolf* was based").

Some cited overrulings involved *both* significant doctrinal developments *and* changed facts or understandings that had together undermined a basic premise of the prior decision. See *Janus* v. *State, County, and Municipal Employees*, 585 U. S. ___, ___, ___–___ (2018) (slip op., at 42, 47–49) (holding that requiring public-sector union dues from nonmembers violates the First Amendment, and overruling *Abood* v. *Detroit Bd. of Ed.*, 431 U. S. 209 (1977), based on "both factual and legal" developments that had "eroded the decision's underpinnings and left it an outlier among our First Amendment cases" (internal quotation marks omitted)); *Obergefell* v. *Hodges*, 576 U. S. 644, 659–663 (2015) (holding that the Fourteenth Amendment protects the right of same-sex couples to marry in light of doctrinal developments, as well as fundamentally changed social understanding); *Lawrence* v. *Texas*, 539 U. S. 558, 572–578 (2003) (overruling *Bowers* v. *Hardwick*, 478 U. S. 186 (1986), after finding anti-sodomy laws to be inconsistent with the Fourteenth Amendment in light of developments in the legal doctrine, as well as changed social understanding of sexuality); *United States* v. *Scott*, 437 U. S. 82, 101 (1978) (overruling *United States* v. *Jenkins*, 420 U. S. 358 (1975), three years after it was decided, because of developments in the Court's double jeopardy case law, and because intervening practice had shown that government appeals from midtrial dismissals requested by the defendant were practicable, desirable, and consistent with double jeopardy values); *Craig* v. *Boren*, 429 U. S. 190, 197–199, 210, n. 23 (1976) (holding that sex-based classifications are subject to intermediate scrutiny under the Fourteenth Amendment's Equal Protection Clause, including because *Reed* v. *Reed*, 404 U. S. 71 (1971), and other equal protection cases and social changes had overtaken any "inconsistent" suggestion in *Goesaert* v. *Cleary*, 335 U. S. 464 (1948)); *Taylor* v. *Louisiana*, 419 U. S. 522, 535–537 (1975) (recognizing as "a foregone conclusion from the pattern of some of the Court's cases over the past 30 years, as well as from legislative developments at both federal and state levels," that women could not be excluded from jury service, and explaining that the prior decision approving such practice, *Hoyt* v. *Florida*, 368 U. S. 57 (1961), had been rendered inconsistent with equal protection jurisprudence).

Other overrulings occurred very close in time to the original decision so did not engender substantial reliance and could not be described as having been "embedded" as "part of our national culture." *Dickerson* v. *United States*, 530 U. S. 428, 443 (2000); see *Payne* v. *Tennessee*, 501 U. S. 808 (1991) (revising procedural rules of evidence that had barred admission of certain victim-impact evidence during the penalty phase of capital cases, and overruling *South Carolina* v. *Gathers*, 490 U. S. 805 (1989), and *Booth* v. *Maryland*, 482 U. S. 496 (1987), which had been decided two and four years prior, respectively); *Seminole Tribe of Fla.* v. *Florida*, 517 U. S. 44 (1996) (holding that Congress cannot abrogate state-sovereign immunity under its Article I commerce power, and rejecting the result in *Pennsylvania* v. *Union Gas Co.*, 491 U. S. 1 (1989), seven years later; the decision in *Union Gas* never garnered a majority); *Garcia* v. *San Antonio Metropolitan Transit Authority*, 469 U. S. 528, 531 (1985) (holding that local governments are not constitutionally immune from federal employment laws, and overruling *National League of Cities* v. *Usery*, 426 U. S. 833 (1976), after "eight years" of experience under that regime showed *Usery*'s standard was unworkable and, in practice, undermined the federalism principles the decision sought

66 DOBBS v. JACKSON WOMEN'S HEALTH ORGANIZATION

highestAppendix to opinion of BREYER, SOTOMAYOR, and KAGAN, JJ.

to protect).

The rest of the cited cases were relatively minor in their effect, modifying part or an application of a prior precedent's test or analysis. See *Montejo* v. *Louisiana*, 556 U. S. 778 (2009) (citing workability and practical concerns with additional layers of prophylactic procedural safeguards for defendants' right to counsel, as had been enshrined in *Michigan* v. *Jackson*, 475 U. S. 625 (1986)); *Illinois* v. *Gates*, 462 U. S. 213, 227–228 (1983) (replacing a two-pronged test under *Aguilar* v. *Texas*, 378 U. S. 108 (1964), and *Spinelli* v. *United States*, 393 U. S. 410 (1969), in favor of a traditional totality-of-the-circumstances approach to evaluate probable cause for issuance of a warrant); *Wesberry* v. *Sanders*, 376 U. S. 1, 4 (1964), and *Baker* v. *Carr*, 369 U. S. 186, 202 (1962) (clarifying that the "political question" passage of the minority opinion in *Colegrove* v. *Green*, 328 U. S. 549 (1946), was not controlling law).

In sum, none of the cases the majority cites is analogous to today's decision to overrule 50- and 30-year-old watershed constitutional precedents that remain unweakened by any changes of law or fact.

Syllabus

NOTE: Where it is feasible, a syllabus (headnote) will be released, as is being done in connection with this case, at the time the opinion is issued. The syllabus constitutes no part of the opinion of the Court but has been prepared by the Reporter of Decisions for the convenience of the reader. See *United States* v. *Detroit Timber & Lumber Co.,* 200 U. S. 321, 337.

SUPREME COURT OF THE UNITED STATES

Syllabus

DOBBS, STATE HEALTH OFFICER OF THE MISSISSIPPI DEPARTMENT OF HEALTH, ET AL. *v.* JACKSON WOMEN'S HEALTH ORGANIZATION ET AL.

CERTIORARI TO THE UNITED STATES COURT OF APPEALS FOR THE FIFTH CIRCUIT

No. 19–1392.   Argued December 1, 2021—Decided June 24, 2022

Mississippi's Gestational Age Act provides that "[e]xcept in a medical emergency or in the case of a severe fetal abnormality, a person shall not intentionally or knowingly perform . . . or induce an abortion of an unborn human being if the probable gestational age of the unborn human being has been determined to be greater than fifteen (15) weeks." Miss. Code Ann. §41–41–191. Respondents—Jackson Women's Health Organization, an abortion clinic, and one of its doctors—challenged the Act in Federal District Court, alleging that it violated this Court's precedents establishing a constitutional right to abortion, in particular *Roe* v. *Wade,* 410 U. S. 113, and *Planned Parenthood of Southeastern Pa.* v. *Casey,* 505 U. S. 833. The District Court granted summary judgment in favor of respondents and permanently enjoined enforcement of the Act, reasoning that Mississippi's 15-week restriction on abortion violates this Court's cases forbidding States to ban abortion pre-viability. The Fifth Circuit affirmed. Before this Court, petitioners defend the Act on the grounds that *Roe* and *Casey* were wrongly decided and that the Act is constitutional because it satisfies rational-basis review.

Held: The Constitution does not confer a right to abortion; *Roe* and *Casey* are overruled; and the authority to regulate abortion is returned to the people and their elected representatives. Pp. 8–79.

    (a) The critical question is whether the Constitution, properly understood, confers a right to obtain an abortion. *Casey*'s controlling opinion skipped over that question and reaffirmed *Roe* solely on the basis of *stare decisis*. A proper application of *stare decisis*, however, requires an assessment of the strength of the grounds on which *Roe* was based. The Court therefore turns to the question that the *Casey* plurality did not consider. Pp. 8–32.

(1) First, the Court reviews the standard that the Court's cases have used to determine whether the Fourteenth Amendment's reference to "liberty" protects a particular right. The Constitution makes no express reference to a right to obtain an abortion, but several constitutional provisions have been offered as potential homes for an implicit constitutional right. *Roe* held that the abortion right is part of a right to privacy that springs from the First, Fourth, Fifth, Ninth, and Fourteenth Amendments. See 410 U. S., at 152–153. The *Casey* Court grounded its decision solely on the theory that the right to obtain an abortion is part of the "liberty" protected by the Fourteenth Amendment's Due Process Clause. Others have suggested that support can be found in the Fourteenth Amendment's Equal Protection Clause, but that theory is squarely foreclosed by the Court's precedents, which establish that a State's regulation of abortion is not a sex-based classification and is thus not subject to the heightened scrutiny that applies to such classifications. See *Geduldig* v. *Aiello*, 417 U. S. 484, 496, n. 20; *Bray* v. *Alexandria Women's Health Clinic*, 506 U. S. 263, 273–274. Rather, regulations and prohibitions of abortion are governed by the same standard of review as other health and safety measures. Pp. 9–11.

(2) Next, the Court examines whether the right to obtain an abortion is rooted in the Nation's history and tradition and whether it is an essential component of "ordered liberty." The Court finds that the right to abortion is not deeply rooted in the Nation's history and tradition. The underlying theory on which *Casey* rested—that the Fourteenth Amendment's Due Process Clause provides substantive, as well as procedural, protection for "liberty"—has long been controversial.

The Court's decisions have held that the Due Process Clause protects two categories of substantive rights—those rights guaranteed by the first eight Amendments to the Constitution and those rights deemed fundamental that are not mentioned anywhere in the Constitution. In deciding whether a right falls into either of these categories, the question is whether the right is "deeply rooted in [our] history and tradition" and whether it is essential to this Nation's "scheme of ordered liberty." *Timbs* v. *Indiana*, 586 U. S. ___, ___ (internal quotation marks omitted). The term "liberty" alone provides little guidance. Thus, historical inquiries are essential whenever the Court is asked to recognize a new component of the "liberty" interest protected by the Due Process Clause. In interpreting what is meant by "liberty," the Court must guard against the natural human tendency to confuse what the Fourteenth Amendment protects with the Court's own ardent views about the liberty that Americans should enjoy. For this reason, the Court has been "reluctant" to recognize rights that are not mentioned in the Constitution. *Collins* v. *Harker Heights*, 503 U. S. 115, 125.

Guided by the history and tradition that map the essential components of the Nation's concept of ordered liberty, the Court finds the Fourteenth Amendment clearly does not protect the right to an abortion. Until the latter part of the 20th century, there was no support in American law for a constitutional right to obtain an abortion. No state constitutional provision had recognized such a right. Until a few years before *Roe*, no federal or state court had recognized such a right. Nor had any scholarly treatise. Indeed, abortion had long been a *crime* in every single State. At common law, abortion was criminal in at least some stages of pregnancy and was regarded as unlawful and could have very serious consequences at all stages. American law followed the common law until a wave of statutory restrictions in the 1800s expanded criminal liability for abortions. By the time the Fourteenth Amendment was adopted, three-quarters of the States had made abortion a crime at any stage of pregnancy. This consensus endured until the day *Roe* was decided. *Roe* either ignored or misstated this history, and *Casey* declined to reconsider *Roe*'s faulty historical analysis.

Respondents' argument that this history does not matter flies in the face of the standard the Court has applied in determining whether an asserted right that is nowhere mentioned in the Constitution is nevertheless protected by the Fourteenth Amendment. The Solicitor General repeats *Roe*'s claim that it is "doubtful . . . abortion was ever firmly established as a common-law crime even with respect to the destruction of a quick fetus," 410 U. S., at 136, but the great common-law authorities—Bracton, Coke, Hale, and Blackstone—all wrote that a post-quickening abortion was a crime. Moreover, many authorities asserted that even a pre-quickening abortion was "unlawful" and that, as a result, an abortionist was guilty of murder if the woman died from the attempt. The Solicitor General suggests that history supports an abortion right because of the common law's failure to criminalize abortion before quickening, but the insistence on quickening was not universal, see *Mills* v. *Commonwealth*, 13 Pa. 631, 633; *State* v. *Slagle*, 83 N. C. 630, 632, and regardless, the fact that many States in the late 18th and early 19th century did not criminalize pre-quickening abortions does not mean that anyone thought the States lacked the authority to do so.

Instead of seriously pressing the argument that the abortion right itself has deep roots, supporters of *Roe* and *Casey* contend that the abortion right is an integral part of a broader entrenched right. *Roe* termed this a right to privacy, 410 U. S., at 154, and *Casey* described it as the freedom to make "intimate and personal choices" that are "central to personal dignity and autonomy," 505 U. S., at 851. Ordered liberty sets limits and defines the boundary between competing interests. *Roe* and *Casey* each struck a particular balance between the interests of a woman who wants an abortion and the interests of what they termed "potential life." *Roe*, 410 U. S., at 150; *Casey*, 505 U. S., at 852. But the people of the various States may evaluate those interests differently. The Nation's historical understanding of ordered liberty does not prevent the people's elected representatives from deciding how abortion should be regulated. Pp. 11–30.

(3) Finally, the Court considers whether a right to obtain an abortion is part of a broader entrenched right that is supported by other precedents. The Court concludes the right to obtain an abortion cannot be justified as a component of such a right. Attempts to justify abortion through appeals to a broader right to autonomy and to define one's "concept of existence" prove too much. *Casey*, 505 U. S., at 851. Those criteria, at a high level of generality, could license fundamental rights to illicit drug use, prostitution, and the like. What sharply distinguishes the abortion right from the rights recognized in the cases on which *Roe* and *Casey* rely is something that both those decisions acknowledged: Abortion is different because it destroys what *Roe* termed "potential life" and what the law challenged in this case calls an "unborn human being." None of the other decisions cited by *Roe* and *Casey* involved the critical moral question posed by abortion. Accordingly, those cases do not support the right to obtain an abortion, and the Court's conclusion that the Constitution does not confer such a right does not undermine them in any way. Pp. 30–32.

(b) The doctrine of *stare decisis* does not counsel continued acceptance of *Roe* and *Casey*. *Stare decisis* plays an important role and protects the interests of those who have taken action in reliance on a past decision. It "reduces incentives for challenging settled precedents, saving parties and courts the expense of endless relitigation." *Kimble* v. *Marvel Entertainment, LLC*, 576 U. S. 446, 455. It "contributes to the actual and perceived integrity of the judicial process." *Payne* v. *Tennessee*, 501 U. S. 808, 827. And it restrains judicial hubris by respecting the judgment of those who grappled with important questions in the past. But *stare decisis* is not an inexorable command, *Pearson* v. *Callahan*, 555 U. S. 223, 233, and "is at its weakest when [the Court] interpret[s] the Constitution," *Agostini* v. *Felton*, 521 U. S. 203, 235. Some of the Court's most important constitutional decisions have overruled prior precedents. See, *e.g.*, *Brown* v. *Board of Education*, 347 U. S. 483, 491 (overruling the infamous decision in *Plessy* v. *Ferguson*, 163 U. S. 537, and its progeny).

The Court's cases have identified factors that should be considered in deciding when a precedent should be overruled. *Janus* v. *State, County, and Municipal Employees*, 585 U. S. ___, ___–___. Five factors

discussed below weigh strongly in favor of overruling *Roe* and *Casey*.
Pp. 39–66.

    (1) *The nature of the Court's error.* Like the infamous decision in
Plessy v. *Ferguson*, *Roe* was also egregiously wrong and on a collision
course with the Constitution from the day it was decided. *Casey* perpetuated its errors, calling both sides of the national controversy to
resolve their debate, but in doing so, *Casey* necessarily declared a winning side. Those on the losing side—those who sought to advance the
State's interest in fetal life—could no longer seek to persuade their
elected representatives to adopt policies consistent with their views.
The Court short-circuited the democratic process by closing it to the
large number of Americans who disagreed with *Roe*. Pp. 43–45.

    (2) *The quality of the reasoning.* Without any grounding in the
constitutional text, history, or precedent, *Roe* imposed on the entire
country a detailed set of rules for pregnancy divided into trimesters
much like those that one might expect to find in a statute or regulation.
See 410 U. S., at 163–164. *Roe*'s failure even to note the overwhelming
consensus of state laws in effect in 1868 is striking, and what it said
about the common law was simply wrong. Then, after surveying history, the opinion spent many paragraphs conducting the sort of fact-
finding that might be undertaken by a legislative committee, and did
not explain why the sources on which it relied shed light on the meaning of the Constitution. As to precedent, citing a broad array of cases,
the Court found support for a constitutional "right of personal privacy."
Id., at 152. But *Roe* conflated the right to shield information from disclosure and the right to make and implement important personal decisions without governmental interference. See *Whalen* v. *Roe*, 429
U. S. 589, 599–600. None of these decisions involved what is distinctive about abortion: its effect on what *Roe* termed "potential life."
When the Court summarized the basis for the scheme it imposed on
the country, it asserted that its rules were "consistent with," among
other things, "the relative weights of the respective interests involved"
and "the demands of the profound problems of the present day." *Roe*,
410 U. S., at 165. These are precisely the sort of considerations that
legislative bodies often take into account when they draw lines that
accommodate competing interests. The scheme *Roe* produced *looked*
like legislation, and the Court provided the sort of explanation that
might be expected from a legislative body. An even more glaring deficiency was *Roe*'s failure to justify the critical distinction it drew between pre- and post-viability abortions. See *id.*, at 163. The arbitrary
viability line, which *Casey* termed *Roe*'s central rule, has not found
much support among philosophers and ethicists who have attempted
to justify a right to abortion. The most obvious problem with any such

argument is that viability has changed over time and is heavily dependent on factors—such as medical advances and the availability of
quality medical care—that have nothing to do with the characteristics
of a fetus.

When *Casey* revisited *Roe* almost 20 years later, it reaffirmed *Roe*'s
central holding, but pointedly refrained from endorsing most of its reasoning. The Court abandoned any reliance on a privacy right and instead grounded the abortion right entirely on the Fourteenth Amendment's Due Process Clause. 505 U. S., at 846. The controlling opinion
criticized and rejected *Roe*'s trimester scheme, 505 U. S., at 872, and
substituted a new and obscure "undue burden" test. *Casey*, in short,
either refused to reaffirm or rejected important aspects of *Roe*'s analysis, failed to remedy glaring deficiencies in *Roe*'s reasoning, endorsed
what it termed *Roe*'s central holding while suggesting that a majority
might not have thought it was correct, provided no new support for the
abortion right other than *Roe*'s status as precedent, and imposed a new
test with no firm grounding in constitutional text, history, or precedent. Pp. 45–56.

(3) *Workability.* Deciding whether a precedent should be overruled depends in part on whether the rule it imposes is workable—that
is, whether it can be understood and applied in a consistent and predictable manner. *Casey*'s "undue burden" test has scored poorly on the
workability scale. The *Casey* plurality tried to put meaning into the
"undue burden" test by setting out three subsidiary rules, but these
rules created their own problems. And the difficulty of applying *Casey*'s new rules surfaced in that very case. Compare 505 U. S., at 881–
887, with *id.*, at 920–922 (Stevens, J., concurring in part and dissenting in part). The experience of the Courts of Appeals provides further
evidence that *Casey*'s "line between" permissible and unconstitutional
restrictions "has proved to be impossible to draw with precision." *Janus*, 585 U. S., at ___. *Casey* has generated a long list of Circuit conflicts. Continued adherence to *Casey*'s unworkable "undue burden"
test would undermine, not advance, the "evenhanded, predictable, and
consistent development of legal principles." *Payne*, 501 U. S., at 827.
Pp. 56–62.

(4) *Effect on other areas of law.* *Roe* and *Casey* have led to the
distortion of many important but unrelated legal doctrines, and that
effect provides further support for overruling those decisions. See *Ramos* v. *Louisiana*, 590 U. S. ___, ___ (KAVANAUGH, J., concurring in
part). Pp. 62–63.

(5) *Reliance interests.* Overruling *Roe* and *Casey* will not upend
concrete reliance interests like those that develop in "cases involving
property and contract rights." *Payne*, 501 U. S., at 828. In *Casey*, the
controlling opinion conceded that traditional reliance interests were

not implicated because getting an abortion is generally "unplanned activity," and "reproductive planning could take virtually immediate account of any sudden restoration of state authority to ban abortions." 505 U. S., at 856. Instead, the opinion perceived a more intangible form of reliance, namely, that "people [had] organized intimate relationships and made choices that define their views of themselves and their places in society . . . in reliance on the availability of abortion in the event that contraception should fail" and that "[t]he ability of women to participate equally in the economic and social life of the Nation has been facilitated by their ability to control their reproductive lives." *Ibid.* The contending sides in this case make impassioned and conflicting arguments about the effects of the abortion right on the lives of women as well as the status of the fetus. The *Casey* plurality's speculative attempt to weigh the relative importance of the interests of the fetus and the mother represent a departure from the "original constitutional proposition" that "courts do not substitute their social and economic beliefs for the judgment of legislative bodies." *Ferguson* v. *Skrupa,* 372 U. S. 726, 729–730.

The Solicitor General suggests that overruling *Roe* and *Casey* would threaten the protection of other rights under the Due Process Clause. The Court emphasizes that this decision concerns the constitutional right to abortion and no other right. Nothing in this opinion should be understood to cast doubt on precedents that do not concern abortion. Pp. 63–66.

(c) *Casey* identified another concern, namely, the danger that the public will perceive a decision overruling a controversial "watershed" decision, such as *Roe,* as influenced by political considerations or public opinion. 505 U. S., at 866–867. But the Court cannot allow its decisions to be affected by such extraneous concerns. A precedent of this Court is subject to the usual principles of *stare decisis* under which adherence to precedent is the norm but not an inexorable command. If the rule were otherwise, erroneous decisions like *Plessy* would still be the law. The Court's job is to interpret the law, apply longstanding principles of *stare decisis,* and decide this case accordingly. Pp. 66–69.

(d) Under the Court's precedents, rational-basis review is the appropriate standard to apply when state abortion regulations undergo constitutional challenge. Given that procuring an abortion is not a fundamental constitutional right, it follows that the States may regulate abortion for legitimate reasons, and when such regulations are challenged under the Constitution, courts cannot "substitute their social and economic beliefs for the judgment of legislative bodies." *Ferguson,* 372 U. S., at 729–730. That applies even when the laws at issue concern matters of great social significance and moral substance. A law regulating abortion, like other health and welfare laws, is entitled to a

Syllabus

"strong presumption of validity." *Heller* v. *Doe,* 509 U. S. 312, 319. It must be sustained if there is a rational basis on which the legislature could have thought that it would serve legitimate state interests. *Id.,* at 320.

Mississippi's Gestational Age Act is supported by the Mississippi Legislature's specific findings, which include the State's asserted interest in "protecting the life of the unborn." §2(b)(i). These legitimate interests provide a rational basis for the Gestational Age Act, and it follows that respondents' constitutional challenge must fail. Pp. 76–78.

(e) Abortion presents a profound moral question. The Constitution does not prohibit the citizens of each State from regulating or prohibiting abortion. *Roe* and *Casey* arrogated that authority. The Court overrules those decisions and returns that authority to the people and their elected representatives. Pp. 78–79.

945 F. 3d 265, reversed and remanded.

ALITO, J., delivered the opinion of the Court, in which THOMAS, GORSUCH, KAVANAUGH, and BARRETT, JJ., joined. THOMAS, J., and KAVANAUGH, J., filed concurring opinions. ROBERTS, C. J., filed an opinion concurring in the judgment. BREYER, SOTOMAYOR, and KAGAN, JJ., filed a dissenting opinion.

SUPREME COURT OF THE UNITED STATES

No. 19–1392

THOMAS E. DOBBS, STATE HEALTH OFFICER OF THE MISSISSIPPI DEPARTMENT OF HEALTH, ET AL., PETITIONERS v. JACKSON WOMEN'S HEALTH ORGANIZATION, ET AL.

ON WRIT OF CERTIORARI TO THE UNITED STATES COURT OF
APPEALS FOR THE FIFTH CIRCUIT

[June 24, 2022]

JUSTICE ALITO delivered the opinion of the Court.

Abortion presents a profound moral issue on which Americans hold sharply conflicting views. Some believe fervently that a human person comes into being at conception and that abortion ends an innocent life. Others feel just as strongly that any regulation of abortion invades a woman's right to control her own body and prevents women from achieving full equality. Still others in a third group think that abortion should be allowed under some but not all circumstances, and those within this group hold a variety of views about the particular restrictions that should be imposed.

For the first 185 years after the adoption of the Constitution, each State was permitted to address this issue in accordance with the views of its citizens. Then, in 1973, this Court decided *Roe* v. *Wade*, 410 U. S. 113. Even though the Constitution makes no mention of abortion, the Court held that it confers a broad right to obtain one. It did not claim that American law or the common law had ever recognized such a right, and its survey of history ranged from the constitutionally irrelevant (*e.g.*, its discussion of abortion in antiquity) to the plainly incorrect (*e.g.*, its assertion that abortion was probably never a crime under the common law). After cataloging a wealth of other information having no bearing on the meaning of the Constitution, the opinion concluded with a numbered set of rules much like those that might be found in a statute enacted by a legislature.

Under this scheme, each trimester of pregnancy was regulated differently, but the most critical line was drawn at roughly the end of the second trimester, which, at the time, corresponded to the point at which a fetus was thought to achieve "viability," *i.e.*, the ability to survive outside the womb. Although the Court acknowledged that States had a legitimate interest in protecting "potential life,"[1] it found that this interest could not justify any restriction on previability abortions. The Court did not explain the basis for this line, and even abortion supporters have found it hard to defend *Roe*'s reasoning. One prominent constitutional scholar wrote that he "would vote for a statute very much like the one the Court end[ed] up drafting" if he were "a legislator," but his assessment of *Roe* was memorable and brutal: *Roe* was "not constitutional law" at all and gave "almost no sense of an obligation to try to be."[2]

At the time of *Roe*, 30 States still prohibited abortion at all stages. In the years prior to that decision, about a third of the States had liberalized their laws, but *Roe* abruptly ended that political process. It imposed the same highly restrictive regime on the entire Nation, and it effectively struck down the abortion laws of every single State.[3] As

---

[1] *Roe* v. *Wade*, 410 U. S. 113, 163 (1973).

[2] J. Ely, The Wages of Crying Wolf: A Comment on *Roe* v. *Wade*, 82 Yale L. J. 920, 926, 947 (1973) (Ely) (emphasis deleted).

[3] L. Tribe, Foreword: Toward a Model of Roles in the Due Process of Life and Law, 87 Harv. L. Rev. 1, 2 (1973) (Tribe).

Justice Byron White aptly put it in his dissent, the decision represented the "exercise of raw judicial power," 410 U. S., at 222, and it sparked a national controversy that has embittered our political culture for a half century.[4]

Eventually, in *Planned Parenthood of Southeastern Pa.* v. *Casey*, 505 U. S. 833 (1992), the Court revisited *Roe*, but the Members of the Court split three ways. Two Justices expressed no desire to change *Roe* in any way.[5] Four others wanted to overrule the decision in its entirety.[6] And the three remaining Justices, who jointly signed the controlling opinion, took a third position.[7] Their opinion did not endorse *Roe*'s reasoning, and it even hinted that one or more of its authors might have "reservations" about whether the Constitution protects a right to abortion.[8] But the opinion concluded that *stare decisis*, which calls for prior decisions to be followed in most instances, required adherence to what it called *Roe*'s "central holding"—that a State may not constitutionally protect fetal life before "viability"—even if that holding was wrong.[9] Anything less, the opinion claimed, would undermine respect for this Court and the rule of law.

Paradoxically, the judgment in *Casey* did a fair amount of overruling. Several important abortion decisions were

---

[4]See R. Ginsburg, Speaking in a Judicial Voice, 67 N. Y. U. L. Rev. 1185, 1208 (1992) ("*Roe* . . . halted a political process that was moving in a reform direction and thereby, I believed, prolonged divisiveness and deferred stable settlement of the issue").

[5]See 505 U. S., at 911 (Stevens, J., concurring in part and dissenting in part); *id.,* at 922 (Blackmun, J., concurring in part, concurring in judgment in part, and dissenting in part).

[6]See *id.,* at 944 (Rehnquist, C. J., concurring in judgment in part and dissenting in part); *id.,* at 979 (Scalia, J., concurring in judgment in part and dissenting in part).

[7]See *id.,* at 843 (joint opinion of O'Connor, Kennedy, and Souter, JJ.).

[8]*Id.,* at 853.

[9]*Id.,* at 860.

Opinion of the Court

overruled *in toto*, and *Roe* itself was overruled in part.[10] *Casey* threw out *Roe*'s trimester scheme and substituted a new rule of uncertain origin under which States were forbidden to adopt any regulation that imposed an "undue burden" on a woman's right to have an abortion.[11] The decision provided no clear guidance about the difference between a "due" and an "undue" burden. But the three Justices who authored the controlling opinion "call[ed] the contending sides of a national controversy to end their national division" by treating the Court's decision as the final settlement of the question of the constitutional right to abortion.[12]

As has become increasingly apparent in the intervening years, *Casey* did not achieve that goal. Americans continue to hold passionate and widely divergent views on abortion, and state legislatures have acted accordingly. Some have recently enacted laws allowing abortion, with few restrictions, at all stages of pregnancy. Others have tightly restricted abortion beginning well before viability. And in this case, 26 States have expressly asked this Court to overrule *Roe* and *Casey* and allow the States to regulate or prohibit pre-viability abortions.

Before us now is one such state law. The State of Mississippi asks us to uphold the constitutionality of a law that generally prohibits an abortion after the 15th week of pregnancy—several weeks before the point at which a fetus is now regarded as "viable" outside the womb. In defending this law, the State's primary argument is that we should reconsider and overrule *Roe* and *Casey* and once again allow each State to regulate abortion as its citizens wish. On the other side, respondents and the Solicitor General ask us to

---

[10] *Id.*, at 861, 870, 873 (overruling *Akron* v. *Akron Center for Reproductive Health, Inc.*, 462 U. S. 416 (1983), and *Thornburgh* v. *American College of Obstetricians and Gynecologists*, 476 U. S. 747 (1986)).

[11] 505 U. S., at 874.

[12] *Id.*, at 867.

reaffirm *Roe* and *Casey*, and they contend that the Mississippi law cannot stand if we do so. Allowing Mississippi to prohibit abortions after 15 weeks of pregnancy, they argue, "would be no different than overruling *Casey* and *Roe* entirely." Brief for Respondents 43. They contend that "no half-measures" are available and that we must either reaffirm or overrule *Roe* and *Casey.* Brief for Respondents 50.

We hold that *Roe* and *Casey* must be overruled. The Constitution makes no reference to abortion, and no such right is implicitly protected by any constitutional provision, including the one on which the defenders of *Roe* and *Casey* now chiefly rely—the Due Process Clause of the Fourteenth Amendment. That provision has been held to guarantee some rights that are not mentioned in the Constitution, but any such right must be "deeply rooted in this Nation's history and tradition" and "implicit in the concept of ordered liberty." *Washington* v. *Glucksberg,* 521 U. S. 702, 721 (1997) (internal quotation marks omitted).

The right to abortion does not fall within this category. Until the latter part of the 20th century, such a right was entirely unknown in American law. Indeed, when the Fourteenth Amendment was adopted, three quarters of the States made abortion a crime at all stages of pregnancy. The abortion right is also critically different from any other right that this Court has held to fall within the Fourteenth Amendment's protection of "liberty." *Roe*'s defenders characterize the abortion right as similar to the rights recognized in past decisions involving matters such as intimate sexual relations, contraception, and marriage, but abortion is fundamentally different, as both *Roe* and *Casey* acknowledged, because it destroys what those decisions called "fetal life" and what the law now before us describes as an "unborn human being."[13]

Stare decisis, the doctrine on which *Casey*'s controlling

_____
[13] Miss. Code Ann. §41–41–191(4)(b) (2018).

opinion was based, does not compel unending adherence to *Roe*'s abuse of judicial authority. *Roe* was egregiously wrong from the start. Its reasoning was exceptionally weak, and the decision has had damaging consequences. And far from bringing about a national settlement of the abortion issue, *Roe* and *Casey* have enflamed debate and deepened division.

It is time to heed the Constitution and return the issue of abortion to the people's elected representatives. "The permissibility of abortion, and the limitations, upon it, are to be resolved like most important questions in our democracy: by citizens trying to persuade one another and then voting." *Casey*, 505 U. S., at 979 (Scalia, J., concurring in judgment in part and dissenting in part). That is what the Constitution and the rule of law demand.

I

The law at issue in this case, Mississippi's Gestational Age Act, see Miss. Code Ann. §41–41–191 (2018), contains this central provision: "Except in a medical emergency or in the case of a severe fetal abnormality, a person shall not intentionally or knowingly perform . . . or induce an abortion of an unborn human being if the probable gestational age of the unborn human being has been determined to be greater than fifteen (15) weeks." §4(b).[14]

To support this Act, the legislature made a series of factual findings. It began by noting that, at the time of enactment, only six countries besides the United States "permit[ted] nontherapeutic or elective abortion-on-demand after the twentieth week of gestation."[15] §2(a). The legisla-

---

[14] The Act defines "gestational age" to be "the age of an unborn human being as calculated from the first day of the last menstrual period of the pregnant woman." §3(f).

[15] Those other six countries were Canada, China, the Netherlands,

Opinion of the Court

ture then found that at 5 or 6 weeks' gestational age an "unborn human being's heart begins beating"; at 8 weeks the "unborn human being begins to move about in the womb"; at 9 weeks "all basic physiological functions are present"; at 10 weeks "vital organs begin to function," and "[h]air, fingernails, and toenails . . . begin to form"; at 11 weeks "an unborn human being's diaphragm is developing," and he or she may "move about freely in the womb"; and at 12 weeks the "unborn human being" has "taken on 'the human form' in all relevant respects." §2(b)(i) (quoting *Gonzales* v. *Carhart*, 550 U. S. 124, 160 (2007)). It found that most abortions after 15 weeks employ "dilation and evacuation procedures which involve the use of surgical instruments to crush and tear the unborn child," and it concluded that the "intentional commitment of such acts for nontherapeutic or elective reasons is a barbaric practice, dangerous for the maternal patient, and demeaning to the medical profession." §2(b)(i)(8).

Respondents are an abortion clinic, Jackson Women's Health Organization, and one of its doctors. On the day the Gestational Age Act was enacted, respondents filed suit in Federal District Court against various Mississippi officials, alleging that the Act violated this Court's precedents establishing a constitutional right to abortion. The District

---

North Korea, Singapore, and Vietnam. See A. Baglini, Charlotte Lozier Institute, Gestational Limits on Abortion in the United States Compared to International Norms 6–7 (2014); M. Lee, Is the United States One of Seven Countries That "Allow Elective Abortions After 20 Weeks of Pregnancy?" Wash. Post (Oct. 8, 2017), www.washingtonpost.com/news/fact-checker/wp/2017/10/09/is-the-united-states-one-of-seven-countries-that-allow-elective-abortions-after-20-weeks-of-preganacy (stating that the claim made by the Mississippi Legislature and the Charlotte Lozier Institute was "backed by data"). A more recent compilation from the Center for Reproductive Rights indicates that Iceland and Guinea-Bissau are now also similarly permissive. See The World's Abortion Laws, Center for Reproductive Rights (Feb. 23, 2021), https://reproductiverights.org/maps/worlds-abortion-laws/.

Court granted summary judgment in favor of respondents and permanently enjoined enforcement of the Act, reasoning that "viability marks the earliest point at which the State's interest in fetal life is constitutionally adequate to justify a legislative ban on nontherapeutic abortions" and that 15 weeks' gestational age is "prior to viability." *Jackson Women's Health Org. v. Currier*, 349 F. Supp. 3d 536, 539–540 (SD Miss. 2019) (internal quotation marks omitted). The Fifth Circuit affirmed. 945 F. 3d 265 (2019).

We granted certiorari, 593 U. S. ___ (2021), to resolve the question whether "all pre-viability prohibitions on elective abortions are unconstitutional," Pet. for Cert. i. Petitioners' primary defense of the Mississippi Gestational Age Act is that *Roe* and *Casey* were wrongly decided and that "the Act is constitutional because it satisfies rational-basis review." Brief for Petitioners 49. Respondents answer that allowing Mississippi to ban pre-viability abortions "would be no different than overruling *Casey* and *Roe* entirely." Brief for Respondents 43. They tell us that "no half-measures" are available: We must either reaffirm or overrule *Roe* and *Casey*. Brief for Respondents 50.

II

We begin by considering the critical question whether the Constitution, properly understood, confers a right to obtain an abortion. Skipping over that question, the controlling opinion in *Casey* reaffirmed *Roe*'s "central holding" based solely on the doctrine of *stare decisis*, but as we will explain, proper application of *stare decisis* required an assessment of the strength of the grounds on which *Roe* was based. See *infra,* at 45–56.

We therefore turn to the question that the *Casey* plurality did not consider, and we address that question in three steps. First, we explain the standard that our cases have used in determining whether the Fourteenth Amendment's reference to "liberty" protects a particular right. Second, we examine whether the right at issue in this case is rooted in our Nation's history and tradition and whether it is an essential component of what we have described as "ordered liberty." Finally, we consider whether a right to obtain an abortion is part of a broader entrenched right that is supported by other precedents.

A

1

Constitutional analysis must begin with "the language of the instrument," *Gibbons* v. *Ogden*, 9 Wheat. 1, 186–189 (1824), which offers a "fixed standard" for ascertaining what our founding document means, 1 J. Story, Commentaries on the Constitution of the United States §399, p. 383 (1833). The Constitution makes no express reference to a right to obtain an abortion, and therefore those who claim that it protects such a right must show that the right is somehow implicit in the constitutional text.

Roe, however, was remarkably loose in its treatment of the constitutional text. It held that the abortion right, which is not mentioned in the Constitution, is part of a right to privacy, which is also not mentioned. See 410 U. S., at 152–153. And that privacy right, *Roe* observed, had been found to spring from no fewer than five different constitutional provisions—the First, Fourth, Fifth, Ninth, and Fourteenth Amendments. *Id.,* at 152.

The Court's discussion left open at least three ways in which some combination of these provisions could protect the abortion right. One possibility was that the right was "founded . . . in the Ninth Amendment's reservation of rights to the people." *Id.,* at 153. Another was that the right was rooted in the First, Fourth, or Fifth Amendment, or in some combination of those provisions, and that this right had been "incorporated" into the Due Process Clause of the Fourteenth Amendment just as many other Bill of Rights provisions had by then been incorporated. *Ibid*; see also *McDonald* v. *Chicago*, 561 U. S. 742, 763–766 (2010) (majority opinion) (discussing incorporation). And a third path was that the First, Fourth, and Fifth Amendments played no role and that the right was simply a component of the "liberty" protected by the Fourteenth Amendment's Due Process Clause. *Roe*, 410 U. S., at 153. *Roe* expressed the "feel[ing]" that the Fourteenth Amendment was the provision that did the work, but its message seemed to be that the abortion right could be found *somewhere* in the Constitution and that specifying its exact location was not of paramount importance.[16] The *Casey* Court did not defend this unfocused analysis and instead grounded its decision solely on the theory that the right to obtain an abortion is part of the "liberty" protected by the Fourteenth Amendment's Due Process Clause.

We discuss this theory in depth below, but before doing so, we briefly address one additional constitutional provision that some of respondents' *amici* have now offered as yet another potential home for the abortion right: the Fourteenth Amendment's Equal Protection Clause. See Brief for United States as *Amicus Curiae* 24 (Brief for United States); see also Brief for Equal Protection Constitutional Law Scholars as *Amici Curiae*. Neither *Roe* nor *Casey* saw fit to invoke this theory, and it is squarely foreclosed by our precedents, which establish that a State's regulation of abortion is not a sex-based classification and is thus not subject to the "heightened scrutiny" that applies to such classifications.[17] The regulation of a medical procedure that

_____

[16] The Court's words were as follows: "This right of privacy, whether it be founded in the Fourteenth Amendment's concept of personal liberty and restrictions upon state action, as we feel it is, or, as the District Court determined, in the Ninth Amendment's reservation of rights to the people, is broad enough to encompass a woman's decision whether or not to terminate her pregnancy." 410 U. S., at 153.

[17] See, *e.g.*, *Sessions* v. *Morales-Santana*, 582 U. S. 47, ___ (2017) (slip op., at 8).

only one sex can undergo does not trigger heightened constitutional scrutiny unless the regulation is a "mere pretex[t] designed to effect an invidious discrimination against members of one sex or the other." *Geduldig* v. *Aiello*, 417 U. S. 484, 496, n. 20 (1974). And as the Court has stated, the "goal of preventing abortion" does not constitute "invidiously discriminatory animus" against women. *Bray* v. *Alexandria Women's Health Clinic*, 506 U. S. 263, 273–274 (1993) (internal quotation marks omitted). Accordingly, laws regulating or prohibiting abortion are not subject to heightened scrutiny. Rather, they are governed by the same standard of review as other health and safety measures.[18]

With this new theory addressed, we turn to *Casey*'s bold assertion that the abortion right is an aspect of the "liberty" protected by the Due Process Clause of the Fourteenth Amendment. 505 U. S., at 846; Brief for Respondents 17; Brief for United States 21–22.

2

The underlying theory on which this argument rests— that the Fourteenth Amendment's Due Process Clause provides substantive, as well as procedural, protection for "liberty"—has long been controversial. But our decisions have held that the Due Process Clause protects two categories of substantive rights.

The first consists of rights guaranteed by the first eight Amendments. Those Amendments originally applied only to the Federal Government, *Barron ex rel. Tiernan* v. *Mayor of Baltimore*, 7 Pet. 243, 247–251 (1833) (opinion for the Court by Marshall, C. J.), but this Court has held that the Due Process Clause of the Fourteenth Amendment "incorporates" the great majority of those rights and thus makes them equally applicable to the States. See *McDonald*, 561

---

[18] We discuss this standard in Part VI of this opinion.

U. S., at 763–767, and nn. 12–13. The second category—which is the one in question here—comprises a select list of fundamental rights that are not mentioned anywhere in the Constitution.

In deciding whether a right falls into either of these categories, the Court has long asked whether the right is "deeply rooted in [our] history and tradition" and whether it is essential to our Nation's "scheme of ordered liberty." *Timbs* v. *Indiana*, 586 U. S. ___, ___ (2019) (slip op., at 3) (internal quotation marks omitted); *McDonald*, 561 U. S., at 764, 767 (internal quotation marks omitted); *Glucksberg*, 521 U. S., at 721 (internal quotation marks omitted).[19] And in conducting this inquiry, we have engaged in a careful analysis of the history of the right at issue.

Justice Ginsburg's opinion for the Court in *Timbs* is a recent example. In concluding that the Eighth Amendment's protection against excessive fines is "fundamental to our scheme of ordered liberty" and "deeply rooted in this Nation's history and tradition," 586 U. S., at ___ (slip op., at 7) (internal quotation marks omitted), her opinion traced the right back to Magna Carta, Blackstone's Commentaries, and 35 of the 37 state constitutions in effect at the ratification of the Fourteenth Amendment. 586 U. S., at ___–___ (slip op., at 3–7).

A similar inquiry was undertaken in *McDonald*, which held that the Fourteenth Amendment protects the right to keep and bear arms. The lead opinion surveyed the origins of the Second Amendment, the debates in Congress about

---

[19] See also, *e.g.*, *Duncan* v. *Louisiana*, 391 U. S. 145, 148 (1968) (asking whether "a right is among those 'fundamental principles of liberty and justice which lie at the base of our civil and political institutions'"); *Palko* v. *Connecticut*, 302 U. S. 319, 325 (1937) (requiring "a 'principle of justice so rooted in the traditions and conscience of our people as to be ranked as fundamental'" (quoting *Snyder* v. *Massachusetts*, 291 U. S. 97, 105 (1934))).

the adoption of the Fourteenth Amendment, the state constitutions in effect when that Amendment was ratified (at least 22 of the 37 States protected the right to keep and bear arms), federal laws enacted during the same period, and other relevant historical evidence. 561 U. S., at 767–777. Only then did the opinion conclude that "the Framers and ratifiers of the Fourteenth Amendment counted the right to keep and bear arms among those fundamental rights necessary to our system of ordered liberty." *Id.*, at 778; see also *id.*, at 822–850 (THOMAS, J., concurring in part and concurring in judgment) (surveying history and reaching the same result under the Fourteenth Amendment's Privileges or Immunities Clause).

Timbs and *McDonald* concerned the question whether the Fourteenth Amendment protects rights that are expressly set out in the Bill of Rights, and it would be anomalous if similar historical support were not required when a putative right is not mentioned anywhere in the Constitution. Thus, in *Glucksberg*, which held that the Due Process Clause does not confer a right to assisted suicide, the Court surveyed more than 700 years of "Anglo-American common law tradition," 521 U. S., at 711, and made clear that a fundamental right must be "objectively, deeply rooted in this Nation's history and tradition," *id.*, at 720–721.

Historical inquiries of this nature are essential whenever we are asked to recognize a new component of the "liberty" protected by the Due Process Clause because the term "liberty" alone provides little guidance. "Liberty" is a capacious term. As Lincoln once said: "We all declare for Liberty; but in using the same word we do not all mean the same thing."[20] In a well-known essay, Isaiah Berlin reported that "[h]istorians of ideas" had cataloged more than

---

[20] Address at Sanitary Fair at Baltimore, Md. (Apr. 18, 1864), reprinted in 7 The Collected Works of Abraham Lincoln 301 (R. Basler ed. 1953).

200 different senses in which the term had been used.[21]

In interpreting what is meant by the Fourteenth Amendment's reference to "liberty," we must guard against the natural human tendency to confuse what that Amendment protects with our own ardent views about the liberty that Americans should enjoy. That is why the Court has long been "reluctant" to recognize rights that are not mentioned in the Constitution. *Collins* v. *Harker Heights*, 503 U. S. 115, 125 (1992). "Substantive due process has at times been a treacherous field for this Court," *Moore* v. *East Cleveland*, 431 U. S. 494, 503 (1977) (plurality opinion), and it has sometimes led the Court to usurp authority that the Constitution entrusts to the people's elected representatives. See *Regents of Univ. of Mich.* v. *Ewing*, 474 U. S. 214, 225– 226 (1985). As the Court cautioned in *Glucksberg*, "[w]e must . . . exercise the utmost care whenever we are asked to break new ground in this field, lest the liberty protected by the Due Process Clause be subtly transformed into the policy preferences of the Members of this Court." 521 U. S., at 720 (internal quotation marks and citation omitted).

On occasion, when the Court has ignored the "[a]ppropriate limits" imposed by "'respect for the teachings of history,'" *Moore*, 431 U. S., at 503 (plurality opinion), it has fallen into the freewheeling judicial policymaking that characterized discredited decisions such as *Lochner* v. *New York*, 198 U. S. 45 (1905). The Court must not fall prey to such an unprincipled approach. Instead, guided by the history and tradition that map the essential components of our Nation's concept of ordered liberty, we must ask what the *Fourteenth Amendment* means by the term "liberty." When we engage in that inquiry in the present case, the clear answer is that the Fourteenth Amendment does not protect

---

[21] Four Essays on Liberty 121 (1969).

the right to an abortion.[22]

B

1

Until the latter part of the 20th century, there was no support in American law for a constitutional right to obtain an abortion. No state constitutional provision had recognized such a right. Until a few years before *Roe* was handed down, no federal or state court had recognized such a right. Nor had any scholarly treatise of which we are aware. And although law review articles are not reticent about advocating new rights, the earliest article proposing a constitutional right to abortion that has come to our attention was published only a few years before *Roe*.[23]

---

[22] That is true regardless of whether we look to the Amendment's Due Process Clause or its Privileges or Immunities Clause. Some scholars and Justices have maintained that the Privileges or Immunities Clause is the provision of the Fourteenth Amendment that guarantees substantive rights. See, *e.g., McDonald* v. *Chicago*, 561 U. S. 742, 813–850 (2010) (THOMAS, J., concurring in part and concurring in judgment); *Duncan*, 391 U. S., at 165–166 (Black, J., concurring); A. Amar, Bill of Rights: Creation and Reconstruction 163–180 (1998) (Amar); J. Ely, Democracy and Distrust 22–30 (1980); 2 W. Crosskey, Politics and the Constitution in the History of the United States 1089–1095 (1953). But even on that view, such a right would need to be rooted in the Nation's history and tradition. See *Corfield* v. *Coryell*, 6 F. Cas. 546, 551–552 (No. 3,230) (CC ED Pa. 1823) (describing unenumerated rights under the Privileges and Immunities Clause, Art. IV, §2, as those "fundamental" rights "which have, at all times, been enjoyed by the citizens of the several states"); Amar 176 (relying on *Corfield* to interpret the Privileges or Immunities Clause); cf. *McDonald*, 561 U. S., at 819–820, 832, 854 (opinion of THOMAS, J.) (reserving the question whether the Privileges or Immunities Clause protects "any rights besides those enumerated in the Constitution").

[23] See R. Lucas, Federal Constitutional Limitations on the Enforcement and Administration of State Abortion Statutes, 46 N. C. L. Rev. 730 (1968) (Lucas); see also D. Garrow, Liberty and Sexuality 334–335 (1994) (Garrow) (stating that Lucas was "undeniably the first person to fully

Not only was there no support for such a constitutional right until shortly before *Roe*, but abortion had long been a *crime* in every single State. At common law, abortion was criminal in at least some stages of pregnancy and was regarded as unlawful and could have very serious consequences at all stages. American law followed the common law until a wave of statutory restrictions in the 1800s expanded criminal liability for abortions. By the time of the adoption of the Fourteenth Amendment, three-quarters of the States had made abortion a crime at any stage of pregnancy, and the remaining States would soon follow.

Roe either ignored or misstated this history, and *Casey* declined to reconsider *Roe*'s faulty historical analysis. It is therefore important to set the record straight.

2

a

We begin with the common law, under which abortion was a crime at least after "quickening"—*i.e.*, the first felt movement of the fetus in the womb, which usually occurs between the 16th and 18th week of pregnancy.[24]

---

articulate on paper" the argument that "a woman's right to choose abortion was a fundamental individual freedom protected by the U. S. Constitution's guarantee of personal liberty").

[24] The exact meaning of "quickening" is subject to some debate. Compare Brief for Scholars of Jurisprudence as *Amici Curiae* 12–14, and n. 32 (emphasis deleted) ("'a quick child'" meant simply a "live" child, and under the era's outdated knowledge of embryology, a fetus was thought to become "quick" at around the sixth week of pregnancy), with Brief for American Historical Association et al. as *Amici Curiae* 6, n. 2 ("quick" and "quickening" consistently meant "the woman's perception of fetal movement"). We need not wade into this debate. First, it suffices for present purposes to show that abortion was criminal by *at least* the 16th or 18th week of pregnancy. Second, as we will show, during the relevant period—*i.e.*, the period surrounding the enactment of the Fourteenth Amendment—the quickening distinction was abandoned as States criminalized abortion at all stages of pregnancy. See *infra*, at 21–

The "eminent common-law authorities (Blackstone, Coke, Hale, and the like)," *Kahler* v. *Kansas*, 589 U. S. ___, ___ (2020) (slip op., at 7), *all* describe abortion after quickening as criminal. Henry de Bracton's 13th-century treatise explained that if a person has "struck a pregnant woman, or has given her poison, whereby he has caused abortion, if the foetus be already formed and animated, and particularly if it be animated, he commits homicide." 2 De Legibus et Consuetudinibus Angliae 279 (T. Twiss ed. 1879); see also 1 Fleta, c. 23, reprinted in 72 Selden Soc. 60–61 (H. Richardson & G. Sayles eds. 1955) (13th-century treatise).[25]

Sir Edward Coke's 17th-century treatise likewise asserted that abortion of a quick child was "murder" if the "childe be born alive" and a "great misprision" if the "childe dieth in her body." 3 Institutes of the Laws of England 50–51 (1644). ("Misprision" referred to "some heynous offence under the degree of felony." *Id.*, at 139.) Two treatises by Sir Matthew Hale likewise described abortion of a quick child who died in the womb as a "great crime" and a "great misprision." Pleas of the Crown 53 (P. Glazebrook ed. 1972); 1 History of the Pleas of the Crown 433 (1736) (Hale). And writing near the time of the adoption of our Constitution, William Blackstone explained that abortion of a "quick" child was "by the ancient law homicide or manslaughter" (citing Bracton), and at least a very "heinous misdemeanor" (citing Coke). 1 Commentaries on the Laws of England 129–130 (7th ed. 1775) (Blackstone).

English cases dating all the way back to the 13th century corroborate the treatises' statements that abortion was a crime. See generally J. Dellapenna, Dispelling the Myths

---

25.

[25] Even before Bracton's time, English law imposed punishment for the killing of a fetus. See Leges Henrici Primi 222–223 (L. Downer ed. 1972) (imposing penalty for any abortion and treating a woman who aborted a "quick" child "as if she were a murderess").

of Abortion History 126, and n. 16, 134–142, 188–194, and
nn. 84–86 (2006) (Dellapenna); J. Keown, Abortion, Doctors
and the Law 3–12 (1988) (Keown). In 1732, for example,
Eleanor Beare was convicted of "destroying the Foetus in
the Womb" of another woman and "thereby causing her to
miscarry."[26] For that crime and another "misdemeanor,"
Beare was sentenced to two days in the pillory and three
years' imprisonment.[27]

   Although a pre-quickening abortion was not itself considered homicide, it does not follow that abortion was *permissible* at common law—much less that abortion was a legal
right. Cf. *Glucksberg*, 521 U. S., at 713 (removal of "common law's harsh sanctions did not represent an acceptance
of suicide"). Quite to the contrary, in the 1732 case mentioned above, the judge said of the charge of abortion (with
no mention of quickening) that he had "never met with a
case so barbarous and unnatural."[28] Similarly, an indictment from 1602, which did not distinguish between a pre-
quickening and post-quickening abortion, described abortion as "pernicious" and "against the peace of our Lady the
Queen, her crown and dignity." Keown 7 (discussing *R.* v.
Webb, Calendar of Assize Records, Surrey Indictments 512
(1980)).

   That the common law did not condone even pre-
quickening abortions is confirmed by what one might call a
proto-felony-murder rule. Hale and Blackstone explained a
way in which a pre-quickening abortion could rise to the
level of a homicide. Hale wrote that if a physician gave a
woman "with child" a "potion" to cause an abortion, and the
woman died, it was "murder" because the potion was given
"*unlawfully* to destroy her child within her." 1 Hale 429–
430 (emphasis added). As Blackstone explained, to be

---

[26] 2 Gentleman's Magazine 931 (Aug. 1732).
[27] *Id.*, at 932.
[28] *Ibid.*

"murder" a killing had to be done with "malice afore-thought, . . . either express or implied." 4 Blackstone 198 (emphasis deleted). In the case of an abortionist, Blackstone wrote, "the law will imply [malice]" for the same reason that it would imply malice if a person who intended to kill one person accidentally killed a different person:

> "[I]f one shoots at A and misses *him*, but kills B, this is murder; because of the previous felonious intent, which the law transfers from one to the other. The same is the case, where one lays poison for A; and B, against whom the prisoner had no malicious intent, takes it, and it kills him; this is likewise murder. *So also*, if one gives *a woman with child* a medicine to procure abortion, and it operates so violently as to kill the woman, *this is murder* in the person who gave it." *Id.*, at 200–201 (emphasis added; footnote omitted).[29]

Notably, Blackstone, like Hale, did not state that this proto-felony-murder rule required that the woman be "with quick child"—only that she be "with child." *Id.*, at 201. And it is revealing that Hale and Blackstone treated abortionists differently from *other* physicians or surgeons who caused the death of a patient "without any intent of doing [the patient] any bodily hurt." Hale 429; see 4 Blackstone 197. These other physicians—even if "unlicensed"—would not be "guilty of murder or manslaughter." Hale 429. But a physician performing an abortion would, precisely because his aim was an "unlawful" one.

In sum, although common-law authorities differed on the severity of punishment for abortions committed at different

---

[29] Other treatises restated the same rule. See 1 W. Russell & C. Greaves, Crimes and Misdemeanors 540 (5th ed. 1845) ("So where a person gave medicine to a woman to procure an abortion, and where a person put skewers into the woman for the same purpose, by which in both cases the women were killed, these acts were clearly held to be murder" (footnotes omitted)); 1 E. East, Pleas of the Crown 230 (1803) (similar).

points in pregnancy, none endorsed the practice. Moreover, we are aware of no common-law case or authority, and the parties have not pointed to any, that remotely suggests a positive *right* to procure an abortion at any stage of pregnancy.

b

In this country, the historical record is similar. The "most important early American edition of Blackstone's Commentaries," *District of Columbia* v. *Heller*, 554 U. S. 570, 594 (2008), reported Blackstone's statement that abortion of a quick child was at least "a heinous misdemeanor," 2 St. George Tucker, Blackstone's Commentaries 129–130 (1803), and that edition also included Blackstone's discussion of the proto-felony-murder rule, 5 *id*., at 200–201. Manuals for justices of the peace printed in the Colonies in the 18th century typically restated the common-law rule on abortion, and some manuals repeated Hale's and Blackstone's statements that anyone who prescribed medication "unlawfully to destroy the child" would be guilty of murder if the woman died. See, *e.g.*, J. Parker, Conductor Generalis 220 (1788); 2 R. Burn, Justice of the Peace, and Parish Officer 221–222 (7th ed. 1762) (English manual stating the same).[30]

---

[30] For manuals restating one or both rules, see J. Davis, Criminal Law 96, 102–103, 339 (1838); Conductor Generalis 194–195 (1801) (printed in Philadelphia); Conductor Generalis 194–195 (1794) (printed in Albany); Conductor Generalis 220 (1788) (printed in New York); Conductor Generalis 198 (1749) (printed in New York); G. Webb, Office and Authority of a Justice of Peace 232 (1736) (printed in Williamsburg); Conductor Generalis 161 (1722) (printed in Philadelphia); see also J. Conley, Doing It by the Book: Justice of the Peace Manuals and English Law in Eighteenth Century America, 6 J. Legal Hist. 257, 265, 267 (1985) (noting that these manuals were the justices' "primary source of legal reference" and of "practical value for a wider audience than the justices").

For cases stating the proto-felony-murder rule, see, *e.g.*, *Commonwealth* v. *Parker*, 50 Mass. 263, 265 (1845); *People* v. *Sessions*, 58 Mich.

The few cases available from the early colonial period corroborate that abortion was a crime. See generally Dellapenna 215–228 (collecting cases). In Maryland in 1652, for example, an indictment charged that a man "Murtherously endeavoured to destroy or Murther the Child by him begotten in the Womb." *Proprietary* v. *Mitchell*, 10 Md. Archives 80, 183 (1652) (W. Browne ed. 1891). And by the 19th century, courts frequently explained that the common law made abortion of a quick child a crime. See, *e.g.*, *Smith* v. *Gaffard*, 31 Ala. 45, 51 (1857); *Smith* v. *State*, 33 Me. 48, 55 (1851); *State* v. *Cooper*, 22 N. J. L. 52, 52–55 (1849); *Commonwealth* v. *Parker*, 50 Mass. 263, 264–268 (1845).

c

The original ground for drawing a distinction between pre- and post-quickening abortions is not entirely clear, but some have attributed the rule to the difficulty of proving that a pre-quickening fetus was alive. At that time, there were no scientific methods for detecting pregnancy in its early stages,[31] and thus, as one court put it in 1872: "[U]ntil the period of quickening there is no *evidence* of life; and whatever may be said of the feotus, the law has fixed upon this period of gestation as the time when the child is endowed with life" because "foetal movements are the first clearly marked and well defined *evidences of life.*" *Evans* v. *People*, 49 N. Y. 86, 90 (emphasis added); *Cooper*, 22 N. J. L., at 56 ("In contemplation of law life commences at the moment of quickening, at that moment when the embryo gives *the first physical proof of life*, no matter when it first received it" (emphasis added)).

594, 595–596, 26 N. W. 291, 292–293 (1886); *State* v. *Moore*, 25 Iowa 128, 131–132 (1868); *Smith* v. *State*, 33 Me. 48, 54–55 (1851).

[31] See E. Rigby, A System of Midwifery 73 (1841) ("Under all circumstances, the diagnosis of pregnancy must ever be difficult and obscure during the early months"); see also *id.*, at 74–80 (discussing rudimentary techniques for detecting early pregnancy); A. Taylor, A Manual of Medical Jurisprudence 418–421 (6th Am. ed. 1866) (same).

The Solicitor General offers a different explanation of the basis for the quickening rule, namely, that before quickening the common law did not regard a fetus "as having a 'separate and independent existence.'" Brief for United States 26 (quoting *Parker*, 50 Mass., at 266). But the case on which the Solicitor General relies for this proposition also suggested that the criminal law's quickening rule was out of step with the treatment of prenatal life in other areas of law, noting that "to many purposes, in reference to civil rights, an infant *in ventre sa mere* is regarded as a person in being." *Ibid.* (citing 1 Blackstone 129); see also *Evans,* 49 N. Y., at 89; *Mills* v. *Commonwealth*, 13 Pa. 631, 633 (1850); *Morrow* v. *Scott*, 7 Ga. 535, 537 (1849); *Hall* v. *Hancock*, 32 Mass. 255, 258 (1834); *Thellusson* v. *Woodford*, 4 Ves. 227, 321–322, 31 Eng. Rep. 117, 163 (1789).

At any rate, the original ground for the quickening rule is of little importance for present purposes because the rule was abandoned in the 19th century. During that period, treatise writers and commentators criticized the quickening distinction as "neither in accordance with the result of medical experience, nor with the principles of the common law." F. Wharton, Criminal Law §1220, p. 606 (rev. 4th ed. 1857) (footnotes omitted); see also J. Beck, Researches in Medicine and Medical Jurisprudence 26–28 (2d ed. 1835) (describing the quickening distinction as "absurd" and "injurious").[32] In 1803, the British Parliament made abortion

---

[32] See *Mitchell* v. *Commonwealth*, 78 Ky. 204, 209–210 (1879) (acknowledging the common-law rule but arguing that "the law should punish abortions and miscarriages, willfully produced, at any time during the period of gestation"); *Mills* v. *Commonwealth*, 13 Pa., 631, 633 (1850) (the quickening rule "never ought to have been the law anywhere"); J. Bishop, Commentaries on the Law of Statutory Crimes §744, p. 471 (1873) ("If we look at the reason of the law, we shall prefer" a rule that "discard[s] this doctrine of the necessity of a quickening"); I. Dana, Report of the Committee on the Production of Abortion, in 5 Transactions

a crime at all stages of pregnancy and authorized the imposition of severe punishment. See Lord Ellenborough's Act, 43 Geo. 3, c. 58 (1803). One scholar has suggested that Parliament's decision "may partly have been attributable to the medical man's concern that fetal life should be protected by the law at all stages of gestation." Keown 22.

In this country during the 19th century, the vast majority of the States enacted statutes criminalizing abortion at all stages of pregnancy. See Appendix A, *infra* (listing state statutory provisions in chronological order).[33] By 1868, the year when the Fourteenth Amendment was ratified, three-quarters of the States, 28 out of 37, had enacted statutes making abortion a crime even if it was performed before quickening.[34] See *ibid.* Of the nine States that had not yet

---

of the Maine Medical Association 37–39 (1866); Report on Criminal Abortion, in 12 Transactions of the American Medical Association 75–77 (1859); W. Guy, Principles of Medical Forensics 133–134 (1845); J. Chitty, Practical Treatise on Medical Jurisprudence 438 (2d Am. ed. 1836); 1 T. Beck & J. Beck, Elements of Medical Jurisprudence 293 (5th ed. 1823); 2 T. Percival, The Works, Literary, Moral and Medical 430 (1807); see also Keown 38–39 (collecting English authorities).

[33] See generally Dellapenna 315–319 (cataloging the development of the law in the States); E. Quay, Justifiable Abortion—Medical and Legal Foundations, 49 Geo. L. J. 395, 435–437, 447–520 (1961) (Quay) (same); J. Witherspoon, Reexamining *Roe*: Nineteenth-Century Abortion Statutes and The Fourteenth Amendment, 17 St. Mary's L. J. 29, 34–36 (1985) (Witherspoon) (same).

[34] Some scholars assert that only 27 States prohibited abortion at all stages. See, *e.g.*, Dellapenna 315; Witherspoon 34–35, and n. 15. Those scholars appear to have overlooked Rhode Island, which criminalized abortion at all stages in 1861. See Acts and Resolves R. I. 1861, ch. 371, §1, p. 133 (criminalizing the attempt to "procure the miscarriage" of "any pregnant woman" or "any woman supposed by such person to be pregnant," without mention of quickening). The *amicus* brief for the American Historical Association asserts that only 26 States prohibited abortion at all stages, but that brief incorrectly excludes West Virginia and Nebraska from its count. Compare Brief for American Historical Association 27–28 (citing Quay), with Appendix A, *infra*.

criminalized abortion at all stages, all but one did so by 1910. See *ibid.*

The trend in the Territories that would become the last 13 States was similar: All of them criminalized abortion at all stages of pregnancy between 1850 (the Kingdom of Hawaii) and 1919 (New Mexico). See Appendix B, *infra*; see also *Casey*, 505 U. S., at 952 (Rehnquist, C. J., concurring in judgment in part and dissenting in part); Dellapenna 317–319. By the end of the 1950s, according to the *Roe* Court's own count, statutes in all but four States and the District of Columbia prohibited abortion "however and whenever performed, unless done to save or preserve the life of the mother." 410 U. S., at 139.[35]

This overwhelming consensus endured until the day *Roe* was decided. At that time, also by the *Roe* Court's own count, a substantial majority—30 States—still prohibited abortion at all stages except to save the life of the mother. See *id.*, at 118, and n. 2 (listing States). And though *Roe* discerned a "trend toward liberalization" in about "one-third of the States," those States still criminalized some abortions and regulated them more stringently than *Roe* would allow. *Id.*, at 140, and n. 37; Tribe 2. In short, the

---

[35] The statutes of three States (Massachusetts, New Jersey, and Pennsylvania) prohibited abortions performed "unlawfully" or "without lawful justification." *Roe*, 410 U. S., at 139 (internal quotation marks omitted). In Massachusetts, case law held that abortion was allowed when, according to the judgment of physicians in the relevant community, the procedure was necessary to preserve the woman's life or her physical or emotional health. *Commonwealth* v. *Wheeler*, 315 Mass. 394, 395, 53 N. E. 2d 4, 5 (1944). In the other two States, however, there is no clear support in case law for the proposition that abortion was lawful where the mother's life was not at risk. See *State* v. *Brandenberg*, 137 N. J. L. 124, 58 A. 2d 709 (1948); *Commonwealth* v. *Trombetta*, 131 Pa. Super. 487, 200 A. 107 (1938).

Statutes in the two remaining jurisdictions (the District of Columbia and Alabama) permitted "abortion to preserve the mother's health." *Roe*, 410 U. S., at 139. Case law in those jurisdictions does not clarify the breadth of these exceptions.

"Court's opinion in *Roe* itself convincingly refutes the notion that the abortion liberty is deeply rooted in the history or tradition of our people." *Thornburgh* v. *American College of Obstetricians and Gynecologists*, 476 U. S. 747, 793 (1986) (White, J., dissenting).

d

The inescapable conclusion is that a right to abortion is not deeply rooted in the Nation's history and traditions. On the contrary, an unbroken tradition of prohibiting abortion on pain of criminal punishment persisted from the earliest days of the common law until 1973. The Court in *Roe* could have said of abortion exactly what *Glucksberg* said of assisted suicide: "Attitudes toward [abortion] have changed since Bracton, but our laws have consistently condemned, and continue to prohibit, [that practice]." 521 U. S., at 719.

3

Respondents and their *amici* have no persuasive answer to this historical evidence.

Neither respondents nor the Solicitor General disputes the fact that by 1868 the vast majority of States criminalized abortion at all stages of pregnancy. See Brief for Petitioners 12–13; see also Brief for American Historical Association et al. as *Amici Curiae* 27–28, and nn. 14–15 (conceding that 26 out of 37 States prohibited abortion before quickening); Tr. of Oral Arg. 74–75 (respondents' counsel conceding the same). Instead, respondents are forced to argue that it "does [not] matter that some States prohibited abortion at the time *Roe* was decided or when the Fourteenth Amendment was adopted." Brief for Respondents 21. But that argument flies in the face of the standard we have applied in determining whether an asserted right that is nowhere mentioned in the Constitution is nevertheless protected by the Fourteenth Amendment.

Not only are respondents and their *amici* unable to show

that a constitutional right to abortion was established when the Fourteenth Amendment was adopted, but they have found no support for the existence of an abortion right that predates the latter part of the 20th century—no state constitutional provision, no statute, no judicial decision, no learned treatise. The earliest sources called to our attention are a few district court and state court decisions decided shortly before *Roe* and a small number of law review articles from the same time period.[36]

A few of respondents' *amici* muster historical arguments, but they are very weak. The Solicitor General repeats *Roe's* claim that it is "'doubtful' . . . 'abortion was ever firmly established as a common-law crime even with respect to the destruction of a quick fetus.'" Brief for United States 26 (quoting *Roe*, 410 U. S., at 136). But as we have seen, great common-law authorities like Bracton, Coke, Hale, and Blackstone all wrote that a post-quickening abortion was a crime—and a serious one at that. Moreover, Hale and Blackstone (and many other authorities following them) asserted that even a pre-quickening abortion was "unlawful" and that, as a result, an abortionist was guilty of murder if the woman died from the attempt.

Instead of following these authorities, *Roe* relied largely on two articles by a pro-abortion advocate who claimed that Coke had intentionally misstated the common law because of his strong anti-abortion views.[37] These articles have

---

[36] See 410 U. S., at 154–155 (collecting cases decided between 1970 and 1973); C. Means, The Phoenix of Abortional Freedom: Is a Penumbral or Ninth-Amendment Right About To Arise From the Nineteenth-Century Legislative Ashes of a Fourteenth-Century Common-Law Liberty? 17 N. Y. L. Forum 335, 337–339 (1971) (Means II); C. Means, The Law of New York Concerning Abortion and the Status of the Foetus, 1664–1968: A Case of Cessation of Constitutionality, 14 N. Y. L. Forum 411 (1968) (Means I); Lucas 730.

[37] See 410 U. S., at 136, n. 26 (citing Means II); 410 U. S., at 132–133, n. 21 (citing Means I).

been discredited,[38] and it has come to light that even members of Jane Roe's legal team did not regard them as serious scholarship. An internal memorandum characterized this author's work as donning "the guise of impartial scholarship while advancing the proper ideological goals."[39] Continued reliance on such scholarship is unsupportable.

The Solicitor General next suggests that history supports an abortion right because the common law's failure to criminalize abortion before quickening means that "at the Founding and for decades thereafter, women generally could terminate a pregnancy, at least in its early stages."[40] Brief for United States 26–27; see also Brief for Respondents 21. But the insistence on quickening was not universal, see *Mills*, 13 Pa., at 633; *State* v. *Slagle*, 83 N. C. 630, 632 (1880), and regardless, the fact that many States in the

---

[38] For critiques of Means's work, see, *e.g.*, Dellapenna 143–152, 325–331; Keown 3–12; J. Finnis, "Shameless Acts" in Colorado: Abuse of Scholarship in Constitutional Cases, 7 Academic Questions 10, 11–12 (1994); R. Destro, Abortion and the Constitution: The Need for a Life-Protective Amendment, 63 Cal. L. Rev. 1250, 1267–1282 (1975); R. Byrn, An American Tragedy: The Supreme Court on Abortion, 41 Ford. L. Rev. 807, 814–829 (1973).

[39] Garrow 500–501, and n. 41 (internal quotation marks omitted).

[40] In any event, *Roe*, *Casey*, and other related abortion decisions imposed substantial restrictions on a State's capacity to regulate abortions performed after quickening. See, *e.g.*, *June Medical Services L. L. C.* v. *Russo*, 591 U. S. ___ (2020) (holding a law requiring doctors performing abortions to secure admitting privileges to be unconstitutional); *Whole Woman's Health* v. *Hellerstedt*, 579 U. S. 582 (2016) (similar); *Casey*, 505 U. S., at 846 (declaring that prohibitions on "abortion before viability" are unconstitutional); *id.*, at 887–898 (holding that a spousal notification provision was unconstitutional). In addition, *Doe* v. *Bolton*, 410 U. S. 179 (1973), has been interpreted by some to protect a broad right to obtain an abortion at any stage of pregnancy provided that a physician is willing to certify that it is needed due to a woman's "emotional" needs or "familial" concerns. *Id.*, at 192. See, *e.g.*, *Women's Medical Professional Corp.* v. *Voinovich*, 130 F. 3d 187, 209 (CA6 1997), cert. denied, 523 U. S. 1036 (1998); but see *id.*, at 1039 (THOMAS, J., dissenting from denial of certiorari).

late 18th and early 19th century did not criminalize pre-quickening abortions does not mean that anyone thought the States lacked the authority to do so. When legislatures began to exercise that authority as the century wore on, no one, as far as we are aware, argued that the laws they enacted violated a fundamental right. That is not surprising since common-law authorities had repeatedly condemned abortion and described it as an "unlawful" act without regard to whether it occurred before or after quickening. See *supra*, at 16–21.

Another *amicus* brief relied upon by respondents (see Brief for Respondents 21) tries to dismiss the significance of the state criminal statutes that were in effect when the Fourteenth Amendment was adopted by suggesting that they were enacted for illegitimate reasons. According to this account, which is based almost entirely on statements made by one prominent proponent of the statutes, important motives for the laws were the fear that Catholic immigrants were having more babies than Protestants and that the availability of abortion was leading White Protestant women to "shir[k their] maternal duties." Brief for American Historical Association et al. as *Amici Curiae* 20.

Resort to this argument is a testament to the lack of any real historical support for the right that *Roe* and *Casey* recognized. This Court has long disfavored arguments based on alleged legislative motives. See, *e.g.*, *Erie* v. *Pap's A. M.*, 529 U. S. 277, 292 (2000) (plurality opinion); *Turner Broadcasting System, Inc.* v. *FCC*, 512 U. S. 622, 652 (1994); *United States* v. *O'Brien*, 391 U. S. 367, 383 (1968); *Arizona* v. *California*, 283 U. S. 423, 455 (1931) (collecting cases). The Court has recognized that inquiries into legislative motives "are a hazardous matter." *O'Brien*, 391 U. S., at 383. Even when an argument about legislative motive is backed by statements made by legislators who voted for a law, we have been reluctant to attribute those motives to the legislative body as a whole. "What motivates one legislator to make a speech about a statute is not necessarily what motivates scores of others to enact it." *Id.*, at 384.

Here, the argument about legislative motive is not even based on statements by legislators, but on statements made by a few supporters of the new 19th-century abortion laws, and it is quite a leap to attribute these motives to all the legislators whose votes were responsible for the enactment of those laws. Recall that at the time of the adoption of the Fourteenth Amendment, over three-quarters of the States had adopted statutes criminalizing abortion (usually at all stages of pregnancy), and that from the early 20th century until the day *Roe* was handed down, every single State had such a law on its books. Are we to believe that the hundreds of lawmakers whose votes were needed to enact these laws were motivated by hostility to Catholics and women?

There is ample evidence that the passage of these laws was instead spurred by a sincere belief that abortion kills a human being. Many judicial decisions from the late 19th and early 20th centuries made that point. See, *e.g.*, *Nash* v. *Meyer*, 54 Idaho 283, 301, 31 P. 2d 273, 280 (1934); *State* v. *Ausplund*, 86 Ore. 121, 131–132, 167 P. 1019, 1022–1023 (1917); *Trent* v. *State*, 15 Ala. App. 485, 488, 73 S. 834, 836 (1916); *State* v. *Miller*, 90 Kan. 230, 233, 133 P. 878, 879 (1913); *State* v. *Tippie*, 89 Ohio St. 35, 39–40, 105 N. E. 75, 77 (1913); *State* v. *Gedicke*, 43 N. J. L. 86, 90 (1881); *Dougherty* v. *People*, 1 Colo. 514, 522–523 (1873); *State* v. *Moore*, 25 Iowa 128, 131–132 (1868); *Smith*, 33 Me., at 57; see also *Memphis Center for Reproductive Health* v. *Slatery*, 14 F. 4th 409, 446, and n. 11 (CA6 2021) (Thapar, J., concurring in judgment in part and dissenting in part) (citing cases).

One may disagree with this belief (and our decision is not based on any view about when a State should regard prenatal life as having rights or legally cognizable interests), but even *Roe* and *Casey* did not question the good faith of abortion opponents. See, *e.g., Casey*, 505 U. S., at 850 ("Men and women of good conscience can disagree . . . about the profound moral and spiritual implications of terminating a pregnancy even in its earliest stage"). And we see no reason to discount the significance of the state laws in question based on these *amici's* suggestions about legislative motive.[41]

C

1

Instead of seriously pressing the argument that the abortion right itself has deep roots, supporters of *Roe* and *Casey* contend that the abortion right is an integral part of a broader entrenched right. *Roe* termed this a right to privacy, 410 U. S., at 154, and *Casey* described it as the freedom to make "intimate and personal choices" that are "central to personal dignity and autonomy," 505 U. S., at 851. *Casey* elaborated: "At the heart of liberty is the right to define one's own concept of existence, of meaning, of the universe, and of the mystery of human life." *Ibid.*

The Court did not claim that this broadly framed right is absolute, and no such claim would be plausible. While individuals are certainly free *to think* and *to say* what they

---

[41] Other *amicus* briefs present arguments about the motives of proponents of liberal access to abortion. They note that some such supporters have been motivated by a desire to suppress the size of the African-American population. See Brief for African-American Organization et al. as *Amici Curiae* 14–21; see also *Box* v. *Planned Parenthood of Ind. and Ky., Inc.*, 587 U. S. ___, ___–___ (2019) (THOMAS, J., concurring) (slip op., at 1–4). And it is beyond dispute that *Roe* has had that demographic effect. A highly disproportionate percentage of aborted fetuses are Black. See, *e.g.*, Dept. of Health and Human Servs., Centers for Disease Control and Prevention (CDC), K. Kortsmit et al., Abortion Surveillance—United States, 2019, 70 Morbidity and Mortality Report, Surveillance Summaries, p. 20 (Nov. 26, 2021) (Table 6). For our part, we do not question the motives of either those who have supported or those who have opposed laws restricting abortions.

wish about "existence," "meaning," the "universe," and "the mystery of human life," they are not always free *to act* in accordance with those thoughts. License to act on the basis of such beliefs may correspond to one of the many understandings of "liberty," but it is certainly not "ordered liberty."

Ordered liberty sets limits and defines the boundary between competing interests. *Roe* and *Casey* each struck a particular balance between the interests of a woman who wants an abortion and the interests of what they termed "potential life." *Roe*, 410 U. S., at 150 (emphasis deleted); *Casey*, 505 U. S., at 852. But the people of the various States may evaluate those interests differently. In some States, voters may believe that the abortion right should be even more extensive than the right that *Roe* and *Casey* recognized. Voters in other States may wish to impose tight restrictions based on their belief that abortion destroys an "unborn human being." Miss. Code Ann. §41–41–191(4)(b). Our Nation's historical understanding of ordered liberty does not prevent the people's elected representatives from deciding how abortion should be regulated.

Nor does the right to obtain an abortion have a sound basis in precedent. *Casey* relied on cases involving the right to marry a person of a different race, *Loving* v. *Virginia*, 388 U. S. 1 (1967); the right to marry while in prison, *Turner* v. *Safley*, 482 U. S. 78 (1987); the right to obtain contraceptives, *Griswold* v. *Connecticut*, 381 U. S. 479 (1965), *Eisenstadt* v. *Baird*, 405 U. S. 438 (1972), *Carey* v. *Population Services Int'l*, 431 U. S. 678 (1977); the right to reside with relatives, *Moore* v. *East Cleveland*, 431 U. S. 494 (1977); the right to make decisions about the education of one's children, *Pierce* v. *Society of Sisters*, 268 U. S. 510 (1925), *Meyer* v. *Nebraska*, 262 U. S. 390 (1923); the right not to be sterilized without consent, *Skinner* v. *Oklahoma ex rel. Williamson*, 316 U. S. 535 (1942); and the right in certain circumstances not to undergo involuntary surgery, forced administration of drugs, or other substantially similar procedures, *Winston* v. *Lee*, 470 U. S. 753 (1985), *Washington* v. *Harper*, 494 U. S. 210 (1990), *Rochin* v. *California*, 342 U. S. 165 (1952). Respondents and the Solicitor General also rely on post-*Casey* decisions like *Lawrence* v. *Texas*, 539 U. S. 558 (2003) (right to engage in private, consensual sexual acts), and *Obergefell* v. *Hodges*, 576 U. S. 644 (2015) (right to marry a person of the same sex). See Brief for Respondents 18; Brief for United States 23–24.

These attempts to justify abortion through appeals to a broader right to autonomy and to define one's "concept of existence" prove too much. *Casey*, 505 U. S., at 851. Those criteria, at a high level of generality, could license fundamental rights to illicit drug use, prostitution, and the like. See *Compassion in Dying* v. *Washington*, 85 F. 3d 1440, 1444 (CA9 1996) (O'Scannlain, J., dissenting from denial of rehearing en banc). None of these rights has any claim to being deeply rooted in history. *Id.*, at 1440, 1445.

What sharply distinguishes the abortion right from the rights recognized in the cases on which *Roe* and *Casey* rely is something that both those decisions acknowledged: Abortion destroys what those decisions call "potential life" and what the law at issue in this case regards as the life of an "unborn human being." See *Roe*, 410 U. S., at 159 (abortion is "inherently different"); *Casey*, 505 U. S., at 852 (abortion is "a unique act"). None of the other decisions cited by *Roe* and *Casey* involved the critical moral question posed by abortion. They are therefore inapposite. They do not support the right to obtain an abortion, and by the same token, our conclusion that the Constitution does not confer such a right does not undermine them in any way.

2

In drawing this critical distinction between the abortion right and other rights, it is not necessary to dispute *Casey*'s claim (which we accept for the sake of argument) that "the specific practices of States at the time of the adoption of the Fourteenth Amendment" do not "mar[k] the outer limits of the substantive sphere of liberty which the Fourteenth Amendment protects." 505 U. S., at 848. Abortion is nothing new. It has been addressed by lawmakers for centuries, and the fundamental moral question that it poses is ageless.

Defenders of *Roe* and *Casey* do not claim that any new scientific learning calls for a different answer to the underlying moral question, but they do contend that changes in society require the recognition of a constitutional right to obtain an abortion. Without the availability of abortion, they maintain, people will be inhibited from exercising their freedom to choose the types of relationships they desire, and women will be unable to compete with men in the workplace and in other endeavors.

Americans who believe that abortion should be restricted press countervailing arguments about modern developments. They note that attitudes about the pregnancy of unmarried women have changed drastically; that federal and state laws ban discrimination on the basis of pregnancy;[42] that leave for pregnancy and childbirth are now guaranteed by law in many cases;[43] that the costs of medical care asso-

---

[42] See, *e.g.*, Pregnancy Discrimination Act, 92 Stat. 2076, 42 U. S. C. §2000e(k) (federal law prohibiting pregnancy discrimination in employment); Dept. of Labor, Women's Bureau, Employment Protections for Workers Who Are Pregnant or Nursing, https://www.dol.gov/agencies/wb/pregnant-nursing-employment-protections (showing that 46 States and the District of Columbia have employment protections against pregnancy discrimination).

[43] See, *e.g.*, Family and Medical Leave Act of 1993, 107 Stat. 9, 29 U. S. C. §2612 (federal law guaranteeing employment leave for pregnancy and birth); Bureau of Labor Statistics, Access to Paid and Unpaid Family Leave in 2018, https://www.bls.gov/opub/ted/2019/access-to-paid-

ciated with pregnancy are covered by insurance or government assistance;[44] that States have increasingly adopted
"safe haven" laws, which generally allow women to drop off
babies anonymously;[45] and that a woman who puts her newborn up for adoption today has little reason to fear that the
baby will not find a suitable home.[46] They also claim that
many people now have a new appreciation of fetal life and
that when prospective parents who want to have a child
view a sonogram, they typically have no doubt that what
they see is their daughter or son.

---

and-unpaid-family-leave-in-2018.htm (showing that 89 percent of civil-
ian workers had access to unpaid family leave in 2018).

[44]The Affordable Care Act (ACA) requires non-grandfathered health
plans in the individual and small group markets to cover certain essential health benefits, which include maternity and newborn care. See 124
Stat. 163, 42 U. S. C. §18022(b)(1)(D). The ACA also prohibits annual
limits, see §300gg–11, and limits annual cost-sharing obligations on such
benefits, §18022(c). State Medicaid plans must provide coverage for
pregnancy-related services—including, but not limited to, prenatal care,
delivery, and postpartum care—as well as services for other conditions
that might complicate the pregnancy.   42 CFR §§440.210(a)(2)(i)–(ii)
(2020). State Medicaid plans are also prohibited from imposing deduc-
tions, cost-sharing, or similar charges for pregnancy-related services for
pregnant women. 42 U. S. C. §§1396o(a)(2)(B), (b)(2)(B).

[45]Since *Casey*, all 50 States and the District of Columbia have enacted
such laws. Dept. of Health and Human Servs., Children's Bureau, Infant
Safe Haven Laws 1–2 (2016), https://www.childwelfare.gov/pubPDFs/
safehaven.pdf (noting that safe haven laws began in Texas in 1999).

[46]See, *e.g.*, CDC, Adoption Experiences of Women and Men and Demand for Children To Adopt by Women 18–44 Years of Age in the United
States 16 (Aug. 2008) ("[N]early 1 million women were seeking to adopt
children in 2002 (*i.e.*, they were in demand for a child), whereas the do-
mestic supply of infants relinquished at birth or within the first month
of life and available to be adopted had become virtually nonexistent");
CDC, National Center for Health Statistics, Adoption and Nonbiological
Parenting, https://www.cdc.gov/nchs/nsfg/key_statistics/a-keystat.htm#
adoption (showing that approximately 3.1 million women between the
ages of 18–49 had ever "[t]aken steps to adopt a child" based on data
collected from 2015–2019).

Both sides make important policy arguments, but supporters of *Roe* and *Casey* must show that this Court has the authority to weigh those arguments and decide how abortion may be regulated in the States. They have failed to make that showing, and we thus return the power to weigh those arguments to the people and their elected representatives.

D

1

The dissent is very candid that it cannot show that a constitutional right to abortion has any foundation, let alone a "'deeply rooted'" one, "'in this Nation's history and tradition.'" *Glucksberg*, 521 U. S., at 721; see *post*, at 12–14 (joint opinion of BREYER, SOTOMAYOR, and KAGAN, JJ.). The dissent does not identify *any* pre-*Roe* authority that supports such a right—no state constitutional provision or statute, no federal or state judicial precedent, not even a scholarly treatise. Compare *post*, at 12–14, n. 2, with *supra*, at 15–16, and n. 23. Nor does the dissent dispute the fact that abortion was illegal at common law at least after quickening; that the 19th century saw a trend toward criminalization of pre-quickening abortions; that by 1868, a supermajority of States (at least 26 of 37) had enacted statutes criminalizing abortion at all stages of pregnancy; that by the late 1950s at least 46 States prohibited abortion "however and whenever performed" except if necessary to save "the life of the mother," *Roe*, 410 U. S., at 139; and that when *Roe* was decided in 1973 similar statutes were still in effect in 30 States. Compare *post*, at 12–14, nn. 2–3, with *supra*, at 23–25, and nn. 33–34.[47]

The dissent's failure to engage with this long tradition is

---

[47] By way of contrast, at the time *Griswold* v. *Connecticut*, 381 U. S. 479 (1965), was decided, the Connecticut statute at issue was an extreme outlier. See Brief for Planned Parenthood Federation of America, Inc. as *Amicus Curiae* in *Griswold* v. *Connecticut*, O. T. 1964, No. 496, p. 27.

devastating to its position. We have held that the "established method of substantive-due-process analysis" requires that an unenumerated right be "'deeply rooted in this Nation's history and tradition'" before it can be recognized as a component of the "liberty" protected in the Due Process Clause. *Glucksberg*, 521 U. S., at 721; cf. *Timbs*, 586 U. S., at ___ (slip op., at 7). But despite the dissent's professed fidelity to *stare decisis*, it fails to seriously engage with that important precedent—which it cannot possibly satisfy.

The dissent attempts to obscure this failure by misrepresenting our application of *Glucksberg*. The dissent suggests that we have focused only on "the legal status of abortion in the 19th century," *post*, at 26, but our review of this Nation's tradition extends well past that period. As explained, for more than a century after 1868—including "another half-century" after women gained the constitutional right to vote in 1920, see *post*, at 15; Amdt. 19—it was firmly established that laws prohibiting abortion like the Texas law at issue in *Roe* were permissible exercises of state regulatory authority. And today, another half century later, more than half of the States have asked us to overrule *Roe* and *Casey*. The dissent cannot establish that a right to abortion has *ever* been part of this Nation's tradition.

2

Because the dissent cannot argue that the abortion right is rooted in this Nation's history and tradition, it contends that the "constitutional tradition" is "not captured whole at a single moment," and that its "meaning gains content from the long sweep of our history and from successive judicial precedents." *Post*, at 18 (internal quotation marks omitted). This vague formulation imposes no clear restraints on what Justice White called the "exercise of raw judicial power," *Roe*, 410 U. S., at 222 (dissenting opinion), and while the dissent claims that its standard "does not mean anything goes," *post*, at 17, any real restraints are hard to discern.

The largely limitless reach of the dissenters' standard is illustrated by the way they apply it here. First, if the "long sweep of history" imposes any restraint on the recognition of unenumerated rights, then *Roe* was surely wrong, since abortion was never allowed (except to save the life of the mother) in a majority of States for over 100 years before that decision was handed down. Second, it is impossible to defend *Roe* based on prior precedent because all of the precedents *Roe* cited, including *Griswold* and *Eisenstadt*, were critically different for a reason that we have explained: None of those cases involved the destruction of what *Roe* called "potential life." See *supra*, at 32.

So without support in history or relevant precedent, *Roe*'s reasoning cannot be defended even under the dissent's proposed test, and the dissent is forced to rely solely on the fact that a constitutional right to abortion was recognized in *Roe* and later decisions that accepted *Roe*'s interpretation. Under the doctrine of *stare decisis*, those precedents are entitled to careful and respectful consideration, and we engage in that analysis below. But as the Court has reiterated time and time again, adherence to precedent is not "'an inexorable command.'" *Kimble* v. *Marvel Entertainment, LLC*, 576 U. S. 446, 455 (2015). There are occasions when past decisions should be overruled, and as we will explain, this is one of them.

3

The most striking feature of the dissent is the absence of any serious discussion of the legitimacy of the States' interest in protecting fetal life. This is evident in the analogy that the dissent draws between the abortion right and the rights recognized in *Griswold* (contraception), *Eisenstadt* (same), *Lawrence* (sexual conduct with member of the same sex), and *Obergefell* (same-sex marriage). Perhaps this is designed to stoke unfounded fear that our decision will imperil those other rights, but the dissent's analogy is objectionable for a more important reason: what it reveals about the dissent's views on the protection of what *Roe* called "potential life." The exercise of the rights at issue in *Griswold, Eisenstadt, Lawrence,* and *Obergefell* does not destroy a "potential life," but an abortion has that effect. So if the rights at issue in those cases are fundamentally the same as the right recognized in *Roe* and *Casey*, the implication is clear: The Constitution does not permit the States to regard the destruction of a "potential life" as a matter of any significance.

That view is evident throughout the dissent. The dissent has much to say about the effects of pregnancy on women, the burdens of motherhood, and the difficulties faced by poor women. These are important concerns. However, the dissent evinces no similar regard for a State's interest in protecting prenatal life. The dissent repeatedly praises the "balance," *post,* at 2, 6, 8, 10, 12, that the viability line strikes between a woman's liberty interest and the State's interest in prenatal life. But for reasons we discuss later, see *infra,* at 50–54, 55–56, and given in the opinion of THE CHIEF JUSTICE, *post,* at 2–5 (opinion concurring in judgment), the viability line makes no sense. It was not adequately justified in *Roe*, and the dissent does not even try to defend it today. Nor does it identify any other point in a pregnancy after which a State is permitted to prohibit the destruction of a fetus.

Our opinion is not based on any view about if and when prenatal life is entitled to any of the rights enjoyed after birth. The dissent, by contrast, would impose on the people a particular theory about when the rights of personhood begin. According to the dissent, the Constitution *requires* the States to regard a fetus as lacking even the most basic human right—to live—at least until an arbitrary point in a pregnancy has passed. Nothing in the Constitution or in our Nation's legal traditions authorizes the Court to adopt that "'theory of life.'" *Post*, at 8.

III

We next consider whether the doctrine of *stare decisis* counsels continued acceptance of *Roe* and *Casey*. *Stare decisis* plays an important role in our case law, and we have explained that it serves many valuable ends. It protects the interests of those who have taken action in reliance on a past decision. See *Casey*, 505 U. S., at 856 (joint opinion); see also *Payne* v. *Tennessee*, 501 U. S. 808, 828 (1991). It "reduces incentives for challenging settled precedents, saving parties and courts the expense of endless relitigation." *Kimble*, 576 U. S., at 455. It fosters "evenhanded" decisionmaking by requiring that like cases be decided in a like manner. *Payne*, 501 U. S., at 827. It "contributes to the actual and perceived integrity of the judicial process." *Ibid.* And it restrains judicial hubris and reminds us to respect the judgment of those who have grappled with important questions in the past. "Precedent is a way of accumulating and passing down the learning of past generations, a font of established wisdom richer than what can be found in any single judge or panel of judges." N. Gorsuch, A Republic, If You Can Keep It 217 (2019).

We have long recognized, however, that *stare decisis* is "not an inexorable command," *Pearson* v. *Callahan*, 555 U. S. 223, 233 (2009) (internal quotation marks omitted), and it "is at its weakest when we interpret the Constitution," *Agostini* v. *Felton*, 521 U. S. 203, 235 (1997). It has been said that it is sometimes more important that an issue "'be settled than that it be settled right.'" *Kimble*, 576 U. S., at 455 (quoting *Burnet* v. *Coronado Oil & Gas Co.*, 285 U. S. 393, 406 (1932) (Brandeis, J., dissenting)). But when it comes to the interpretation of the Constitution— the "great charter of our liberties," which was meant "to endure through a long lapse of ages," *Martin* v. *Hunter's Lessee,* 1 Wheat. 304, 326 (1816) (opinion for the Court by Story, J.)—we place a high value on having the matter "settled right." In addition, when one of our constitutional decisions goes astray, the country is usually stuck with the bad decision unless we correct our own mistake. An erroneous constitutional decision can be fixed by amending the Constitution, but our Constitution is notoriously hard to amend. See Art. V; *Kimble,* 576 U. S., at 456. Therefore, in appropriate circumstances we must be willing to reconsider and, if necessary, overrule constitutional decisions.

Some of our most important constitutional decisions have overruled prior precedents. We mention three. In *Brown* v. *Board of Education,* 347 U. S. 483 (1954), the Court repudiated the "separate but equal" doctrine, which had allowed States to maintain racially segregated schools and other facilities. *Id.,* at 488 (internal quotation marks omitted). In so doing, the Court overruled the infamous decision in *Plessy* v. *Ferguson,* 163 U. S. 537 (1896), along with six other Supreme Court precedents that had applied the separate-but-equal rule. See *Brown,* 347 U. S., at 491.

In *West Coast Hotel Co.* v. *Parrish,* 300 U. S. 379 (1937), the Court overruled *Adkins* v. *Children's Hospital of D. C.,* 261 U. S. 525 (1923), which had held that a law setting minimum wages for women violated the "liberty" protected by the Fifth Amendment's Due Process Clause. *Id.,* at 545. *West Coast Hotel* signaled the demise of an entire line of important precedents that had protected an individual liberty right against state and federal health and welfare legislation. See *Lochner* v. *New York,* 198 U. S. 45 (1905) (holding invalid a law setting maximum working hours); *Coppage* v. *Kansas,* 236 U. S. 1 (1915) (holding invalid a law banning contracts forbidding employees to join a union); *Jay Burns Baking Co.* v. *Bryan,* 264 U. S. 504 (1924) (holding invalid laws fixing the weight of loaves of bread).

Finally, in *West Virginia Bd. of Ed.* v. *Barnette,* 319 U. S.

624 (1943), after the lapse of only three years, the Court overruled *Minersville School Dist.* v. *Gobitis*, 310 U. S. 586 (1940), and held that public school students could not be compelled to salute the flag in violation of their sincere beliefs. *Barnette* stands out because nothing had changed during the intervening period other than the Court's belated recognition that its earlier decision had been seriously wrong.

On many other occasions, this Court has overruled important constitutional decisions. (We include a partial list in the footnote that follows.[48]) Without these decisions,

---

[48]See, *e.g.*, *Obergefell* v. *Hodges*, 576 U. S. 644 (2015) (right to same-sex marriage), overruling *Baker* v. *Nelson*, 409 U. S. 810 (1972); *Citizens United* v. *Federal Election Comm'n*, 558 U. S. 310 (2010) (right to engage in campaign-related speech), overruling *Austin* v. *Michigan Chamber of Commerce*, 494 U. S. 652 (1990), and partially overruling *McConnell* v. *Federal Election Comm'n*, 540 U. S. 93 (2003); *Montejo* v. *Louisiana*, 556 U. S. 778 (2009) (Sixth Amendment right to counsel), overruling *Michigan* v. *Jackson*, 475 U. S. 625 (1986); *Crawford* v. *Washington*, 541 U. S. 36 (2004) (Sixth Amendment right to confront witnesses), overruling *Ohio* v. *Roberts*, 448 U. S. 56 (1980); *Lawrence* v. *Texas*, 539 U. S. 558 (2003) (right to engage in consensual, same-sex intimacy in one's home), overruling *Bowers* v. *Hardwick*, 478 U. S. 186 (1986); *Ring* v. *Arizona*, 536 U. S. 584 (2002) (Sixth Amendment right to a jury trial in capital prosecutions), overruling *Walton* v. *Arizona*, 497 U. S. 639 (1990); *Agostini* v. *Felton*, 521 U. S. 203 (1997) (evaluating whether government aid violates the Establishment Clause), overruling *Aguilar* v. *Felton*, 473 U. S. 402 (1985), and *School Dist. of Grand Rapids* v. *Ball*, 473 U. S. 373 (1985); *Seminole Tribe of Fla.* v. *Florida*, 517 U. S. 44 (1996) (lack of congressional power under the Indian Commerce Clause to abrogate States' Eleventh Amendment immunity), overruling *Pennsylvania* v. *Union Gas Co.*, 491 U. S. 1 (1989); *Payne* v. *Tennessee*, 501 U. S. 808 (1991) (the Eighth Amendment does not erect a *per se* bar to the admission of victim impact evidence during the penalty phase of a capital trial), overruling *Booth* v. *Maryland*, 482 U. S. 496 (1987), and *South Carolina* v. *Gathers*, 490 U. S. 805 (1989); *Batson* v. *Kentucky*, 476 U. S. 79 (1986) (the Equal Protection Clause guarantees the defendant that the State will not exclude members of his race from the jury venire on account of race), overruling *Swain* v. *Alabama*, 380 U. S. 202 (1965); *Garcia* v. *San Antonio*

42   DOBBS *v.* JACKSON WOMEN'S HEALTH ORGANIZATION

Opinion of the Court

Metropolitan Transit Authority, 469 U. S. 528, 530 (1985) (rejecting the
principle that the Commerce Clause does not empower Congress to enforce requirements, such as minimum wage laws, against the States "'in
areas of traditional governmental functions'"), overruling *National
League of Cities* v. *Usery,* 426 U. S. 833 (1976); *Illinois* v. *Gates,* 462 U. S.
213 (1983) (the Fourth Amendment requires a totality of the circumstances approach for determining whether an informant's tip establishes
probable cause), overruling *Aguilar* v. *Texas,* 378 U. S. 108 (1964), and
Spinelli v. *United States,* 393 U. S. 410 (1969); *United States* v. *Scott,* 437
U. S. 82 (1978) (the Double Jeopardy Clause does not apply to Government appeals from orders granting defense motions to terminate a trial
before verdict), overruling *United States* v. *Jenkins,* 420 U. S. 358 (1975);
Craig v. *Boren,* 429 U. S. 190 (1976) (gender-based classifications are
subject to intermediate scrutiny under the Equal Protection Clause),
overruling *Goesaert* v. *Cleary,* 335 U. S. 464 (1948); *Taylor* v. *Louisiana,*
419 U. S. 522 (1975) (jury system which operates to exclude women from
jury service violates the defendant's Sixth and Fourteenth Amendment
right to an impartial jury), overruling *Hoyt* v. *Florida,* 368 U. S. 57
(1961); *Brandenburg* v. *Ohio,* 395 U. S. 444 (1969) (*per curiam*) (the mere
advocacy of violence is protected under the First Amendment unless it is
directed to incite or produce imminent lawless action), overruling *Whitney* v. *California,* 274 U. S. 357 (1927); *Katz* v. *United States,* 389 U. S.
347, 351 (1967) (Fourth Amendment "protects people, not places," and
extends to what a person "seeks to preserve as private"), overruling
Olmstead v. *United States,* 277 U. S. 438 (1928), and *Goldman* v. *United
States,* 316 U. S. 129 (1942); *Miranda* v. *Arizona,* 384 U. S. 436 (1966)
(procedural safeguards to protect the Fifth Amendment privilege against
self-incrimination), overruling *Crooker* v. *California,* 357 U. S. 433
(1958), and *Cicenia* v. *Lagay,* 357 U. S. 504 (1958); *Malloy* v. *Hogan,* 378
U. S. 1 (1964) (the Fifth Amendment privilege against self-incrimination
is also protected by the Fourteenth Amendment against abridgment by
the States), overruling *Twining* v. *New Jersey,* 211 U. S. 78 (1908), and
Adamson v. *California,* 332 U. S. 46 (1947); *Wesberry* v. *Sanders,* 376
U. S. 1, 7–8 (1964) (congressional districts should be apportioned so that
"as nearly as is practicable one man's vote in a congressional election is
to be worth as much as another's"), overruling in effect *Colegrove* v.
Green, 328 U. S. 549 (1946); *Gideon* v. *Wainwright,* 372 U. S. 335 (1963)
(right to counsel for indigent defendant in a criminal prosecution in state
court under the Sixth and Fourteenth Amendments), overruling *Betts* v.
Brady, 316 U. S. 455 (1942); *Baker* v. *Carr,* 369 U. S. 186 (1962) (federal
courts have jurisdiction to consider constitutional challenges to state re-
districting plans), effectively overruling in part *Colegrove,* 328 U. S. 549;

American constitutional law as we know it would be unrecognizable, and this would be a different country.

No Justice of this Court has ever argued that the Court should *never* overrule a constitutional decision, but overruling a precedent is a serious matter. It is not a step that should be taken lightly. Our cases have attempted to provide a framework for deciding when a precedent should be overruled, and they have identified factors that should be considered in making such a decision. *Janus* v. *State, County, and Municipal Employees*, 585 U. S. ___, ___–___ (2018) (slip op., at 34–35); *Ramos* v. *Louisiana*, 590 U. S. ___, ___–___ (2020) (KAVANAUGH, J., concurring in part) (slip op., at 7–9).

In this case, five factors weigh strongly in favor of overruling *Roe* and *Casey*: the nature of their error, the quality of their reasoning, the "workability" of the rules they imposed on the country, their disruptive effect on other areas of the law, and the absence of concrete reliance.

A

The nature of the Court's error. An erroneous interpretation of the Constitution is always important, but some are more damaging than others.

The infamous decision in *Plessy* v. *Ferguson*, was one

Mapp v. *Ohio*, 367 U. S. 643 (1961) (the exclusionary rule regarding the inadmissibility of evidence obtained in violation of the Fourth Amendment applies to the States), overruling *Wolf* v. *Colorado*, 338 U. S. 25 (1949); *Smith* v. *Allwright*, 321 U. S. 649 (1944) (racial restrictions on the right to vote in primary elections violates the Equal Protection Clause of the Fourteenth Amendment), overruling *Grovey* v. *Townsend*, 295 U. S. 45 (1935); *United States* v. *Darby*, 312 U. S. 100 (1941) (congressional power to regulate employment conditions under the Commerce Clause), overruling *Hammer* v. *Dagenhart*, 247 U. S. 251 (1918); *Erie R. Co.* v. *Tompkins*, 304 U. S. 64 (1938) (Congress does not have the power to declare substantive rules of common law; a federal court sitting in diversity jurisdiction must apply the substantive state law), overruling *Swift* v. *Tyson*, 16 Pet. 1 (1842).

such decision. It betrayed our commitment to "equality before the law." 163 U. S., at 562 (Harlan, J., dissenting). It was "egregiously wrong" on the day it was decided, see *Ramos*, 590 U. S., at ___ (opinion of KAVANAUGH, J.) (slip op., at 7), and as the Solicitor General agreed at oral argument, it should have been overruled at the earliest opportunity, see Tr. of Oral Arg. 92–93.

Roe was also egregiously wrong and deeply damaging. For reasons already explained, *Roe*'s constitutional analysis was far outside the bounds of any reasonable interpretation of the various constitutional provisions to which it vaguely pointed.

Roe was on a collision course with the Constitution from the day it was decided, *Casey* perpetuated its errors, and those errors do not concern some arcane corner of the law of little importance to the American people. Rather, wielding nothing but "raw judicial power," *Roe*, 410 U. S., at 222 (White, J., dissenting), the Court usurped the power to address a question of profound moral and social importance that the Constitution unequivocally leaves for the people. *Casey* described itself as calling both sides of the national controversy to resolve their debate, but in doing so, *Casey* necessarily declared a winning side. Those on the losing side—those who sought to advance the State's interest in fetal life—could no longer seek to persuade their elected representatives to adopt policies consistent with their views. The Court short-circuited the democratic process by closing it to the large number of Americans who dissented in any respect from *Roe*. "*Roe* fanned into life an issue that has inflamed our national politics in general, and has obscured with its smoke the selection of Justices to this Court in particular, ever since." *Casey*, 505 U. S., at 995–996 (opinion of Scalia, J.). Together, *Roe* and *Casey* represent an error that cannot be allowed to stand.

As the Court's landmark decision in *West Coast Hotel* illustrates, the Court has previously overruled decisions that wrongly removed an issue from the people and the democratic process. As Justice White later explained, "decisions that find in the Constitution principles or values that cannot fairly be read into that document usurp the people's authority, for such decisions represent choices that the people have never made and that they cannot disavow through corrective legislation. For this reason, it is essential that this Court maintain the power to restore authority to its proper possessors by correcting constitutional decisions that, on reconsideration, are found to be mistaken." *Thornburgh*, 476 U. S., at 787 (dissenting opinion).

B

The quality of the reasoning. Under our precedents, the quality of the reasoning in a prior case has an important bearing on whether it should be reconsidered. See *Janus*, 585 U. S., at ___ (slip op., at 38); *Ramos*, 590 U. S., at ___–___ (opinion of KAVANAUGH, J.) (slip op., at 7–8). In Part II, *supra*, we explained why *Roe* was incorrectly decided, but that decision was more than just wrong. It stood on exceptionally weak grounds.

Roe found that the Constitution implicitly conferred a right to obtain an abortion, but it failed to ground its decision in text, history, or precedent. It relied on an erroneous historical narrative; it devoted great attention to and presumably relied on matters that have no bearing on the meaning of the Constitution; it disregarded the fundamental difference between the precedents on which it relied and the question before the Court; it concocted an elaborate set of rules, with different restrictions for each trimester of pregnancy, but it did not explain how this veritable code could be teased out of anything in the Constitution, the history of abortion laws, prior precedent, or any other cited source; and its most important rule (that States cannot protect fetal life prior to "viability") was never raised by any party and has never been plausibly explained. *Roe*'s reasoning quickly drew scathing scholarly criticism, even from supporters of broad access to abortion.

The *Casey* plurality, while reaffirming *Roe*'s central holding, pointedly refrained from endorsing most of its reasoning. It revised the textual basis for the abortion right, silently abandoned *Roe*'s erroneous historical narrative, and jettisoned the trimester framework. But it replaced that scheme with an arbitrary "undue burden" test and relied on an exceptional version of *stare decisis* that, as explained below, this Court had never before applied and has never invoked since.

1

a

The weaknesses in *Roe*'s reasoning are well-known. Without any grounding in the constitutional text, history, or precedent, it imposed on the entire country a detailed set of rules much like those that one might expect to find in a statute or regulation. See 410 U. S., at 163–164. Dividing pregnancy into three trimesters, the Court imposed special rules for each. During the first trimester, the Court announced, "the abortion decision and its effectuation must be left to the medical judgment of the pregnant woman's attending physician." *Id.*, at 164. After that point, a State's interest in regulating abortion for the sake of a woman's health became compelling, and accordingly, a State could "regulate the abortion procedure in ways that are reasonably related to maternal health." *Ibid.* Finally, in "the stage subsequent to viability," which in 1973 roughly coincided with the beginning of the third trimester, the State's interest in "the potentiality of human life" became compelling, and therefore a State could "regulate, and even proscribe, abortion except where it is necessary, in appropriate medical judgment, for the preservation of the life or health of the mother." *Id.*, at 164–165.

This elaborate scheme was the Court's own brainchild. Neither party advocated the trimester framework; nor did either party or any *amicus* argue that "viability" should mark the point at which the scope of the abortion right and a State's regulatory authority should be substantially transformed. See Brief for Appellant and Brief for Appellee in *Roe* v. *Wade*, O. T. 1972, No. 70–18; see also C. Forsythe, Abuse of Discretion: The Inside Story of *Roe* v. *Wade* 127, 141 (2012).

b

Not only did this scheme resemble the work of a legislature, but the Court made little effort to explain how these rules could be deduced from any of the sources on which constitutional decisions are usually based. We have already discussed *Roe*'s treatment of constitutional text, and the opinion failed to show that history, precedent, or any other cited source supported its scheme.

Roe featured a lengthy survey of history, but much of its discussion was irrelevant, and the Court made no effort to explain why it was included. For example, multiple paragraphs were devoted to an account of the views and practices of ancient civilizations where infanticide was widely accepted. See 410 U. S., at 130–132 (discussing ancient Greek and Roman practices).[49] When it came to the most important historical fact—how the States regulated abortion when the Fourteenth Amendment was adopted—the Court said almost nothing. It allowed that States had tightened their abortion laws "in the middle and late 19th century," *id.*, at 139, but it implied that these laws might have

_____

[49] See, *e.g.*, C. Patterson, "Not Worth the Rearing": The Causes of Infant Exposure in Ancient Greece, 115 Transactions Am. Philosophical Assn. 103, 111–123 (1985); A. Cameron, The Exposure of Children and Greek Ethics, 46 Classical Rev. 105–108 (1932); H. Bennett, The Exposure of Infants in Ancient Rome, 18 Classical J. 341–351 (1923); W. Harris, Child-Exposure in the Roman Empire, 84 J. Roman Studies 1 (1994).

been enacted not to protect fetal life but to further "a Victorian social concern" about "illicit sexual conduct," id., at 148.

Roe's failure even to note the overwhelming consensus of state laws in effect in 1868 is striking, and what it said about the common law was simply wrong. Relying on two discredited articles by an abortion advocate, the Court erroneously suggested—contrary to Bracton, Coke, Hale, Blackstone, and a wealth of other authority—that the common law had probably never really treated post-quickening abortion as a crime. See id., at 136 ("[I]t now appear[s] doubtful that abortion was ever firmly established as a common-law crime even with respect to the destruction of a quick fetus"). This erroneous understanding appears to have played an important part in the Court's thinking because the opinion cited "the lenity of the common law" as one of the four factors that informed its decision. Id., at 165.

After surveying history, the opinion spent many paragraphs conducting the sort of fact-finding that might be undertaken by a legislative committee. This included a lengthy account of the "position of the American Medical Association" and "[t]he position of the American Public Health Association," as well as the vote by the American Bar Association's House of Delegates in February 1972 on proposed abortion legislation. Id., at 141, 144, 146 (emphasis deleted). Also noted were a British judicial decision handed down in 1939 and a new British abortion law enacted in 1967. Id., at 137–138. The Court did not explain why these sources shed light on the meaning of the Constitution, and not one of them adopted or advocated anything like the scheme that Roe imposed on the country.

Finally, after all this, the Court turned to precedent. Citing a broad array of cases, the Court found support for a constitutional "right of personal privacy," id., at 152, but it conflated two very different meanings of the term: the right to shield information from disclosure and the right to make and implement important personal decisions without governmental interference. See *Whalen* v. *Roe*, 429 U. S. 589, 599–600 (1977). Only the cases involving this second sense of the term could have any possible relevance to the abortion issue, and some of the cases in that category involved personal decisions that were obviously very, very far afield. See *Pierce*, 268 U. S. 510 (right to send children to religious school); *Meyer*, 262 U. S. 390 (right to have children receive German language instruction).

What remained was a handful of cases having something to do with marriage, *Loving*, 388 U. S. 1 (right to marry a person of a different race), or procreation, *Skinner*, 316 U. S. 535 (right not to be sterilized); *Griswold*, 381 U. S. 479 (right of married persons to obtain contraceptives); *Eisenstadt*, 405 U. S. 438 (same, for unmarried persons). But none of these decisions involved what is distinctive about abortion: its effect on what *Roe* termed "potential life."

When the Court summarized the basis for the scheme it imposed on the country, it asserted that its rules were "consistent with" the following: (1) "the relative weights of the respective interests involved," (2) "the lessons and examples of medical and legal history," (3) "the lenity of the common law," and (4) "the demands of the profound problems of the present day." *Roe*, 410 U. S., at 165. Put aside the second and third factors, which were based on the Court's flawed account of history, and what remains are precisely the sort of considerations that legislative bodies often take into account when they draw lines that accommodate competing interests. The scheme *Roe* produced *looked* like legislation, and the Court provided the sort of explanation that might be expected from a legislative body.

c

What *Roe* did not provide was any cogent justification for the lines it drew. Why, for example, does a State have no

authority to regulate first trimester abortions for the purpose of protecting a woman's health? The Court's only explanation was that mortality rates for abortion at that stage
were lower than the mortality rates for childbirth. *Id.*, at
163. But the Court did not explain why mortality rates
were the only factor that a State could legitimately consider. Many health and safety regulations aim to avoid ad-
verse health consequences short of death. And the Court
did not explain why it departed from the normal rule that
courts defer to the judgments of legislatures "in areas
fraught with medical and scientific uncertainties." *Marshall* v. *United States*, 414 U. S. 417, 427 (1974).

An even more glaring deficiency was *Roe*'s failure to justify the critical distinction it drew between pre- and post-
viability abortions. Here is the Court's entire explanation:

> "With respect to the State's important and legitimate
> interest in potential life, the 'compelling' point is at vi-
> ability. This is so because the fetus then presumably
> has the capability of meaningful life outside the womb."
> 410 U. S., at 163.

As Professor Laurence Tribe has written, "[c]learly, this
mistakes 'a definition for a syllogism.'" Tribe 4 (quoting Ely
924). The definition of a "viable" fetus is one that is capable
of surviving outside the womb, but why is this the point at
which the State's interest becomes compelling? If, as *Roe*
held, a State's interest in protecting prenatal life is compelling "after viability," 410 U. S., at 163, why isn't that interest "equally compelling before viability"? *Webster* v. *Reproductive Health Services*, 492 U. S. 490, 519 (1989) (plurality
opinion) (quoting *Thornburgh*, 476 U. S., at 795 (White, J.,
dissenting)). *Roe* did not say, and no explanation is apparent.

This arbitrary line has not found much support among
philosophers and ethicists who have attempted to justify a
right to abortion. Some have argued that a fetus should not

be entitled to legal protection until it acquires the characteristics that they regard as defining what it means to be a "person." Among the characteristics that have been offered as essential attributes of "personhood" are sentience, self-awareness, the ability to reason, or some combination thereof.[50] By this logic, it would be an open question whether even born individuals, including young children or those afflicted with certain developmental or medical conditions, merit protection as "persons." But even if one takes the view that "personhood" begins when a certain attribute or combination of attributes is acquired, it is very hard to see why viability should mark the point where "personhood" begins.

The most obvious problem with any such argument is that viability is heavily dependent on factors that have nothing to do with the characteristics of a fetus. One is the

---

[50] See, e.g., P. Singer, Rethinking Life & Death 218 (1994) (defining a person as "a being with awareness of her or his own existence over time, and the capacity to have wants and plans for the future"); B. Steinbock, Life Before Birth: The Moral and Legal Status of Embryos and Fetuses 9–13 (1992) (arguing that "the possession of interests is both necessary and sufficient for moral status" and that the "capacity for conscious awareness is a necessary condition for the possession of interests" (emphasis deleted)); M. Warren, On the Moral and Legal Status of Abortion, 57 The Monist 1, 5 (1973) (arguing that, to qualify as a person, a being must have at least one of five traits that are "central to the concept of personhood": (1) "consciousness (of objects and events external and/or internal to the being), and in particular the capacity to feel pain"; (2) "reasoning (the developed capacity to solve new and relatively complex problems)"; (3) "self-motivated activity (activity which is relatively independent of either genetic or direct external control)"; (4) "the capacity to communicate, by whatever means, messages of an indefinite variety of types"; and (5) "the presence of self-concepts, and self-awareness, either individual or racial, or both" (emphasis deleted)); M. Tooley, Abortion & Infanticide, 2 Philosophy & Pub. Affairs 37, 49 (Autumn 1972) (arguing that "having a right to life presupposes that one is capable of desiring to continue existing as a subject of experiences and other mental states").

state of neonatal care at a particular point in time. Due to the development of new equipment and improved practices, the viability line has changed over the years. In the 19th century, a fetus may not have been viable until the 32d or 33d week of pregnancy or even later.[51] When *Roe* was decided, viability was gauged at roughly 28 weeks. See 410 U. S., at 160. Today, respondents draw the line at 23 or 24 weeks. Brief for Respondents 8. So, according to *Roe*'s logic, States now have a compelling interest in protecting a fetus with a gestational age of, say, 26 weeks, but in 1973 States did not have an interest in protecting an identical fetus. How can that be?

Viability also depends on the "quality of the available medical facilities." *Colautti* v. *Franklin*, 439 U. S. 379, 396 (1979). Thus, a 24-week-old fetus may be viable if a woman gives birth in a city with hospitals that provide advanced care for very premature babies, but if the woman travels to a remote area far from any such hospital, the fetus may no longer be viable. On what ground could the constitutional status of a fetus depend on the pregnant woman's location? And if viability is meant to mark a line having universal moral significance, can it be that a fetus that is viable in a big city in the United States has a privileged moral status

---

[51] See W. Lusk, Science and the Art of Midwifery 74–75 (1882) (explaining that "[w]ith care, the life of a child born within [the eighth month of pregnancy] may be preserved"); *id.*, at 326 ("Where the choice lies with the physician, the provocation of labor is usually deferred until the thirty-third or thirty-fourth week"); J. Beck, Researches in Medicine and Medical Jurisprudence 68 (2d ed. 1835) ("Although children born before the completion of the seventh month have occasionally survived, and been reared, yet in a medico-legal point of view, no child ought to be considered as capable of sustaining an independent existence until the seventh month has been fully completed"); see also J. Baker, The Incubator and the Medical Discovery of the Premature Infant, J. Perinatology 322 (2000) (explaining that, in the 19th century, infants born at seven to eight months' gestation were unlikely to survive beyond "the first days of life").

not enjoyed by an identical fetus in a remote area of a poor country?

In addition, as the Court once explained, viability is not really a hard-and-fast line. *Ibid.* A physician determining a particular fetus's odds of surviving outside the womb must consider "a number of variables," including "gestational age," "fetal weight," a woman's "general health and nutrition," the "quality of the available medical facilities," and other factors. *Id.*, at 395–396. It is thus "only with difficulty" that a physician can estimate the "probability" of a particular fetus's survival. *Id.*, at 396. And even if each fetus's probability of survival could be ascertained with certainty, settling on a "probabilit[y] of survival" that should count as "viability" is another matter. *Ibid.* Is a fetus viable with a 10 percent chance of survival? 25 percent? 50 percent? Can such a judgment be made by a State? And can a State specify a gestational age limit that applies in all cases? Or must these difficult questions be left entirely to the individual "attending physician on the particular facts of the case before him"? *Id.*, at 388.

The viability line, which *Casey* termed *Roe*'s central rule, makes no sense, and it is telling that other countries almost uniformly eschew such a line.[52] The Court thus asserted raw judicial power to impose, as a matter of constitutional law, a uniform viability rule that allowed the States less freedom to regulate abortion than the majority of western democracies enjoy.

d

All in all, *Roe*'s reasoning was exceedingly weak, and academic commentators, including those who agreed with the

---

[52] According to the Center for Reproductive Rights, only the United States and the Netherlands use viability as a gestational limit on the availability of abortion on-request. See Center for Reproductive Rights, The World's Abortion Laws (Feb. 23, 2021), https://reproductiverights .org/maps/worlds-abortion-laws.

decision as a matter of policy, were unsparing in their criticism. John Hart Ely famously wrote that *Roe* was "not constitutional law and g[ave] almost no sense of an obligation to try to be." Ely 947 (emphasis deleted). Archibald Cox, who served as Solicitor General under President Kennedy, commented that *Roe* "read[s] like a set of hospital rules and regulations" that "[n]either historian, layman, nor lawyer will be persuaded . . . are part of . . . the Constitution." The Role of the Supreme Court in American Government 113–114 (1976). Laurence Tribe wrote that "even if there is a need to divide pregnancy into several segments with lines that clearly identify the limits of governmental power, 'interest-balancing' of the form the Court pursues fails to justify any of the lines actually drawn." Tribe 4–5. Mark Tushnet termed *Roe* a "totally unreasoned judicial opinion." Red, White, and Blue: A Critical Analysis of Constitutional Law 54 (1988). See also P. Bobbitt, Constitutional Fate 157 (1982); A. Amar, Foreword: The Document and the Doctrine, 114 Harv. L. Rev. 26, 110 (2000).

Despite *Roe*'s weaknesses, its reach was steadily extended in the years that followed. The Court struck down laws requiring that second-trimester abortions be performed only in hospitals, *Akron v. Akron Center for Reproductive Health, Inc.*, 462 U. S. 416, 433–439 (1983); that minors obtain parental consent, *Planned Parenthood of Central Mo. v. Danforth*, 428 U. S. 52, 74 (1976); that women give written consent after being informed of the status of the developing prenatal life and the risks of abortion, *Akron*, 462 U. S., at 442–445; that women wait 24 hours for an abortion, *id.*, at 449–451; that a physician determine viability in a particular manner, *Colautti*, 439 U. S., at 390–397; that a physician performing a post-viability abortion use the technique most likely to preserve the life of the fetus, *id.*, at 397–401; and that fetal remains be treated in a humane and sanitary manner, *Akron*, 462 U. S., at 451–452.

Justice White complained that the Court was engaging in "unrestrained imposition of its own extraconstitutional value preferences." *Thornburgh*, 476 U. S., at 794 (dissenting opinion). And the United States as *amicus curiae* asked the Court to overrule *Roe* five times in the decade before *Casey*, see 505 U. S., at 844 (joint opinion), and then asked the Court to overrule it once more in *Casey* itself.

2

When *Casey* revisited *Roe* almost 20 years later, very little of *Roe*'s reasoning was defended or preserved. The Court abandoned any reliance on a privacy right and instead grounded the abortion right entirely on the Fourteenth Amendment's Due Process Clause. 505 U. S., at 846. The Court did not reaffirm *Roe*'s erroneous account of abortion history. In fact, none of the Justices in the majority said anything about the history of the abortion right. And as for precedent, the Court relied on essentially the same body of cases that *Roe* had cited. Thus, with respect to the standard grounds for constitutional decisionmaking—text, history, and precedent—*Casey* did not attempt to bolster *Roe*'s reasoning.

The Court also made no real effort to remedy one of the greatest weaknesses in *Roe*'s analysis: its much-criticized discussion of viability. The Court retained what it called *Roe*'s "central holding"—that a State may not regulate previability abortions for the purpose of protecting fetal life— but it provided no principled defense of the viability line. 505 U. S., at 860, 870–871. Instead, it merely rephrased what *Roe* had said, stating that viability marked the point at which "the independent existence of a second life can in reason and fairness be the object of state protection that now overrides the rights of the woman." 505 U. S., at 870. Why "reason and fairness" demanded that the line be drawn at viability the Court did not explain. And the Justices who authored the controlling opinion conspicuously failed to say that they agreed with the viability rule; instead, they candidly acknowledged "the reservations [some] of us may have in reaffirming [that] holding of *Roe.*" *Id.*, at 853.

The controlling opinion criticized and rejected *Roe*'s trimester scheme, 505 U. S., at 872, and substituted a new "undue burden" test, but the basis for this test was obscure. And as we will explain, the test is full of ambiguities and is difficult to apply.

Casey, in short, either refused to reaffirm or rejected important aspects of *Roe*'s analysis, failed to remedy glaring deficiencies in *Roe*'s reasoning, endorsed what it termed *Roe*'s central holding while suggesting that a majority might not have thought it was correct, provided no new support for the abortion right other than *Roe*'s status as precedent, and imposed a new and problematic test with no firm grounding in constitutional text, history, or precedent.

As discussed below, *Casey* also deployed a novel version of the doctrine of *stare decisis*. See *infra*, at 64–69. This new doctrine did not account for the profound wrongness of the decision in *Roe*, and placed great weight on an intangible form of reliance with little if any basis in prior case law. *Stare decisis* does not command the preservation of such a decision.

C

Workability.   Our precedents counsel that another important consideration in deciding whether a precedent should be overruled is whether the rule it imposes is workable—that is, whether it can be understood and applied in a consistent and predictable manner. *Montejo* v. *Louisiana*, 556 U. S. 778, 792 (2009); *Patterson* v. *McLean Credit Union*, 491 U. S. 164, 173 (1989); *Gulfstream Aerospace Corp.* v. *Mayacamas Corp.*, 485 U. S. 271, 283–284 (1988).   *Casey*'s "undue burden" test has scored poorly on the workability scale.

1

Problems begin with the very concept of an "undue burden." As Justice Scalia noted in his *Casey* partial dissent, determining whether a burden is "due" or "undue" is "inherently standardless." 505 U. S., at 992; see also *June Medical Services L. L. C.* v. *Russo*, 591 U. S. ___, ___ (2020) (GORSUCH, J., dissenting) (slip op., at 17) ("[W]hether a burden is deemed undue depends heavily on which factors the judge considers and how much weight he accords each of them" (internal quotation marks and alterations omitted)).

The *Casey* plurality tried to put meaning into the "undue burden" test by setting out three subsidiary rules, but these rules created their own problems. The first rule is that "a provision of law is invalid, if its purpose or effect is to place a *substantial obstacle* in the path of a woman seeking an abortion before the fetus attains viability." 505 U. S., at 878 (emphasis added); see also *id.*, at 877. But whether a particular obstacle qualifies as "substantial" is often open to reasonable debate. In the sense relevant here, "substantial" means "of ample or considerable amount, quantity, or size." Random House Webster's Unabridged Dictionary 1897 (2d ed. 2001). Huge burdens are plainly "substantial," and trivial ones are not, but in between these extremes, there is a wide gray area.

This ambiguity is a problem, and the second rule, which applies at all stages of a pregnancy, muddies things further. It states that measures designed "to ensure that the woman's choice is informed" are constitutional so long as they do not impose "an undue burden on the right." *Casey*, 505 U. S., at 878. To the extent that this rule applies to pre-viability abortions, it overlaps with the first rule and appears to impose a different standard. Consider a law that imposes an insubstantial obstacle but serves little purpose. As applied to a pre-viability abortion, would such a regulation be constitutional on the ground that it does not impose a *"substantial* obstacle"? Or would it be unconstitutional on the ground that it creates an *"undue* burden" because the burden it imposes, though slight, outweighs its negligible benefits? *Casey* does not say, and this ambiguity would lead to confusion down the line. Compare *June Medical*, 591 U. S., at ___–___ (plurality opinion) (slip op., at 1–2), with *id.*, at ___–___ (ROBERTS, C. J., concurring) (slip op., at 5–6).

The third rule complicates the picture even more. Under that rule, *"[u]nnecessary health* regulations that have the purpose or effect of presenting a *substantial obstacle* to a woman seeking an abortion impose an *undue burden* on the right." *Casey*, 505 U. S., at 878 (emphasis added). This rule contains no fewer than three vague terms. It includes the two already discussed—"undue burden" and "substantial obstacle"—even though they are inconsistent. And it adds a third ambiguous term when it refers to *"unnecessary* health regulations." The term "necessary" has a range of meanings—from "essential" to merely "useful." See Black's Law Dictionary 928 (5th ed. 1979); American Heritage Dictionary of the English Language 877 (1971). *Casey* did not explain the sense in which the term is used in this rule.

In addition to these problems, one more applies to all three rules. They all call on courts to examine a law's effect on women, but a regulation may have a very different impact on different women for a variety of reasons, including their places of residence, financial resources, family situations, work and personal obligations, knowledge about fetal development and abortion, psychological and emotional disposition and condition, and the firmness of their desire to obtain abortions. In order to determine whether a regulation presents a substantial obstacle to women, a court needs to know which set of women it should have in mind and how many of the women in this set must find that an obstacle is "substantial."

Casey provided no clear answer to these questions. It said that a regulation is unconstitutional if it imposes a substantial obstacle "in a large fraction of cases in which [it] is relevant," 505 U. S., at 895, but there is obviously no clear line between a fraction that is "large" and one that is not. Nor is it clear what the Court meant by "cases in which" a regulation is "relevant." These ambiguities have caused confusion and disagreement. Compare *Whole Woman's Health* v. *Hellerstedt*, 579 U. S. 582, 627–628 (2016), with *id.*, at 666–667, and n. 11 (ALITO, J., dissenting).

2

The difficulty of applying *Casey*'s new rules surfaced in that very case. The controlling opinion found that Pennsylvania's 24-hour waiting period requirement and its informed-consent provision did not impose "undue burden[s]," *Casey*, 505 U. S., at 881–887, but Justice Stevens, applying the same test, reached the opposite result, *id.*, at 920–922 (opinion concurring in part and dissenting in part). That did not bode well, and then-Chief Justice Rehnquist aptly observed that "the undue burden standard presents nothing more workable than the trimester framework." *Id.*, at 964–966 (dissenting opinion).

The ambiguity of the "undue burden" test also produced disagreement in later cases. In *Whole Woman's Health*, the Court adopted the cost-benefit interpretation of the test, stating that "[t]he rule announced in *Casey* . . . requires that courts consider the burdens a law imposes on abortion access *together with the benefits those laws confer.*" 579 U. S., at 607 (emphasis added). But five years later, a majority of the Justices rejected that interpretation. See *June Medical*, 591 U. S. ___. Four Justices reaffirmed *Whole Woman's Health*'s instruction to "weigh" a law's "benefits" against "the burdens it imposes on abortion access." 591 U. S., at ___ (plurality opinion) (slip op., at 2) (internal quotation marks omitted). But THE CHIEF JUSTICE—who cast the deciding vote—argued that "[n]othing about *Casey* suggested that a weighing of costs and benefits of an abortion regulation was a job for the courts." *Id.*, at ___ (opinion concurring in judgment) (slip op., at 6). And the four Justices in dissent rejected the plurality's interpretation of *Casey*. See 591 U. S., at ___ (opinion of ALITO, J., joined in relevant part by THOMAS, GORSUCH, and KAVANAUGH, JJ.) (slip op., at 4); *id.*, at ___-___ (opinion of GORSUCH, J.) (slip op., at 15–18); *id.*, at ___-___ (opinion of KAVANAUGH, J.) (slip op., at 1–2) ("[F]ive Members of the Court reject the *Whole Woman's Health* cost-benefit standard").

This Court's experience applying *Casey* has confirmed Chief Justice Rehnquist's prescient diagnosis that the undue-burden standard was "not built to last." *Casey*, 505 U. S., at 965 (opinion concurring in judgment in part and dissenting in part).

3

The experience of the Courts of Appeals provides further evidence that *Casey*'s "line between" permissible and unconstitutional restrictions "has proved to be impossible to draw with precision." *Janus*, 585 U. S., at ___ (slip op., at 38).

Casey has generated a long list of Circuit conflicts. Most recently, the Courts of Appeals have disagreed about whether the balancing test from *Whole Woman's Health* correctly states the undue-burden framework.[53] They have disagreed on the legality of parental notification rules.[54]

---

[53] Compare *Whole Woman's Health* v. *Paxton*, 10 F. 4th 430, 440 (CA5 2021), *EMW Women's Surgical Center, P.S.C.* v. *Friedlander*, 978 F. 3d 418, 437 (CA6 2020), and *Hopkins* v. *Jegley*, 968 F. 3d 912, 915 (CA8 2020) (*per curiam*), with *Planned Parenthood of Ind. & Ky., Inc.* v. *Box*, 991 F. 3d 740, 751–752 (CA7 2021).

[54] Compare *Planned Parenthood of Blue Ridge* v. *Camblos*, 155 F. 3d 352, 367 (CA4 1998), with *Planned Parenthood of Ind. & Ky., Inc.* v. *Ad-*

Opinion of the Court

They have disagreed about bans on certain dilation and evacuation procedures.[55] They have disagreed about when an increase in the time needed to reach a clinic constitutes an undue burden.[56] And they have disagreed on whether a State may regulate abortions performed because of the fetus's race, sex, or disability.[57]

The Courts of Appeals have experienced particular difficulty in applying the large-fraction-of-relevant-cases test. They have criticized the assignment while reaching unpredictable results.[58] And they have candidly outlined *Casey's* many other problems.[59]

---

ams, 937 F. 3d 973, 985–990 (CA7 2019), cert. granted, judgment vacated, 591 U. S. ___ (2020), and *Planned Parenthood, Sioux Falls Clinic* v. *Miller*, 63 F. 3d 1452, 1460 (CA8 1995).

[55] Compare *Whole Woman's Health* v. *Paxton*, 10 F. 4th, at 435–436, with *West Ala. Women's Center* v. *Williamson*, 900 F. 3d 1310, 1319, 1327 (CA11 2018), and *EMW Women's Surgical Center, P.S.C.* v. *Friedlander*, 960 F. 3d 785, 806–808 (CA6 2020).

[56] Compare *Tucson Woman's Clinic* v. *Eden*, 379 F. 3d 531, 541 (CA9 2004), with *Women's Medical Professional Corp.* v. *Baird*, 438 F. 3d 595, 605 (CA6 2006), and *Greenville Women's Clinic* v. *Bryant*, 222 F. 3d 157, 171–172 (CA4 2000).

[57] Compare *Preterm-Cleveland* v. *McCloud*, 994 F. 3d 512, 520–535 (CA6 2021), with *Little Rock Family Planning Servs.* v. *Rutledge*, 984 F. 3d 682, 688–690 (CA8 2021).

[58] See, *e.g., Bristol Regional Women's Center, P.C.* v. *Slatery*, 7 F. 4th 478, 485 (CA6 2021); *Reproductive Health Servs.* v. *Strange*, 3 F. 4th 1240, 1269 (CA11 2021) (*per curiam*); *June Medical Servs., L.L.C.* v. *Gee*, 905 F. 3d 787, 814 (CA5 2020), rev'd, 591 U. S. ___; *Preterm-Cleveland*, 994 F. 3d, at 534; *Planned Parenthood of Ark. & Eastern Okla.* v. *Jegley*, 864 F. 3d 953, 958–960 (CA8 2017); *McCormack* v. *Hertzog*, 788 F. 3d 1017, 1029–1030 (CA9 2015); compare *A Womans Choice–East Side Womens Clinic* v. *Newman*, 305 F. 3d 684, 699 (CA7 2002) (Coffey, J., concurring), with *id.*, at 708 (Wood, J., dissenting).

[59] See, *e.g., Memphis Center for Reproductive Health* v. *Slatery*, 14 F. 4th 409, 451 (CA6 2021) (Thapar, J., concurring in judgment in part and dissenting in part); *Preterm-Cleveland*, 994 F. 3d, at 524; *Planned Parenthood of Ind. & Ky., Inc.* v. *Commissioner of Ind. State Dept. of*

Casey's "undue burden" test has proved to be unworkable. "[P]lucked from nowhere," 505 U. S., at 965 (opinion of Rehnquist, C. J.), it "seems calculated to perpetuate give-it-a-try litigation" before judges assigned an unwieldy and inappropriate task. *Lehnert* v. *Ferris Faculty Assn.*, 500 U. S. 507, 551 (1991) (Scalia, J., concurring in judgment in part and dissenting in part). Continued adherence to that standard would undermine, not advance, the "evenhanded, predictable, and consistent development of legal principles." *Payne*, 501 U. S., at 827.

D

Effect on other areas of law. *Roe* and *Casey* have led to the distortion of many important but unrelated legal doctrines, and that effect provides further support for overruling those decisions. See *Ramos*, 590 U. S., at ___ (opinion of KAVANAUGH, J.) (slip op., at 8); *Janus*, 585 U. S., at ___ (slip op., at 34).

Members of this Court have repeatedly lamented that "no legal rule or doctrine is safe from ad hoc nullification by this Court when an occasion for its application arises in a case involving state regulation of abortion." *Thornburgh*, 476 U. S., at 814 (O'Connor, J., dissenting); see *Madsen* v. *Women's Health Center, Inc.*, 512 U. S. 753, 785 (1994) (Scalia, J., concurring in judgment in part and dissenting

---

Health, 888 F. 3d 300, 313 (CA7 2018) (Manion, J., concurring in judgment in part and dissenting in part); *Planned Parenthood of Ind. & Ky., Inc.* v. *Box*, 949 F. 3d 997, 999 (CA7 2019) (Easterbrook, J., concurring in denial of reh'g en banc) ("How much burden is 'undue' is a matter of judgment, which depends on what the burden would be . . . and whether that burden is excessive (a matter of weighing costs against benefits, which one judge is apt to do differently from another, and which judges as a group are apt to do differently from state legislators)"); *National Abortion Federation* v. *Gonzales*, 437 F. 3d 278, 290–296 (CA2 2006) (Walker, C. J., concurring); *Planned Parenthood of Rocky Mountains Servs. Corp.* v. *Owens*, 287 F. 3d 910, 931 (CA10 2002) (Baldock, J., dissenting).

in part); *Whole Woman's Health,* 579 U. S., at 631–633 (THOMAS, J., dissenting); *id.,* at 645–666, 678–684 (ALITO, J., dissenting); *June Medical,* 591 U. S., at ___–___ (GORSUCH, J., dissenting) (slip op., at 1–15).

The Court's abortion cases have diluted the strict standard for facial constitutional challenges.[60] They have ignored the Court's third-party standing doctrine.[61] They have disregarded standard *res judicata* principles.[62] They have flouted the ordinary rules on the severability of unconstitutional provisions,[63] as well as the rule that statutes should be read where possible to avoid unconstitutionality.[64] And they have distorted First Amendment doctrines.[65]

When vindicating a doctrinal innovation requires courts to engineer exceptions to longstanding background rules, the doctrine "has failed to deliver the 'principled and intelligible' development of the law that *stare decisis* purports to secure." *Id.,* at ___ (THOMAS, J., dissenting) (slip op., at 19) (quoting *Vasquez* v. *Hillery,* 474 U. S. 254, 265 (1986)).

E

Reliance interests. We last consider whether overruling *Roe* and *Casey* will upend substantial reliance interests.

---

[60] Compare *United States* v. *Salerno,* 481 U. S. 739, 745 (1987), with *Casey,* 505 U. S., at 895; see also *supra,* at 56–59.

[61] Compare *Warth* v. *Seldin,* 422 U. S. 490, 499 (1975), and *Elk Grove Unified School Dist.* v. *Newdow,* 542 U. S. 1, 15, 17–18 (2004), with *June Medical,* 591 U. S., at ___ (ALITO, J., dissenting) (slip op., at 28), *id.,* at ___–___ (GORSUCH, J., dissenting) (slip op., at 6–7) (collecting cases), and *Whole Woman's Health,* 579 U. S., at 632, n. 1 (THOMAS, J., dissenting).

[62] Compare *id.,* at 598–606 (majority opinion), with *id.,* at 645–666 (ALITO, J., dissenting).

[63] Compare *id.,* at 623–626 (majority opinion), with *id.,* at 644–645 (ALITO, J., dissenting).

[64] See *Stenberg* v. *Carhart,* 530 U. S. 914, 977–978 (2000) (Kennedy, J., dissenting); *id.,* at 996–997 (THOMAS, J., dissenting).

[65] See *Hill* v. *Colorado,* 530 U. S. 703, 741–742 (2000) (Scalia, J., dissenting); *id.,* at 765 (Kennedy, J., dissenting).

See *Ramos*, 590 U. S., at ___ (opinion of KAVANAUGH, J.) (slip op., at 15); *Janus*, 585 U. S., at ___–___ (slip op., at 34–35).

1

Traditional reliance interests arise "where advance planning of great precision is most obviously a necessity." *Casey*, 505 U. S., at 856 (joint opinion); see also *Payne*, 501 U. S., at 828. In *Casey*, the controlling opinion conceded that those traditional reliance interests were not implicated because getting an abortion is generally "unplanned activity," and "reproductive planning could take virtually immediate account of any sudden restoration of state authority to ban abortions." 505 U. S., at 856. For these reasons, we agree with the *Casey* plurality that conventional, concrete reliance interests are not present here.

2

Unable to find reliance in the conventional sense, the controlling opinion in *Casey* perceived a more intangible form of reliance. It wrote that "people [had] organized intimate relationships and made choices that define their views of themselves and their places in society . . . in reliance on the availability of abortion in the event that contraception should fail" and that "[t]he ability of women to participate equally in the economic and social life of the Nation has been facilitated by their ability to control their reproductive lives." *Ibid.* But this Court is ill-equipped to assess "generalized assertions about the national psyche." *Id.*, at 957 (opinion of Rehnquist, C. J.). *Casey*'s notion of reliance thus finds little support in our cases, which instead emphasize very concrete reliance interests, like those that develop in "cases involving property and contract rights." *Payne*, 501 U. S., at 828.

When a concrete reliance interest is asserted, courts are equipped to evaluate the claim, but assessing the novel and

Opinion of the Court

intangible form of reliance endorsed by the *Casey* plurality is another matter. That form of reliance depends on an empirical question that is hard for anyone—and in particular, for a court—to assess, namely, the effect of the abortion right on society and in particular on the lives of women. The contending sides in this case make impassioned and conflicting arguments about the effects of the abortion right on the lives of women. Compare Brief for Petitioners 34–36; Brief for Women Scholars et al. as *Amici Curiae* 13–20, 29–41, with Brief for Respondents 36–41; Brief for National Women's Law Center et al. as *Amici Curiae* 15–32. The contending sides also make conflicting arguments about the status of the fetus. This Court has neither the authority nor the expertise to adjudicate those disputes, and the *Casey* plurality's speculations and weighing of the relative importance of the fetus and mother represent a departure from the "original constitutional proposition" that "courts do not substitute their social and economic beliefs for the judgment of legislative bodies." *Ferguson* v. *Skrupa*, 372 U. S. 726, 729–730 (1963).

Our decision returns the issue of abortion to those legislative bodies, and it allows women on both sides of the abortion issue to seek to affect the legislative process by influencing public opinion, lobbying legislators, voting, and running for office. Women are not without electoral or political power. It is noteworthy that the percentage of women who register to vote and cast ballots is consistently higher than the percentage of men who do so.[66] In the last election in November 2020, women, who make up around 51.5 percent of the population of Mississippi,[67] constituted

---

[66] See Dept. of Commerce, U. S. Census Bureau (Census Bureau), An Analysis of the 2018 Congressional Election 6 (Dec. 2021) (Fig. 5) (showing that women made up over 50 percent of the voting population in every congressional election between 1978 and 2018).

[67] Census Bureau, QuickFacts, Mississippi (July 1, 2021), https://www.

55.5 percent of the voters who cast ballots.[68]

3

Unable to show concrete reliance on *Roe* and *Casey* themselves, the Solicitor General suggests that overruling those decisions would "threaten the Court's precedents holding that the Due Process Clause protects other rights." Brief for United States 26 (citing *Obergefell*, 576 U. S. 644; *Lawrence*, 539 U. S. 558; *Griswold*, 381 U. S. 479). That is not correct for reasons we have already discussed. As even the *Casey* plurality recognized, "[a]bortion is a unique act" because it terminates "life or potential life." 505 U. S., at 852; see also *Roe*, 410 U. S., at 159 (abortion is "inherently different from marital intimacy," "marriage," or "procreation"). And to ensure that our decision is not misunderstood or mischaracterized, we emphasize that our decision concerns the constitutional right to abortion and no other right. Nothing in this opinion should be understood to cast doubt on precedents that do not concern abortion.

IV

Having shown that traditional *stare decisis* factors do not weigh in favor of retaining *Roe* or *Casey*, we must address one final argument that featured prominently in the *Casey* plurality opinion.

The argument was cast in different terms, but stated simply, it was essentially as follows. The American people's belief in the rule of law would be shaken if they lost respect for this Court as an institution that decides important cases based on principle, not "social and political pressures." 505 U. S., at 865. There is a special danger that the public will

---

census.gov/quickfacts/MS.

[68] Census Bureau, Voting and Registration in the Election of November 2020, Table 4b: Reported Voting and Registration, by Sex, Race and Hispanic Origin, for States: November 2020, https://www.census.gov/data/tables/time-series/demo/voting-and-registration/p20-585.html.

perceive a decision as having been made for unprincipled reasons when the Court overrules a controversial "watershed" decision, such as *Roe*. 505 U. S., at 866–867. A decision overruling *Roe* would be perceived as having been made "under fire" and as a "surrender to political pressure," 505 U. S., at 867, and therefore the preservation of public approval of the Court weighs heavily in favor of retaining *Roe*, see 505 U. S., at 869.

This analysis starts out on the right foot but ultimately veers off course. The *Casey* plurality was certainly right that it is important for the public to perceive that our decisions are based on principle, and we should make every effort to achieve that objective by issuing opinions that carefully show how a proper understanding of the law leads to the results we reach. But we cannot exceed the scope of our authority under the Constitution, and we cannot allow our decisions to be affected by any extraneous influences such as concern about the public's reaction to our work. Cf. *Texas* v. *Johnson*, 491 U. S. 397 (1989); *Brown*, 347 U. S. 483. That is true both when we initially decide a constitutional issue *and* when we consider whether to overrule a prior decision. As Chief Justice Rehnquist explained, "The Judicial Branch derives its legitimacy, not from following public opinion, but from deciding by its best lights whether legislative enactments of the popular branches of Government comport with the Constitution. The doctrine of *stare decisis* is an adjunct of this duty, and should be no more subject to the vagaries of public opinion than is the basic judicial task." *Casey*, 505 U. S., at 963 (opinion concurring in judgment in part and dissenting in part). In suggesting otherwise, the *Casey* plurality went beyond this Court's role in our constitutional system.

The *Casey* plurality "call[ed] the contending sides of a national controversy to end their national division," and claimed the authority to impose a permanent settlement of the issue of a constitutional abortion right simply by saying that the matter was closed. *Id.*, at 867. That unprecedented claim exceeded the power vested in us by the Constitution. As Alexander Hamilton famously put it, the Constitution gives the judiciary "neither Force nor Will." The Federalist No. 78, p. 523 (J. Cooke ed. 1961). Our sole authority is to exercise "judgment"—which is to say, the authority to judge what the law means and how it should apply to the case at hand. *Ibid.* The Court has no authority to decree that an erroneous precedent is *permanently* exempt from evaluation under traditional *stare decisis* principles. A precedent of this Court is subject to the usual principles of *stare decisis* under which adherence to precedent is the norm but not an inexorable command. If the rule were otherwise, erroneous decisions like *Plessy* and *Lochner* would still be the law. That is not how *stare decisis* operates.

The *Casey* plurality also misjudged the practical limits of this Court's influence. *Roe* certainly did not succeed in ending division on the issue of abortion. On the contrary, *Roe* "inflamed" a national issue that has remained bitterly divisive for the past half century. *Casey*, 505 U. S., at 995 (opinion of Scalia, J.); see also R. Ginsburg, Speaking in a Judicial Voice, 67 N. Y. U. L. Rev. 1185, 1208 (1992) (*Roe* may have "halted a political process," "prolonged divisiveness," and "deferred stable settlement of the issue"). And for the past 30 years, *Casey* has done the same.

Neither decision has ended debate over the issue of a constitutional right to obtain an abortion. Indeed, in this case, 26 States expressly ask us to overrule *Roe* and *Casey* and to return the issue of abortion to the people and their elected representatives. This Court's inability to end debate on the issue should not have been surprising. This Court cannot bring about the permanent resolution of a rancorous national controversy simply by dictating a settlement and telling the people to move on. Whatever influence the Court may have on public attitudes must stem from the strength of our opinions, not an attempt to exercise "raw judicial power." *Roe*, 410 U. S., at 222 (White, J., dissenting).

We do not pretend to know how our political system or society will respond to today's decision overruling *Roe* and *Casey*. And even if we could foresee what will happen, we would have no authority to let that knowledge influence our decision. We can only do our job, which is to interpret the law, apply longstanding principles of *stare decisis*, and decide this case accordingly.

We therefore hold that the Constitution does not confer a right to abortion. *Roe* and *Casey* must be overruled, and the authority to regulate abortion must be returned to the people and their elected representatives.

V

A

1

The dissent argues that we have "abandon[ed]" *stare decisis, post,* at 30, but we have done no such thing, and it is the dissent's understanding of *stare decisis* that breaks with tradition. The dissent's foundational contention is that the Court should never (or perhaps almost never) overrule an egregiously wrong constitutional precedent unless the Court can "poin[t] to major legal or factual changes undermining [the] decision's original basis." *Post*, at 37. To support this contention, the dissent claims that *Brown* v. *Board of Education*, 347 U. S. 483, and other landmark cases overruling prior precedents "responded to changed law and to changed facts and attitudes that had taken hold throughout society." *Post,* at 43. The unmistakable implication of this argument is that only the passage of time and new developments justified those decisions. Recognition that the cases they overruled were egregiously wrong on the day they were handed down was not enough.

The Court has never adopted this strange new version of

stare decisis—and with good reason. Does the dissent really maintain that overruling *Plessy* was not justified until the country had experienced more than a half-century of state-sanctioned segregation and generations of Black school children had suffered all its effects? *Post,* at 44–45.

Here is another example. On the dissent's view, it must have been wrong for *West Virginia Bd. of Ed.* v. *Barnette,* 319 U. S. 624, to overrule *Minersville School Dist.* v. *Gobitis,* 310 U. S. 586, a bare three years after it was handed down. In both cases, children who were Jehovah's Witnesses refused on religious grounds to salute the flag or recite the pledge of allegiance. The *Barnette* Court did not claim that its reexamination of the issue was prompted by any intervening legal or factual developments, so if the Court had followed the dissent's new version of *stare decisis,* it would have been compelled to adhere to *Gobitis* and countenance continued First Amendment violations for some unspecified period.

Precedents should be respected, but sometimes the Court errs, and occasionally the Court issues an important decision that is egregiously wrong. When that happens, *stare decisis* is not a straitjacket. And indeed, the dissent eventually admits that a decision *could* "be overruled just because it is terribly wrong," though the dissent does not explain when that would be so. *Post,* at 45.

2

Even if the dissent were correct in arguing that an egregiously wrong decision should (almost) never be overruled unless its mistake is later highlighted by "major legal or factual changes," reexamination of *Roe* and *Casey* would be amply justified. We have already mentioned a number of post-*Casey* developments, see *supra,* at 33–34, 59–63, but the most profound change may be the failure of the *Casey* plurality's call for "the contending sides" in the controversy about abortion "to end their national division," 505 U. S., at

867. That has not happened, and there is no reason to think that another decision sticking with *Roe* would achieve what *Casey* could not.

The dissent, however, is undeterred. It contends that the "very controversy surrounding *Roe* and *Casey*" is an important *stare decisis* consideration that requires upholding those precedents. See *post,* at 55–57. The dissent characterizes *Casey* as a "precedent about precedent" that is permanently shielded from further evaluation under traditional *stare decisis* principles. See *post,* at 57. But as we have explained, *Casey* broke new ground when it treated the national controversy provoked by *Roe* as a ground for refusing to reconsider that decision, and no subsequent case has relied on that factor. Our decision today simply applies longstanding *stare decisis* factors instead of applying a version of the doctrine that seems to apply only in abortion cases.

3

Finally, the dissent suggests that our decision calls into question *Griswold, Eisenstadt, Lawrence,* and *Obergefell.* *Post,* at 4–5, 26–27, n. 8. But we have stated unequivocally that "[n]othing in this opinion should be understood to cast doubt on precedents that do not concern abortion." *Supra,* at 66. We have also explained why that is so: rights regarding contraception and same-sex relationships are inherently different from the right to abortion because the latter (as we have stressed) uniquely involves what *Roe* and *Casey* termed "potential life." *Roe,* 410 U. S., at 150 (emphasis deleted); *Casey,* 505 U. S., at 852. Therefore, a right to abortion cannot be justified by a purported analogy to the rights recognized in those other cases or by "appeals to a broader right to autonomy." *Supra,* at 32. It is hard to see how we could be clearer. Moreover, even putting aside that these cases are distinguishable, there is a further point that the dissent ignores: Each precedent is subject to its own *stare decisis* analysis, and the factors that our doctrine instructs us to consider like reliance and workability are different for these cases than for our abortion jurisprudence.

B

1

We now turn to the concurrence in the judgment, which reproves us for deciding whether *Roe* and *Casey* should be retained or overruled. That opinion (which for convenience we will call simply "the concurrence") recommends a "more measured course," which it defends based on what it claims is "a straightforward *stare decisis* analysis." *Post*, at 1 (opinion of ROBERTS, C. J.). The concurrence would "leave for another day whether to reject any right to an abortion at all," *post*, at 7, and would hold only that if the Constitution protects any such right, the right ends once women have had "a reasonable opportunity" to obtain an abortion, *post*, at 1. The concurrence does not specify what period of time is sufficient to provide such an opportunity, but it would hold that 15 weeks, the period allowed under Mississippi's law, is enough—at least "absent rare circumstances." *Post*, at 2, 10.

There are serious problems with this approach, and it is revealing that nothing like it was recommended by either party. As we have recounted, both parties and the Solicitor General have urged us either to reaffirm or overrule *Roe* and *Casey*. See *supra*, at 4–5. And when the specific approach advanced by the concurrence was broached at oral argument, both respondents and the Solicitor General emphatically rejected it. Respondents' counsel termed it "completely unworkable" and "less principled and less workable than viability." Tr. of Oral Arg. 54. The Solicitor General argued that abandoning the viability line would leave courts and others with "no continued guidance." *Id.*, at 101. What is more, the concurrence has not identified any of the more than 130 *amicus* briefs filed in this case that advocated its approach. The concurrence would do exactly what it criticizes *Roe* for doing: pulling "out of thin air" a test that "[n]o party or *amicus* asked the Court to adopt." *Post*, at 3.

2

The concurrence's most fundamental defect is its failure to offer any principled basis for its approach. The concurrence would "discar[d]" "the rule from *Roe* and *Casey* that a woman's right to terminate her pregnancy extends up to the point that the fetus is regarded as 'viable' outside the womb." *Post*, at 2. But this rule was a critical component of the holdings in *Roe* and *Casey*, and *stare decisis* is "a doctrine of preservation, not transformation," *Citizens United* v. *Federal Election Comm'n*, 558 U. S. 310, 384 (2010) (ROBERTS, C. J., concurring). Therefore, a new rule that discards the viability rule cannot be defended on *stare decisis* grounds.

The concurrence concedes that its approach would "not be available" if "the rationale of *Roe* and *Casey* were inextricably entangled with and dependent upon the viability standard." *Post*, at 7. But the concurrence asserts that the viability line is separable from the constitutional right they recognized, and can therefore be "discarded" without disturbing any past precedent. *Post*, at 7–8. That is simply incorrect.

Roe's trimester rule was expressly tied to viability, see 410 U. S., at 163–164, and viability played a critical role in later abortion decisions. For example, in *Planned Parenthood of Central Mo.* v. *Danforth*, 428 U. S. 52, the Court reiterated *Roe*'s rule that a "State may regulate an abortion to protect the life of the fetus and even may proscribe abortion" at "the stage *subsequent to viability*." 428 U. S., at 61 (emphasis added). The Court then rejected a challenge to Missouri's definition of viability, holding that the State's definition was consistent with *Roe*'s. 428 U. S., at 63–64. If viability was not an essential part of the rule adopted in *Roe*, the Court would have had no need to make that comparison.

The holding in *Colautti* v. *Franklin*, 439 U. S. 379, is even more instructive. In that case, the Court noted that prior cases had "stressed viability" and reiterated that "[v]iability is the critical point" under *Roe*. 439 U. S., at 388–389. It then struck down Pennsylvania's definition of viability, *id.*, at 389–394, and it is hard to see how the Court could have done that if *Roe*'s discussion of viability was not part of its holding.

When the Court reconsidered *Roe* in *Casey*, it left no doubt about the importance of the viability rule. It described the rule as *Roe*'s "central holding," 505 U. S., at 860, and repeatedly stated that the right it reaffirmed was "the right of the woman to choose to have an abortion *before viability*." *Id.*, at 846 (emphasis added). See *id.*, at 871 ("The woman's right to terminate her pregnancy *before viability* is the most central principle of *Roe* v. *Wade*. It is a rule of law and a component of liberty we cannot renounce" (emphasis added)); *id.*, at 872 (A "woman has a right to choose to terminate or continue her pregnancy *before viability*" (emphasis added)); *id.*, at 879 ("[A] State may not prohibit any woman from making the ultimate decision to terminate her pregnancy *before viability*" (emphasis added)).

Our subsequent cases have continued to recognize the centrality of the viability rule. See *Whole Women's Health*, 579 U. S., at 589–590 ("[A] provision of law is constitutionally invalid, if the 'purpose or effect' of the provision 'is to place a substantial obstacle in the path of a woman seeking an abortion *before the fetus attains viability*'" (emphasis deleted and added)); *id.*, at 627 ("[W]e now use '*viability*' as the relevant point at which a State may begin limiting women's access to abortion for reasons unrelated to maternal health" (emphasis added)).

Not only is the new rule proposed by the concurrence inconsistent with *Casey*'s unambiguous "language," *post*, at 8, it is also contrary to the judgment in that case and later abortion cases. In *Casey*, the Court held that Pennsylvania's spousal-notification provision was facially unconstitutional, not just that it was unconstitutional as applied to abortions sought prior to the time when a woman has had a reasonable opportunity to choose. See 505 U. S., at 887–898. The same is true of *Whole Women's Health*, which held that certain rules that required physicians performing abortions to have admitting privileges at a nearby hospital were facially unconstitutional because they placed "a substantial obstacle in the path of women seeking *a previability abortion*." 579 U. S., at 591 (emphasis added).

For all these reasons, *stare decisis* cannot justify the new "reasonable opportunity" rule propounded by the concurrence. If that rule is to become the law of the land, it must stand on its own, but the concurrence makes no attempt to show that this rule represents a correct interpretation of the Constitution. The concurrence does not claim that the right to a reasonable opportunity to obtain an abortion is "'deeply rooted in this Nation's history and tradition'" and "'implicit in the concept of ordered liberty.'" *Glucksberg*, 521 U. S., at 720–721. Nor does it propound any other theory that could show that the Constitution supports its new rule. And if the Constitution protects a woman's right to obtain an abortion, the opinion does not explain why that right should end after the point at which all "reasonable" women will have decided whether to seek an abortion. While the concurrence is moved by a desire for judicial minimalism, "we cannot embrace a narrow ground of decision simply because it is narrow; it must also be right." *Citizens United*, 558 U. S., at 375 (ROBERTS, C. J., concurring). For the reasons that we have explained, the concurrence's approach is not.

3

The concurrence would "leave for another day whether to reject any right to an abortion at all," *post*, at 7, but "another day" would not be long in coming. Some States have set deadlines for obtaining an abortion that are shorter than Mississippi's. See, *e.g.*, *Memphis Center for Reproductive Health* v. *Slatery*, 14 F. 4th, at 414 (considering law with bans "at cascading intervals of two to three weeks" beginning at six weeks), reh'g en banc granted, 14 F. 4th 550 (CA6 2021). If we held only that Mississippi's 15-week rule is constitutional, we would soon be called upon to pass on the constitutionality of a panoply of laws with shorter deadlines or no deadline at all. The "measured course" charted by the concurrence would be fraught with turmoil until the Court answered the question that the concurrence seeks to defer.

Even if the Court ultimately adopted the new rule suggested by the concurrence, we would be faced with the difficult problem of spelling out what it means. For example, if the period required to give women a "reasonable" opportunity to obtain an abortion were pegged, as the concurrence seems to suggest, at the point when a certain percentage of women make that choice, see *post*, at 1–2, 9–10, we would have to identify the relevant percentage. It would also be necessary to explain what the concurrence means when it refers to "rare circumstances" that might justify an exception. *Post*, at 10. And if this new right aims to give women a reasonable opportunity to get an abortion, it would be necessary to decide whether factors other than promptness in deciding might have a bearing on whether such an opportunity was available.

In sum, the concurrence's quest for a middle way would only put off the day when we would be forced to confront the question we now decide. The turmoil wrought by *Roe* and *Casey* would be prolonged. It is far better—for this Court and the country—to face up to the real issue without further delay.

VI

We must now decide what standard will govern if state abortion regulations undergo constitutional challenge and whether the law before us satisfies the appropriate standard.

A

Under our precedents, rational-basis review is the appropriate standard for such challenges. As we have explained, procuring an abortion is not a fundamental constitutional right because such a right has no basis in the Constitution's text or in our Nation's history. See *supra,* at 8–39.

It follows that the States may regulate abortion for legitimate reasons, and when such regulations are challenged under the Constitution, courts cannot "substitute their social and economic beliefs for the judgment of legislative bodies." *Ferguson,* 372 U. S., at 729–730; see also *Dandridge* v. *Williams,* 397 U. S. 471, 484–486 (1970); *United States* v. *Carolene Products Co.,* 304 U. S. 144, 152 (1938). That respect for a legislature's judgment applies even when the laws at issue concern matters of great social significance and moral substance. See, *e.g., Board of Trustees of Univ. of Ala.* v. *Garrett,* 531 U. S. 356, 365–368 (2001) ("treatment of the disabled"); *Glucksberg,* 521 U. S., at 728 ("assisted suicide"); *San Antonio Independent School Dist.* v. *Rodriguez,* 411 U. S. 1, 32–35, 55 (1973) ("financing public education").

A law regulating abortion, like other health and welfare laws, is entitled to a "strong presumption of validity." *Heller* v. *Doe,* 509 U. S. 312, 319 (1993). It must be sustained if there is a rational basis on which the legislature could have thought that it would serve legitimate state interests. *Id.,* at 320; *FCC* v. *Beach Communications, Inc.,* 508 U. S.

307, 313 (1993); *New Orleans* v. *Dukes,* 427 U. S. 297, 303 (1976) (*per curiam*); *Williamson* v. *Lee Optical of Okla., Inc.,* 348 U. S. 483, 491 (1955). These legitimate interests include respect for and preservation of prenatal life at all stages of development, *Gonzales,* 550 U. S., at 157–158; the protection of maternal health and safety; the elimination of particularly gruesome or barbaric medical procedures; the preservation of the integrity of the medical profession; the mitigation of fetal pain; and the prevention of discrimination on the basis of race, sex, or disability. See *id.,* at 156–157; *Roe,* 410 U. S., at 150; cf. *Glucksberg,* 521 U. S., at 728–731 (identifying similar interests).

B

These legitimate interests justify Mississippi's Gestational Age Act. Except "in a medical emergency or in the case of a severe fetal abnormality," the statute prohibits abortion "if the probable gestational age of the unborn human being has been determined to be greater than fifteen (15) weeks." Miss. Code Ann. §41–41–191(4)(b). The Mississippi Legislature's findings recount the stages of "human prenatal development" and assert the State's interest in "protecting the life of the unborn." §2(b)(i). The legislature also found that abortions performed after 15 weeks typically use the dilation and evacuation procedure, and the legislature found the use of this procedure "for nontherapeutic or elective reasons [to be] a barbaric practice, dangerous for the maternal patient, and demeaning to the medical profession." §2(b)(i)(8); see also *Gonzales,* 550 U. S., at 135–143 (describing such procedures). These legitimate interests provide a rational basis for the Gestational Age Act, and it follows that respondents' constitutional challenge must fail.

VII

We end this opinion where we began. Abortion presents

a profound moral question. The Constitution does not prohibit the citizens of each State from regulating or prohibiting abortion. *Roe* and *Casey* arrogated that authority. We now overrule those decisions and return that authority to the people and their elected representatives.

The judgment of the Fifth Circuit is reversed, and the case is remanded for further proceedings consistent with this opinion.

It is so ordered.

APPENDICES
A

This appendix contains statutes criminalizing abortion at all stages of pregnancy in the States existing in 1868. The statutes appear in chronological order.

1. Missouri (1825):

Sec. 12. "That every person who shall wilfully and maliciously administer or cause to be administered to or taken by any person, any poison, or other noxious, poisonous or destructive substance or liquid, with an intention to harm him or her thereby to murder, or thereby *to cause or procure the miscarriage of any woman then being with child*, and shall thereof be duly convicted, shall suffer imprisonment not exceeding seven years, and be fined not exceeding three thousand dollars."[69]

2. Illinois (1827):

Sec. 46. "Every person who shall wilfully and maliciously administer, or cause to be administered to, or taken by any person, any poison, or other noxious or

---

[69] 1825 Mo. Laws p. 283 (emphasis added); see also, Mo. Rev. Stat., Art. II, §§10, 36 (1835) (extending liability to abortions performed by instrument and establishing differential penalties for pre- and post-quickening abortion) (emphasis added).

destructive substance or liquid, with an intention to cause the death of such person, *or to procure the miscarriage of any woman, then being with child,* and shall thereof be duly convicted, shall be imprisoned for a term not exceeding three years, and be fined in a sum not exceeding one thousand dollars." [70]

3. New York (1828):

Sec. 9. "Every person who shall administer *to any woman pregnant with a quick child,* any medicine, drug or substance whatever, or shall use or employ any instrument or other means, with intent thereby to destroy such child, unless the same shall have been necessary to preserve the life of such mother, or shall have been advised by two physicians to be necessary for such purpose, shall, in case the death of such child or of such mother be thereby produced, be deemed guilty of manslaughter in the second degree."

Sec. 21. "Every person who shall willfully administer *to any pregnant woman,* any medicine, drug, substance or thing whatever, or shall use or employ any instrument of other means whatever, with intent thereby to procure the miscarriage of any such woman, unless the same shall have been necessary to preserve the life of such woman, or shall have been advised by two physicians to be necessary for that purpose; shall, upon conviction, be punished by imprisonment in a county jail not more than one year, or by fine not exceeding five hundred dollars, or by both such fine and imprisonment." [71]

---

[70] Ill. Rev. Code §46 (1827) (emphasis added); see also Ill. Rev. Code §46 (1833) (same); 1867 Ill. Laws p. 89 (extending liability to abortions "by means of any instrument[s]" and raising penalties to imprisonment "not less than two nor more than ten years").

[71] N. Y. Rev. Stat., pt. 4, ch. 1, Tit. 2, §9 (emphasis added); Tit. 6, §21

4. Ohio (1834):

Sec. 1. "Be it enacted by the General Assembly of State of Ohio, That any physician, or other person, who shall wilfully administer *to any pregnant woman* any medicine, drug, substance, or thing whatever, or shall use any instrument or other means whatever, with intent thereby to procure the miscarriage of any such woman, unless the same shall have been necessary to preserve the life of such woman, or shall have been advised by two physicians to be necessary for that purpose, shall, upon conviction, be punished by imprisonment in the county jail not more than one year, or by fine not exceeding five hundred dollars, or by both such fine and imprisonment."

Sec. 2. "That any physician, or other person, who shall administer *to any woman pregnant with a quick child*, any medicine, drug, or substance whatever, or shall use or employ any instrument, or other means, with intent thereby to destroy such child, unless the same shall have been necessary to preserve the life of such mother, or shall have been advised by two physicians to be necessary for such purpose, shall, in case of the death of such child or mother in consequence thereof, be deemed guilty of high misdemeanor, and, upon conviction thereof, shall be imprisoned in the penitentiary not more than seven years, nor less than one year."[72]

5. Indiana (1835):

Sec. 3. "That every person who shall wilfully administer *to any pregnant woman*, any medicine, drug, substance or thing whatever, or shall use or employ any instrument or other means whatever, with intent

_____

(1828) (emphasis added); 1829 N. Y. Laws p. 19 (codifying these provisions in the revised statutes).

[72] 1834 Ohio Laws pp. 20–21 (emphasis deleted and added).

thereby to procure the miscarriage of any such woman, unless the same shall have been necessary to preserve the life of such woman, shall upon conviction be punished by imprisonment in the county jail any term of [time] not exceeding twelve months and be fined any sum not exceeding five hundred dollars."[73]

6. Maine (1840):

Sec. 13. "Every person, who shall administer *to any woman pregnant with child, whether such child be quick or not,* any medicine, drug or substance whatever, or shall use or employ any instrument or other means whatever, with intent to destroy such child, and shall thereby destroy such child before its birth, unless the same shall have been done as necessary to preserve the life of the mother, shall be punished by imprisonment in the state prison, not more than five years, or by fine, not exceeding one thousand dollars, and imprisonment in the county jail, not more than one year."

Sec. 14. "Every person, who shall administer *to any woman, pregnant with child, whether such child shall be quick or not,* any medicine, drug or substance whatever, or shall use or employ any instrument or other means whatever, with intent thereby to procure the miscarriage of such woman, unless the same shall have been done, as necessary to preserve her life, shall be punished by imprisonment in the county jail, not more than one year, or by fine, not exceeding one thousand dollars."[74]

7. Alabama (1841):

Sec. 2. "Every person who shall wilfully administer *to any pregnant woman* any medicines, drugs, substance or thing whatever, or shall use and employ any

---

[73] 1835 Ind. Laws p. 66 (emphasis added).
[74] Me. Rev. Stat., Tit. 12, ch. 160, §§13–14 (1840) (emphasis added).

instrument or means whatever with intent thereby to procure the miscarriage of such woman, unless the same shall be necessary to preserve her life, or shall have been advised by a respectable physician to be necessary for that purpose, shall upon conviction, be punished by fine not exceeding five hundred dollars, and by imprisonment in the county jail, not less than three, and not exceeding six months."[75]

8. **Massachusetts (1845):**

Ch. 27. "Whoever, maliciously or without lawful justification, with intent to cause and procure the miscarriage *of a woman then pregnant with child*, shall administer to her, prescribe for her, or advise or direct her to take or swallow, any poison, drug, medicine or noxious thing, or shall cause or procure her with like intent, to take or swallow any poison, drug, medicine or noxious thing; and whoever maliciously and without lawful justification, shall use any instrument or means whatever with the like intent, and every person, with the like intent, knowingly aiding and assisting such offender or offenders, shall be deemed guilty of felony, if the woman die in consequence thereof, and shall be imprisoned not more than twenty years, nor less than five years in the State Prison; and if the woman doth not die in consequence thereof, such offender shall be guilty of a misdemeanor, and shall be punished by imprisonment not exceeding seven years, nor less than one year, in the state prison or house of correction, or common jail, and by fine not exceeding two thousand dollars."[76]

9. **Michigan (1846):**

Sec. 33. "Every person who shall administer *to any*

---

[75] 1841 Ala. Acts p. 143 (emphasis added).
[76] 1845 Mass. Acts p. 406 (emphasis added).

woman pregnant with a quick child, any medicine, drug or substance whatever, or shall use or employ any instrument or other means, with intent thereby to destroy such child, unless the same shall have been necessary to preserve the life of such mother, or shall have been advised by two physicians to be necessary for such purpose, shall, in case the death of such child or of such mother be thereby produced, be deemed guilty of manslaughter."

Sec. 34. "Every person who shall wilfully administer *to any pregnant woman* any medicine, drug, substance or thing whatever, or shall employ any instrument or other means whatever, with intent thereby to procure the miscarriage of any such woman, unless the same shall have been necessary to preserve the life of such woman, or shall have been advised by two physicians to be necessary for that purpose, shall, upon conviction, be punished by imprisonment in a county jail not more than one year, or by a fine not exceeding five hundred dollars, or by both such fine and imprisonment."[77]

10. Vermont (1846):

Sec. 1. "Whoever maliciously, or without lawful justification with intent to cause and procure the miscarriage *of a woman, then pregnant with child,* shall administer to her, prescribe for her, or advise or direct her to take or swallow any poison, drug, medicine or noxious thing, or shall cause or procure her, with like intent, to take or swallow any poison, drug, medicine or noxious thing, and whoever maliciously and without lawful justification, shall use any instrument or means whatever, with the like intent, and every person, with the like intent, knowingly aiding and assisting such offenders, shall be deemed guilty of felony, if the woman die in consequence thereof, and shall be imprisoned in

---

[77]Mich. Rev. Stat., Tit. 30, ch. 153, §§33–34 (1846) (emphasis added).

the state prison, not more than ten years, nor less than five years; and if the woman does not die in consequence thereof, such offenders shall be deemed guilty of a misdemeanor; and shall be punished by imprisonment in the state prison not exceeding three years, nor less than one year, and pay a fine not exceeding two hundred dollars."[78]

11. Virginia (1848):

Sec. 9. "Any free person who shall administer *to any pregnant woman*, any medicine, drug or substance whatever, or use or employ any instrument or other means with intent thereby to destroy the child with which such woman may be pregnant, or to produce abortion or miscarriage, and shall thereby destroy such child, or produce such abortion or miscarriage, unless the same shall have been done to preserve the life of such woman, shall be punished, if the death of a quick child be thereby produced, by confinement in the penitentiary, for not less than one nor more than five years, or if the death of a child, not quick, be thereby produced, by confinement in the jail for not less than one nor more than twelve months."[79]

12. New Hampshire (1849):

Sec. 1. "That every person, who shall wilfully administer *to any pregnant woman*, any medicine, drug, substance or thing whatever, or shall use or employ any instrument or means whatever with intent thereby to procure the miscarriage of any such woman, unless the same shall have been necessary to preserve the life of such woman, or shall have been advised by two physicians to be necessary for that purpose, shall, upon conviction, be punished by imprisonment in the county jail

_____

[78] 1846 Vt. Acts & Resolves pp. 34–35 (emphasis added).
[79] 1848 Va. Acts p. 96 (emphasis added).

not more than one year, or by a fine not exceeding one thousand dollars, or by both such fine and imprisonment at the discretion of the Court."

Sec. 2. "Every person who shall administer *to any woman pregnant with a quick child*, any medicine, drug or substance whatever, or shall use or employ any instrument or means whatever, with intent thereby to destroy such child, unless the same shall have been necessary to preserve the life of such woman, or shall have been advised by two physicians to be necessary for such purpose, shall, upon conviction, be punished by fine not exceeding one thousand dollars, and by confinement to hard labor not less than one year, nor more than ten years."[80]

13. New Jersey (1849):

"That if any person or persons, maliciously or without lawful justification, with intent to cause and procure the miscarriage *of a woman then pregnant with child*, shall administer to her, prescribe for her, or advise or direct her to take or swallow any poison, drug, medicine, or noxious thing; and if any person or persons maliciously, and without lawful justification, shall use any instrument or means whatever, with the like intent; and every person, with the like intent, knowingly aiding and assisting such offender or offenders, shall, on conviction thereof, be adjudged guilty of a high misdemeanor; and if the woman die in consequence thereof, shall be punished by fine, not exceeding one thousand dollars, or imprisonment at hard labour for any term not exceeding fifteen years, or both; and if the woman doth not die in consequence thereof, such offender shall, on conviction thereof, be adjudged guilty of a misdemeanor, and be punished by fine, not exceed-

---

[80] 1849 N. H. Laws p. 708 (emphasis added).

ing five hundred dollars, or imprisonment at hard labour, for any term not exceeding seven years, or
both."[81]

14. California (1850):

Sec. 45. "And every person who shall administer or
cause to be administered or taken, any medical substances, or shall use or cause to be used any instruments whatever, with the intention *to procure the miscarriage of any woman then being with child,* and shall
be thereof duly convicted, shall be punished by imprisonment in the State Prison for a term not less than two
years, nor more than five years: Provided, that no physician shall be affected by the last clause of this section,
who, in the discharge of his professional duties, deems
it necessary to produce the miscarriage of any woman
in order to save her life."[82]

15. Texas (1854):

Sec. 1. "If any person, with the intent to procure the
miscarriage *of any woman being with child,* unlawfully
and maliciously shall administer to her or cause to be
taken by her any poison or other noxious thing, or shall
use any instrument or any means whatever, with like
intent, every such offender, and every person counsel-
ling or aiding or abetting such offender, shall be punished by confinement to hard labor in the Penitentiary
not exceeding ten years."[83]

16. Louisiana (1856):

Sec. 24. "Whoever shall feloniously administer or
cause to be administered any drug, potion, or any other
thing to any woman, for the purpose of procuring a
premature delivery, and whoever shall administer or

---

[81] 1849 N. J. Laws pp. 266–267 (emphasis added).
[82] 1850 Cal. Stats. p. 233 (emphasis added and deleted).
[83] 1854 Tex. Gen. Laws p. 58 (emphasis added).

cause to be administered *to any woman pregnant with child*, any drug, potion, or any other thing, for the purpose of procuring abortion, or a premature delivery, shall be imprisoned at hard labor, for not less than one, nor more than ten years."[84]

17. Iowa (1858):

Sec. 1. "That every person who shall willfully administer *to any pregnant woman*, any medicine, drug, substance or thing whatever, or shall use or employ any instrument or other means whatever, with the intent thereby to procure the miscarriage of any such woman, unless the same shall be necessary to preserve the life of such woman, shall upon conviction thereof, be punished by imprisonment in the county jail for a term of not exceeding one year, and be fined in a sum not exceeding one thousand dollars."[85]

18. Wisconsin (1858):

Sec. 11. "Every person who shall administer *to any woman pregnant with a child* any medicine, drug, or substance whatever, or shall use or employ any instrument or other means, with intent thereby to destroy such child, unless the same shall have been necessary to preserve the life of such mother, or shall have been advised by two physicians to be necessary for such purpose, shall, in case the death of such child or of such mother be thereby produced, be deemed guilty of manslaughter in the second degree."[86]

Sec. 58. "Every person who shall administer *to any pregnant woman*, or prescribe for any such woman, or advise or procure any such woman to take, any medicine, drug, or substance or thing whatever, or shall use

---

[84] La. Rev. Stat. §24 (1856) (emphasis added).

[85] 1858 Iowa Acts p. 93 (codified in Iowa Rev. Laws §4221) (emphasis added).

[86] Wis. Rev. Stat., ch. 164, §11, ch. 169, §58 (1858) (emphasis added).

or employ any instrument or other means whatever, or advise or procure the same to be used, with intent thereby to procure the miscarriage of any such woman, shall upon conviction be punished by imprisonment in a county jail, not more than one year nor less than three months, or by fine, not exceeding five hundred dollars, or by both fine and imprisonment, at the discretion of the court.' "

19. Kansas (1859):

Sec. 10. "Every person who shall administer *to any woman, pregnant with a quick child*, any medicine, drug or substance whatsoever, or shall use or employ any instrument or other means, with intent thereby to destroy such child, unless the same shall have been necessary to preserve the life of such mother, or shall have been advised by a physician to be necessary for that purpose, shall be deemed guilty of manslaughter in the second degree."

Sec. 37. "Every physician or other person who shall wilfully administer *to any pregnant woman* any medicine, drug or substance whatsoever, or shall use or employ any instrument or means whatsoever, with intent thereby to procure abortion or the miscarriage of any such woman, unless the same shall have been necessary to preserve the life of such woman, or shall have been advised by a physician to be necessary for that purpose, shall, upon conviction, be adjudged guilty of a misdemeanor, and punished by imprisonment in a county jail not exceeding one year, or by fine not exceeding five hundred dollars, or by both such fine and imprisonment."[87]

20. Connecticut (1860):

Sec. 1. "That any person with intent *to procure the*

_____
[87] 1859 Kan. Laws pp. 233, 237 (emphasis added).

miscarriage or abortion of any woman, shall give or administer to her, prescribe for her, or advise, or direct, or cause or procure her to take, any medicine, drug or substance whatever, or use or advise the use of any instrument, or other means whatever, with the like intent, unless the same shall have been necessary to preserve the life of such woman, or of her unborn child, shall be deemed guilty of felony, and upon due conviction thereof shall be punished by imprisonment in the Connecticut state prison, not more than five years or less than one year, or by a fine of one thousand dollars, or both, at the discretion of the court."[88]

21. Pennsylvania (1860):

Sec. 87. "If any person shall unlawfully administer *to any woman, pregnant or quick with child, or supposed and believed to be pregnant or quick with child*, any drug, poison, or other substance whatsoever, or shall unlawfully use any instrument or other means whatsoever, with the intent to procure the miscarriage of such woman, and such woman, or any child with which she may be quick, shall die in consequence of either of said unlawful acts, the person so offending shall be guilty of felony, and shall be sentenced to pay a fine not exceeding five hundred dollars, and to undergo an imprisonment, by separate or solitary confinement at labor, not exceeding seven years."

Sec. 88. "If any person, with intent *to procure the miscarriage of any woman*, shall unlawfully administer to her any poison, drug or substance whatsoever, or shall unlawfully use any instrument, or other means whatsoever, with the like intent, such person shall be guilty of felony, and being thereof convicted, shall be sentenced to pay a fine not exceeding five hundred dol-

---

[88] 1860 Conn. Pub. Acts p. 65 (emphasis added).

lars, and undergo an imprisonment, by separate or solitary confinement at labor, not exceeding three years."[89]

22. Rhode Island (1861):

Sec. 1. "Every person who shall be convicted of wilfully administering *to any pregnant woman, or to any woman supposed by such person to be pregnant,* anything whatever, or shall employ any means whatever, with intent thereby to procure the miscarriage of such woman, unless the same is necessary to preserve her life, shall be imprisoned not exceeding one year, or fined not exceeding one thousand dollars."[90]

23. Nevada (1861):

Sec. 42. "[E]very person who shall administer, or cause to be administered or taken, any medicinal substance, or shall use, or cause to be used, any instruments whatever, with the intention *to procure the miscarriage of any woman then being with child,* and shall be thereof duly convicted, shall be punished by imprisonment in the Territorial prison, for a term not less than two years, nor more than five years; provided, that no physician shall be affected by the last clause of this section, who, in the discharge of his professional duties, deems it necessary to produce the miscarriage of any woman in order to save her life."[91]

24. West Virginia (1863):

West Virginia's Constitution adopted the laws of Virginia when it became its own State:

"Such parts of the common law and of the laws of the State of Virginia as are in force within the boundaries

---

[89] 1861 Pa. Laws pp. 404–405 (emphasis added).

[90] R. I. Acts & Resolves p. 133 (emphasis added).

[91] 1861 Nev. Laws p. 63 (emphasis added and deleted).

of the State of West Virginia, when this Constitution goes into operation, and are not repugnant thereto, shall be and continue the law of this State until altered or repealed by the Legislature."[92]

The Virginia law in force in 1863 stated:

Sec. 8. "Any free person who shall administer to, or cause to be taken, *by a woman*, any drug or other thing, or use any means, with intent to destroy her unborn child, or to produce abortion or miscarriage, and shall thereby destroy such child, or produce such abortion or miscarriage, shall be confined in the penitentiary not less than one, nor more than five years. No person, by reason of any act mentioned in this section, shall be punishable where such act is done in good faith, with the intention of saving the life of such woman or child."[93]

25. Oregon (1864):

Sec. 509. "If any person shall administer *to any woman pregnant with child*, any medicine, drug or substance whatever, or shall use or employ any instrument or other means, with intent thereby to destroy such child, unless the same shall be necessary to preserve the life of such mother, such person shall, in case the death of such child or mother be thereby produced, be deemed guilty of manslaughter."[94]

26. Nebraska (1866):

Sec. 42. "Every person who shall willfully and maliciously administer or cause to be administered to or taken by any person, any poison or other noxious or destructive substance or liquid, with the intention to

---

[92] W. Va. Const., Art. XI, §8 (1862).
[93] Va. Code, Tit. 54, ch. 191, §8 (1849) (emphasis added); see also W. Va. Code, ch. 144, §8 (1870) (similar).
[94] Ore. Gen. Laws, Crim. Code, ch. 43, §509 (1865).

cause the death of such person, and being thereof duly convicted, shall be punished by confinement in the penitentiary for a term not less than one year and not more than seven years. And every person who shall administer or cause to be administered or taken, any such poison, substance or liquid, with the intention *to procure the miscarriage of any woman then being with child*, and shall thereof be duly convicted, shall be imprisoned for a term not exceeding three years in the penitentiary, and fined in a sum not exceeding one thousand dollars."[95]

27. **Maryland (1868):**
Sec. 2. "And be it enacted, That any person who shall knowingly advertise, print, publish, distribute or circulate, or knowingly cause to be advertised, printed, published, distributed or circulated, any pamphlet, printed paper, book, newspaper notice, advertisement or reference containing words or language, giving or conveying any notice, hint or reference to any person, or to the name of any person real or fictitious, from whom; or to any place, house, shop or office, when any poison, drug, mixture, preparation, medicine or noxious thing, or any instrument or means whatever; for the purpose of producing abortion, or who shall knowingly sell, or cause to be sold any such poison, drug, mixture, preparation, medicine or noxious thing or instrument of any kind whatever; or where any advice, direction, information or knowledge may be obtained *for the purpose of causing the miscarriage or abortion of any woman pregnant with child, at any period of her pregnancy*, or shall knowingly sell or cause to be sold any medicine, or who shall knowingly use or cause to be used any means

---

[95] Neb. Rev. Stat., Tit. 4, ch. 4, §42 (1866) (emphasis added); see also Neb. Gen. Stat., ch. 58, §§6, 39 (1873) (expanding criminal liability for abortions by other means, including instruments).

whatsoever for that purpose, shall be punished by imprisonment in the penitentiary for not less than three years, or by a fine of not less than five hundred nor more than one thousand dollars, or by both, in the discretion of the Court; and in case of fine being imposed, one half thereof shall be paid to the State of Maryland, and one-half to the School Fund of the city or county where the offence was committed; provided, however, that nothing herein contained shall be construed so as to prohibit the supervision and management by a regular practitioner of medicine of all cases of abortion occurring spontaneously, either as the result of accident, constitutional debility, or any other natural cause, or the production of abortion by a regular practitioner of medicine when, after consulting with one or more respectable physicians, he shall be satisfied that the foetus is dead, or that no other method will secure the safety of the mother."[96]

28. Florida (1868):

Ch. 3, Sec. 11. "Every person who shall administer *to any woman pregnant with a quick child* any medicine, drug, or substance whatever, or shall use or employ any instrument, or other means, with intent thereby to destroy such child, unless the same shall have been necessary to preserve the life of such mother, or shall have been advised by two physicians to be necessary for such purpose, shall, in case the death of such child or of such mother be thereby produced, be deemed guilty of manslaughter in the second degree."

Ch. 8, Sec. 9. "Whoever, with intent *to procure miscarriage of any woman*, unlawfully administers to her, or advises, or prescribes for her, or causes to be taken by her, any poison, drug, medicine, or other noxious thing, or unlawfully uses any instrument or other

---

[96] 1868 Md. Laws p. 315 (emphasis deleted and added).

means whatever with the like intent, or with like intent aids or assists therein, shall, if the woman does not die in consequence thereof, be punished by imprisonment in the State penittentiary not exceeding seven years, nor less than one year, or by fine not exceeding one thousand dollars."[97]

29. Minnesota (1873):

Sec. 1. "That any person who shall administer *to any woman with child*, or prescribe for any such woman, or suggest to, or advise, or procure her to take any medicine, drug, substance or thing whatever, or who shall use or employ, or advise or suggest the use or employment of any instrument or other means or force whatever, with intent thereby to cause or procure the miscarriage or abortion or premature labor of any such woman, unless the same shall have been necessary to preserve her life, or the life of such child, shall, in case the death of such child or of such woman results in whole or in part therefrom, be deemed guilty of a felony, and upon conviction thereof, shall be punished by imprisonment in the state prison for a term not more than ten (10) years nor less than three (3) years."

Sec. 2. "Any person who shall administer *to any woman with child*, or prescribe, or procure, or provide for any such woman, or suggest to, or advise, or procure any such woman to take any medicine, drug, substance or thing whatever, or shall use or employ, or suggest, or advise the use or employment of any instrument or other means or force whatever, with intent thereby to cause or procure the miscarriage or abortion or premature labor of any such woman, shall upon conviction thereof be punished by imprisonment in the state prison for a term not more than two years nor less than

---

[97] 1868 Fla. Laws, ch. 1637, pp. 64, 97 (emphasis added).

one year, or by fine not more than five thousand dollars nor less than five hundred dollars, or by such fine and imprisonment both, at the discretion of the court."[98]

30. Arkansas (1875):

Sec. 1. "That it shall be unlawful for any one to administer or prescribe any medicine or drugs *to any woman with child*, with intent to produce an abortion, or premature delivery of any foetus before the period of quickening, or to produce or attempt to produce such abortion by any other means; and any person offending against the provision of this section, shall be fined in any sum not exceeding one thousand ($1000) dollars, and imprisoned in the penitentiary not less than one (1) nor more than five (5) years; provided, that this section shall not apply to any abortion produced by any regular practicing physician, for the purpose of saving the mother's life."[99]

31. Georgia (1876):

Sec. 2. "That every person who shall administer *to any woman pregnant with a child*, any medicine, drug, or substance whatever, or shall use or employ any instrument or other means, with intent thereby to destroy such child, unless the same shall have been necessary to preserve the life of such mother, or shall have been advised by two physicians to be necessary for such purpose, shall, in case the death of such child or mother be thereby produced, be declared guilty of an assault with intent to murder."

Sec. 3. "That any person who shall wilfully administer *to any pregnant woman* any medicine, drug or substance, or anything whatever, or shall employ any instrument or means whatever, with intent thereby to

---

[98] 1873 Minn. Laws pp. 117–118 (emphasis added).
[99] 1875 Ark. Acts p. 5 (emphasis added and deleted).

procure the miscarriage or abortion of any such woman, unless the same shall have been necessary to preserve the life of such woman, or shall have been advised by two physicians to be necessary for that purpose, shall, upon conviction, be punished as prescribed in section 4310 of the Revised Code of Georgia."[100]

32. North Carolina (1881):

Sec. 1. "That every person who shall wilfully administer *to any woman either pregnant or quick with child,* or prescribe for any such woman, or advise or procure any such woman to take any medicine, drug or substance whatever, or shall use or employ any instrument or other means with intent thereby to destroy said child, unless the same shall have been necessary to preserve the life of such mother, shall be guilty of a felony, and shall be imprisoned in the state penitentiary for not less than one year nor more than ten years, and be fined at the discretion of the court."

Sec. 2. "That every person who shall administer *to any pregnant woman,* or prescribe for any such woman, or advise and procure such woman to take any medicine, drug or any thing whatsoever, with intent thereby to procure the miscarriage of any such woman, or to injure or destroy such woman, or shall use any instrument or application for any of the above purposes, shall be guilty of a misdemeanor, and, on conviction, shall be imprisoned in the jail or state penitentiary for not less than one year or more than five years, and fined at the discretion of the court."[101]

33. Delaware (1883):

Sec. 2. "Every person who, with the intent to procure

---

[100] 1876 Ga. Acts & Resolutions p. 113 (emphasis added).

[101] 1881 N. C. Sess. Laws pp. 584–585 (emphasis added).

the miscarriage *of any pregnant woman or women supposed by such person to be pregnant,* unless the same be necessary to preserve her life, shall administer to her, advise, or prescribe for her, or cause to be taken by her any poison, drug, medicine, or other noxious thing, or shall use any instrument or other means whatsoever, or shall aid, assist, or counsel any person so intending to procure a miscarriage, whether said miscarriage be accomplished or not, shall be guilty of a felony, and upon conviction thereof shall be fined not less than one hundred dollars nor more than five hundred dollars and be imprisoned for a term not exceeding five years nor less than one year."[102]

34. Tennessee (1883):

Sec. 1. "That every person who shall administer *to any woman pregnant with child, whether such child be quick or not,* any medicine, drug or substance whatever, or shall use or employ any instrument, or other means whatever with intent to destroy such child, and shall thereby destroy such child before its birth, unless the same shall have been done with a view to preserve the life of the mother, shall be punished by imprisonment in the penitentiary not less than one nor more than five years."

Sec. 2. "Every person who shall administer any substance with the intention *to procure the miscarriage of a woman then being with child,* or shall use or employ any instrument or other means with such intent, unless the same shall have been done with a view to preserve the life of such mother, shall be punished by imprisonment in the penitentiary not less than one nor more than three years."[103]

---

[102] 1883 Del. Laws, ch. 226 (emphasis added).
[103] 1883 Tenn. Acts pp. 188–189 (emphasis added).

35. South Carolina (1883):

Sec. 1. "That any person who shall administer *to any woman with child*, or prescribe for any such woman, or suggest to or advise or procure her to take, any medicine, substance, drug or thing whatever, or who shall use or employ, or advise the use or employment of, any instrument or other means of force whatever, with intent thereby to cause or procure the miscarriage or abortion or premature labor of any such woman, unless the same shall have been necessary to preserve her life, or the life of such child, shall, in case the death of such child or of such woman results in whole or in part therefrom, be deemed guilty of a felony, and, upon conviction thereof, shall be punished by imprisonment in the Penitentiary for a term not more than twenty years nor less than five years."

Sec. 2. "That any person who shall administer *to any woman with child*, or prescribe or procure or provide for any such woman, or advise or procure any such woman to take, any medicine, drug, substance or thing whatever, or shall use or employ or advise the use or employment of, any instrument or other means of force whatever, with intent thereby to cause or procure the miscarriage or abortion or premature labor of any such woman, shall, upon conviction thereof, be punished by imprisonment in the Penitentiary for a term not more than five years, or by fine not more than five thousand dollars, or by such fine and imprisonment both, at the discretion of the Court; but no conviction shall be had under the provisions of Section 1 or 2 of this Act upon the uncorroborated evidence of such woman."[104]

36. Kentucky (1910):

Sec. 1. "It shall be unlawful for any person to prescribe or administer *to any pregnant woman, or to any*

------

[104] 1883 S. C. Acts pp. 547–548 (emphasis added).

woman whom he has reason to believe pregnant, at any time during the period of gestation, any drug, medicine or substance, whatsoever, with the intent thereby to procure the miscarriage of such woman, or with like intent, to use any instrument or means whatsoever, unless such miscarriage is necessary to preserve her life; and any person so offending, shall be punished by a fine of not less than five hundred nor more than one thousand dollars, and imprisoned in the State prison for not less than one nor more than ten years."

Sec. 2. "If by reason of any of the acts described in Section 1 hereof, the miscarriage of such woman is procured, and she does miscarry, causing the death of the unborn child, whether before or after quickening time, the person so offending shall be guilty of a felony, and confined in the penitentiary for not less than two, nor more than twenty-one years."

Sec. 3. "If, by reason of the commission of any of the acts described in Section 1 hereof, the woman to whom such drug or substance has been administered, or upon whom such instrument has been used, shall die, the person offending shall be punished as now prescribed by law, for the offense of murder or manslaughter, as the facts may justify."

Sec. 4. "The consent of the woman to the performance of the operation or administering of the medicines or substances, referred to, shall be no defense, and she shall be a competent witness in any prosecution under this act, and for that purpose she shall not be considered an accomplice."[105]

37. Mississippi (1952):

Sec. 1. "Whoever, by means of any instrument, medicine, drug, or other means whatever shall willfully and

---

[105] 1910 Ky. Acts pp. 189–190 (emphasis added).

knowingly cause *any woman pregnant with child* to abort or miscarry, or attempts to procure or produce an abortion or miscarriage, unless the same were done as necessary for the preservation of the mother's life, shall be imprisoned in the state penitentiary no less than one (1) year, nor more than ten (10) years; or if the death of the mother results therefrom, the person procuring, causing, or attempting to procure or cause the abortion or miscarriage shall be guilty of murder."

Sec. 2. "No act prohibited in section 1 hereof shall be considered as necessary for the preservation of the mother's life unless upon the prior advice, in writing, of two reputable licensed physicians."

Sec. 3. "The license of any physician or nurse shall be automatically revoked upon conviction under the provisions of this act."[106]

B

This appendix contains statutes criminalizing abortion at all stages in each of the Territories that became States and in the District of Columbia. The statutes appear in chronological order of enactment.

1. Hawaii (1850):

Sec. 1. "Whoever maliciously, without lawful justification, administers, or causes or procures to be administered any poison or noxious thing *to a woman then with child,* in order to produce her mis-carriage, or maliciously uses any instrument or other means with like intent, shall, if such woman be then quick with child, be punished by fine not exceeding one thousand dollars and imprisonment at hard labor not more than five years. And if she be then not quick with child, shall be punished by a fine not exceeding five hundred dollars,

----

[106] 1952 Miss. Laws p. 289 (codified at Miss. Code Ann. §2223 (1956) (emphasis added)).

and imprisonment at hard labor not more than two years."

Sec. 2. "Where means of causing abortion are used for the purpose of saving the life of the woman, the surgeon or other person using such means is lawfully justified."[107]

2. Washington (1854):

Sec. 37. "Every person who shall administer *to any woman pregnant with a quick child,* any medicine, drug, or substance whatever, or shall use or employ any instrument, or other means, with intent thereby to destroy such child, unless the same shall have been necessary to preserve the life of such mother, shall, in case the death of such child or of such mother be thereby produced, on conviction thereof, be imprisoned in the penitentiary not more than twenty years, nor less than one year."

Sec. 38. "Every person who shall administer *to any pregnant woman, or to any woman who he supposes to be pregnant,* any medicine, drug, or substance whatever, or shall use or employ any instrument, or other means, thereby to procure the miscarriage of such woman, unless the same is necessary to preserve her life, shall on conviction thereof, be imprisoned in the penitentiary not more than five years, nor less than one year, or be imprisoned in the county jail not more than twelve months, nor less than one month, and be fined in any sum not exceeding one thousand dollars."[108]

3. Colorado (1861):

---

[107] Haw. Penal Code, ch. 12, §§1–2 (1850) (emphasis added). Hawaii became a State in 1959. See Presidential Proclamation No. 3309, 73 Stat. c74–c75.

[108] Terr. of Wash. Stat., ch. 2, §§37–38, p. 81 (1854) (emphasis added). Washington became a State in 1889. See Presidential Proclamation No. 8, 26 Stat. 1552–1553.

Sec. 42. "[E]very person who shall administer substance or liquid, or who shall use or cause to be used any instrument, of whatsoever kind, with the intention *to procure the miscarriage of any woman then being with child*, and shall thereof be duly convicted, shall be imprisoned for a term not exceeding three years, and fined in a sum not exceeding one thousand dollars; and if any woman, by reason of such treatment, shall die, the person or persons administering, or causing to be administered, such poison, substance or liquid, or using or causing to be used, any instrument, as aforesaid, shall be deemed guilty of manslaughter, and if convicted, be punished accordingly."[109]

4. Idaho (1864):

Sec. 42. "[E]very person who shall administer or cause to be administered, or taken, any medicinal substance, or shall use or cause to be used, any instruments whatever, with the intention *to procure the miscarriage of any woman then being with child*, and shall be thereof duly convicted, shall be punished by imprisonment in the territorial prison for a term not less than two years, nor more than five years: *Provided*, That no physician shall be effected by the last clause of this section, who in the discharge of his professional duties, deems it necessary to produce the miscarriage of any woman in order to save her life."[110]

5. Montana (1864):

Sec. 41. "[E]very person who shall administer, or cause to be administered, or taken, any medicinal substance, or shall use, or cause to be used, any instru-

---

[109] 1861 Terr. of Colo. Gen. Laws pp. 296–297. Colorado became a State in 1876. See Presidential Proclamation No. 7, 19 Stat. 665–666.

[110] 1863–1864 Terr. of Idaho Laws p. 443. Idaho became a State in 1890. See 26 Stat. 215–219.

ments whatever, with the intention *to produce the miscarriage of any woman then being with child*, and shall be thereof duly convicted, shall be punished by imprisonment in the Territorial prison for a term not less than two years nor more than five years. *Provided*, That no physician shall be affected by the last clause of this section, who in the discharge of his professional duties deems it necessary to produce the miscarriage of any woman in order to save her life."[111]

6. Arizona (1865):

Sec. 45. "[E]very person who shall administer or cause to be administered or taken, any medicinal substances, or shall use or cause to be used any instruments whatever, with the intention *to procure the miscarriage of any woman then being with child*, and shall be thereof duly convicted, shall be punished by imprisonment in the Territorial prison for a term not less than two years nor more than five years: Provided, that no physician shall be affected by the last clause of this section, who in the discharge of his professional duties, deems it necessary to produce the miscarriage of any woman in order to save her life."[112]

7. Wyoming (1869):

Sec. 25. "[A]ny person who shall administer, or cause to be administered, or taken, any such poison, substance or liquid, or who shall use, or cause to be used, any instrument of whatsoever kind, with the intention *to procure the miscarriage of any woman then being with child*, and shall thereof be duly convicted, shall be imprisoned for a term not exceeding three

---

[111] 1864 Terr. of Mont. Laws p. 184. Montana became a State in 1889. See Presidential Proclamation No. 7, 26 Stat. 1551–1552.

[112] Howell Code, ch. 10, §45 (1865). Arizona became a State in 1912. See Presidential Proclamation of Feb. 14, 1912, 37 Stat. 1728–1729.

Appendix B to opinion of the Court

years, in the penitentiary, and fined in a sum not exceeding one thousand dollars; and if any woman by reason of such treatment shall die, the person, or persons, administering, or causing to be administered such poison, substance, or liquid, or using or causing to be used, any instrument, as aforesaid, shall be deemed guilty of manslaughter, and if convicted, be punished by imprisonment for a term not less than three years in the penitentiary, and fined in a sum not exceeding one thousand dollars, unless it appear that such miscarriage was procured or attempted by, or under advice of a physician or surgeon, with intent to save the life of such woman, or to prevent serious and permanent bodily injury to her."[113]

8. Utah (1876):

Sec. 142. "Every person who provides, supplies, or administers *to any pregnant woman*, or procures any such woman to take any medicine, drug, or substance, or uses or employs any instrument or other means whatever, with intent thereby to procure the miscarriage of such woman, unless the same is necessary to preserve her life, is punishable by imprisonment in the penitentiary not less than two nor more than ten years."[114]

9. North Dakota (1877):

Sec. 337. "Every person who administers *to any pregnant woman*, or who prescribes for any such woman, or advises or procures any such woman to take any medicine, drug or substance, or uses or employs

---

[113] 1869 Terr. of Wyo. Gen. Laws p. 104 (emphasis added). Wyoming became a State in 1889. See 26 Stat. 222–226.

[114] Terr. of Utah Comp. Laws §1972 (1876) (emphasis added). Utah became a State in 1896. See Presidential Proclamation No. 9, 29 Stat. 876–877.

any instrument, or other means whatever with intent thereby to procure the miscarriage of such woman, unless the same is necessary to preserve her life, is punishable by imprisonment in the territorial prison not exceeding three years, or in a county jail not exceeding one year."[115]

10. South Dakota (1877): *Same as North Dakota.*

11. Oklahoma (1890):

Sec. 2187. "Every person who administers *to any pregnant woman*, or who prescribes for any such woman, or advises or procures any such woman to take any medicine, drug or substance, or uses or employs any instrument, or other means whatever, with intent thereby to procure the miscarriage of such woman, unless the same is necessary to preserve her life, is punishable by imprisonment in the Territorial prison not exceeding three years, or in a county jail not exceeding one year."[116]

12. Alaska (1899):

Sec. 8. "That if any person shall administer *to any woman pregnant with a child* any medicine, drug, or substance whatever, or shall use any instrument or other means, with intent thereby to destroy such child, unless the same shall be necessary to preserve the life of such mother, such person shall, in case the death of such child or mother be thereby produced, be deemed

---

[115] Dakota Penal Code §337 (1877) (codified at N. D. Rev. Code §7177 (1895)), and S. D. Rev. Penal Code Ann. §337 (1883). North and South Dakota became States in 1889. See Presidential Proclamation No. 5, 26 Stat. 1548–1551.

[116] Okla. Stat. §2187 (1890) (emphasis added). Oklahoma became a State in 1907. See Presidential Proclamation of Nov. 16, 1907, 35 Stat. 2160–2161.

guilty of manslaughter, and shall be punished accordingly."[117]

13. New Mexico (1919):

Sec. 1. "Any person who shall administer *to any pregnant woman any medicine*, drug or substance whatever, or attempt by operation or any other method or means to produce an abortion or miscarriage upon such woman, shall be guilty of a felony, and, upon conviction thereof, shall be fined not more than two thousand ($2,000.00) Dollars, nor less than five hundred ($500.00) Dollars, or imprisoned in the penitentiary for a period of not less than one nor more than five years, or by both such fine and imprisonment in the discretion of the court trying the case."

Sec. 2. "Any person committing such act or acts mentioned in section one hereof which shall culminate in the death of the woman shall be deemed guilty of murder in the second degree; *Provided,* however, an abortion may be produced when two physicians licensed to practice in the State of New Mexico, in consultation, deem it necessary to preserve the life of the woman, or to prevent serious and permanent bodily injury."

Sec. 3. "For the purpose of the act, the term "pregnancy" is defined as that condition of a woman *from the date of conception to the birth of her child.*"[118]

* * *

District of Columbia (1901):

Sec. 809. "Whoever, with intent *to procure the miscarriage of any woman*, prescribes or administers to her

---

[117] 1899 Alaska Sess. Laws ch. 2, p. 3 (emphasis added). Alaska became a State in 1959. See Presidential Proclamation No. 3269, 73 Stat. c16.

[118] N. M. Laws p. 6 (emphasis added). New Mexico became a State in 1912. See Presidential Proclamation of Jan. 6, 1912, 37 Stat. 1723–1724.

Appendix B to opinion of the Court

any medicine, drug, or substance whatever, or with like intent uses any instrument or means, unless when necessary to preserve her life or health and under the direction of a competent licensed practitioner of medicine, shall be imprisoned for not more than five years; or if the woman or her child dies in consequence of such act, by imprisonment for not less than three nor more than twenty years."[119]

---

[119] §809, 31 Stat. 1322 (1901) (emphasis added).

SUPREME COURT OF THE UNITED STATES

No. 19–1392

THOMAS E. DOBBS, STATE HEALTH OFFICER OF THE MISSISSIPPI DEPARTMENT OF HEALTH, ET AL., PETITIONERS v. JACKSON WOMEN'S HEALTH ORGANIZATION, ET AL.

ON WRIT OF CERTIORARI TO THE UNITED STATES COURT OF APPEALS FOR THE FIFTH CIRCUIT

[June 24, 2022]

JUSTICE THOMAS, concurring.

I join the opinion of the Court because it correctly holds that there is no constitutional right to abortion. Respondents invoke one source for that right: the Fourteenth Amendment's guarantee that no State shall "deprive any person of life, liberty, or property without due process of law." The Court well explains why, under our substantive due process precedents, the purported right to abortion is not a form of "liberty" protected by the Due Process Clause. Such a right is neither "deeply rooted in this Nation's history and tradition" nor "implicit in the concept of ordered liberty." *Washington* v. *Glucksberg*, 521 U. S. 702, 721 (1997) (internal quotation marks omitted). "[T]he idea that the Framers of the Fourteenth Amendment understood the Due Process Clause to protect a right to abortion is farcical." *June Medical Services L. L. C.* v. *Russo*, 591 U. S. ＿＿, ＿＿ (2020) (THOMAS, J., dissenting) (slip op., at 17).

I write separately to emphasize a second, more fundamental reason why there is no abortion guarantee lurking in the Due Process Clause. Considerable historical evidence indicates that "due process of law" merely required executive and judicial actors to comply with legislative enactments and the common law when depriving a person of life, liberty, or property. See, *e.g.*, *Johnson* v. *United States*, 576 U. S. 591, 623 (2015) (THOMAS, J., concurring in judgment). Other sources, by contrast, suggest that "due process of law" prohibited legislatures "from authorizing the deprivation of a person's life, liberty, or property without providing him the customary procedures to which freemen were entitled by the old law of England." *United States* v. *Vaello Madero*, 596 U. S. ___, ___ (2022) (THOMAS, J., concurring) (slip op., at 3) (internal quotation marks omitted). Either way, the Due Process Clause at most guarantees *process*. It does not, as the Court's substantive due process cases suppose, "forbi[d] the government to infringe certain 'fundamental' liberty interests *at all*, no matter what process is provided." *Reno* v. *Flores*, 507 U. S. 292, 302 (1993); see also, *e.g.*, *Collins* v. *Harker Heights*, 503 U. S. 115, 125 (1992).

As I have previously explained, "substantive due process" is an oxymoron that "lack[s] any basis in the Constitution." *Johnson*, 576 U. S., at 607–608 (opinion of THOMAS, J.); see also, *e.g.*, *Vaello Madero*, 596 U. S., at ___ (THOMAS, J., concurring) (slip op., at 3) ("[T]ext and history provide little support for modern substantive due process doctrine"). "The notion that a constitutional provision that guarantees only 'process' before a person is deprived of life, liberty, or property could define the substance of those rights strains credulity for even the most casual user of words." *McDonald* v. *Chicago*, 561 U. S. 742, 811 (2010) (THOMAS, J., concurring in part and concurring in judgment); see also *United States* v. *Carlton*, 512 U. S. 26, 40 (1994) (Scalia, J., concurring in judgment). The resolution of this case is thus straightforward. Because the Due Process Clause does not secure *any* substantive rights, it does not secure a right to abortion.

The Court today declines to disturb substantive due process jurisprudence generally or the doctrine's application in other, specific contexts. Cases like *Griswold* v. *Connecticut*,

381 U. S. 479 (1965) (right of married persons to obtain contraceptives)*; *Lawrence* v. *Texas*, 539 U. S. 558 (2003) (right
to engage in private, consensual sexual acts); and *Obergefell* v. *Hodges*, 576 U. S. 644 (2015) (right to same-sex marriage), are not at issue. The Court's abortion cases are
unique, see *ante,* at 31–32, 66, 71–72, and no party has
asked us to decide "whether our entire Fourteenth Amendment jurisprudence must be preserved or revised," *McDonald*, 561 U. S., at 813 (opinion of THOMAS, J.). Thus, I agree
that "[n]othing in [the Court's] opinion should be understood to cast doubt on precedents that do not concern abortion." *Ante*, at 66.

For that reason, in future cases, we should reconsider all
of this Court's substantive due process precedents, including *Griswold, Lawrence*, and *Obergefell*. Because any substantive due process decision is "demonstrably erroneous,"
Ramos v. *Louisiana*, 590 U. S. ___, ___ (2020) (THOMAS, J.,
concurring in judgment) (slip op., at 7), we have a duty to
"correct the error" established in those precedents, *Gamble*
v. *United States*, 587 U. S. ___, ___ (2019) (THOMAS, J., concurring) (slip op., at 9). After overruling these demonstrably erroneous decisions, the question would remain
whether other constitutional provisions guarantee the myriad rights that our substantive due process cases have generated. For example, we could consider whether any of the
rights announced in this Court's substantive due process
cases are "privileges or immunities of citizens of the United
States" protected by the Fourteenth Amendment. Amdt.

---

*Griswold v. *Connecticut* purported not to rely on the Due Process
Clause, but rather reasoned "that specific guarantees in the Bill of
Rights"—including rights enumerated in the First, Third, Fourth, Fifth,
and Ninth Amendments—"have penumbras, formed by emanations,"
that create "zones of privacy." 381 U. S., at 484. Since *Griswold,* the
Court, perhaps recognizing the facial absurdity of *Griswold*'s penumbral
argument, has characterized the decision as one rooted in substantive
due process. See, *e.g., Obergefell* v. *Hodges*, 576 U. S. 644, 663 (2015);
Washington v. *Glucksberg*, 521 U. S. 702, 720 (1997).

14, §1; see *McDonald*, 561 U. S., at 806 (opinion of THOMAS, J.). To answer that question, we would need to decide important antecedent questions, including whether the Privileges or Immunities Clause protects *any* rights that are not enumerated in the Constitution and, if so, how to identify those rights. See *id.*, at 854. That said, even if the Clause does protect unenumerated rights, the Court conclusively demonstrates that abortion is not one of them under any plausible interpretive approach. See *ante*, at 15, n. 22.

Moreover, apart from being a demonstrably incorrect reading of the Due Process Clause, the "legal fiction" of substantive due process is "particularly dangerous." *McDonald*, 561 U. S., at 811 (opinion of THOMAS, J.); accord, *Obergefell*, 576 U. S., at 722 (THOMAS, J., dissenting). At least three dangers favor jettisoning the doctrine entirely.

First, "substantive due process exalts judges at the expense of the People from whom they derive their authority." *Ibid.* Because the Due Process Clause "speaks only to 'process,' the Court has long struggled to define what substantive rights it protects." *Timbs* v. *Indiana*, 586 U. S. ___, ___ (2019) (THOMAS, J., concurring in judgment) (slip op., at 2) (internal quotation marks omitted). In practice, the Court's approach for identifying those "fundamental" rights "unquestionably involves policymaking rather than neutral legal analysis." *Carlton*, 512 U. S., at 41–42 (opinion of Scalia, J.); see also *McDonald*, 561 U. S., at 812 (opinion of THOMAS, J.) (substantive due process is "a jurisprudence devoid of a guiding principle"). The Court divines new rights in line with "its own, extraconstitutional value preferences" and nullifies state laws that do not align with the judicially created guarantees. *Thornburgh* v. *American College of Obstetricians and Gynecologists*, 476 U. S. 747, 794 (1986) (White, J., dissenting).

Nowhere is this exaltation of judicial policymaking clearer than this Court's abortion jurisprudence. In *Roe* v. *Wade*, 410 U. S. 113 (1973), the Court divined a right to

abortion because it "fe[lt]" that "the Fourteenth Amendment's concept of personal liberty" included a "right of privacy" that "is broad enough to encompass a woman's decision whether or not to terminate her pregnancy." *Id.,* at
153. In *Planned Parenthood of Southeastern Pa.* v. *Casey,*
505 U. S. 833 (1992), the Court likewise identified an abortion guarantee in "the liberty protected by the Fourteenth
Amendment," but, rather than a "right of privacy," it invoked an ethereal "right to define one's own concept of existence, of meaning, of the universe, and of the mystery of
human life." *Id.,* at 851. As the Court's preferred manifes-
tation of "liberty" changed, so, too, did the test used to protect it, as *Roe*'s author lamented. See *Casey,* 505 U. S., at
930 (Blackmun, J., concurring in part and dissenting in
part) ("[T]he *Roe* framework is far more administrable, and
far less manipulable, than the 'undue burden' standard").

Now, in this case, the nature of the purported "liberty"
supporting the abortion right has shifted yet again. Respondents and the United States propose no fewer than
three different interests that supposedly spring from the
Due Process Clause. They include "bodily integrity," "personal autonomy in matters of family, medical care, and
faith," Brief for Respondents 21, and "women's equal citizenship," Brief for United States as *Amicus Curiae* 24. That
50 years have passed since *Roe* and abortion advocates still
cannot coherently articulate the right (or rights) at stake
proves the obvious: The right to abortion is ultimately a policy goal in desperate search of a constitutional justification.

Second, substantive due process distorts other areas of
constitutional law. For example, once this Court identifies
a "fundamental" right for one class of individuals, it invokes
the Equal Protection Clause to demand exacting scrutiny of
statutes that deny the right to others. See, *e.g., Eisenstadt*
v. *Baird,* 405 U. S. 438, 453–454 (1972) (relying on *Griswold* to invalidate a state statute prohibiting distribution

of contraceptives to unmarried persons). Statutory classifications implicating certain "nonfundamental" rights, meanwhile, receive only cursory review. See, *e.g.*, *Armour* v. *Indianapolis*, 566 U. S. 673, 680 (2012). Similarly, this Court deems unconstitutionally "vague" or "overbroad" those laws that impinge on its preferred rights, while letting slide those laws that implicate supposedly lesser values. See, *e.g.*, *Johnson*, 576 U. S., at 618–621 (opinion of THOMAS, J.); *United States* v. *Sineneng-Smith*, 590 U. S. ___, ___–___ (2020) (THOMAS, J., concurring) (slip op., at 3–5). "In fact, our vagueness doctrine served as the basis for the first draft of the majority opinion in *Roe* v. *Wade*," and it since has been "deployed . . . to nullify even mild regulations of the abortion industry." *Johnson*, 576 U. S., at 620–621 (opinion of THOMAS, J.). Therefore, regardless of the doctrinal context, the Court often "demand[s] extra justifications for encroachments" on "preferred rights" while "relax[ing] purportedly higher standards of review for lesspreferred rights." *Whole Woman's Health* v. *Hellerstedt*, 579 U. S. 582, 640–642 (2016) (THOMAS, J., dissenting). Substantive due process is the core inspiration for many of the Court's constitutionally unmoored policy judgments.

Third, substantive due process is often wielded to "disastrous ends." *Gamble*, 587 U. S., at ___ (THOMAS, J., concurring) (slip op., at 16). For instance, in *Dred Scott* v. *Sandford*, 19 How. 393 (1857), the Court invoked a species of substantive due process to announce that Congress was powerless to emancipate slaves brought into the federal territories. See *id.*, at 452. While *Dred Scott* "was overruled on the battlefields of the Civil War and by constitutional amendment after Appomattox," *Obergefell*, 576 U. S., at 696 (ROBERTS, C. J., dissenting), that overruling was "[p]urchased at the price of immeasurable human suffering," *Adarand Constructors, Inc.* v. *Peña*, 515 U. S. 200, 240 (1995) (THOMAS, J., concurring in part and concurring in judgment). Now today, the Court rightly overrules *Roe* and

Casey—two of this Court's "most notoriously incorrect" substantive due process decisions, *Timbs*, 586 U. S., at ___ (opinion of THOMAS, J.) (slip op., at 2)—after more than 63 million abortions have been performed, see National Right to Life Committee, Abortion Statistics (Jan. 2022), https:// www.nrlc.org/uploads/factsheets/FS01AbortionintheUS.pdf. The harm caused by this Court's forays into substantive due process remains immeasurable.

*   *   *

Because the Court properly applies our substantive due process precedents to reject the fabrication of a constitutional right to abortion, and because this case does not present the opportunity to reject substantive due process entirely, I join the Court's opinion. But, in future cases, we should "follow the text of the Constitution, which sets forth certain substantive rights that cannot be taken away, and adds, beyond that, a right to due process when life, liberty, or property is to be taken away." *Carlton*, 512 U. S., at 42 (opinion of Scalia, J.). Substantive due process conflicts with that textual command and has harmed our country in many ways. Accordingly, we should eliminate it from our jurisprudence at the earliest opportunity.

SUPREME COURT OF THE UNITED STATES

No. 19–1392

THOMAS E. DOBBS, STATE HEALTH OFFICER OF THE MISSISSIPPI DEPARTMENT OF HEALTH, ET AL., PETITIONERS v. JACKSON WOMEN'S HEALTH ORGANIZATION, ET AL.

ON WRIT OF CERTIORARI TO THE UNITED STATES COURT OF APPEALS FOR THE FIFTH CIRCUIT

[June 24, 2022]

JUSTICE KAVANAUGH, concurring.

I write separately to explain my additional views about why *Roe* was wrongly decided, why *Roe* should be overruled at this time, and the future implications of today's decision.

I

Abortion is a profoundly difficult and contentious issue because it presents an irreconcilable conflict between the interests of a pregnant woman who seeks an abortion and the interests in protecting fetal life. The interests on both sides of the abortion issue are extraordinarily weighty.

On the one side, many pro-choice advocates forcefully argue that the ability to obtain an abortion is critically important for women's personal and professional lives, and for women's health. They contend that the widespread availability of abortion has been essential for women to advance in society and to achieve greater equality over the last 50 years. And they maintain that women must have the freedom to choose for themselves whether to have an abortion.

On the other side, many pro-life advocates forcefully argue that a fetus is a human life. They contend that all human life should be protected as a matter of human dignity and fundamental morality. And they stress that a significant percentage of Americans with pro-life views are women.

When it comes to abortion, one interest must prevail over the other at any given point in a pregnancy. Many Americans of good faith would prioritize the interests of the pregnant woman. Many other Americans of good faith instead would prioritize the interests in protecting fetal life—at least unless, for example, an abortion is necessary to save the life of the mother. Of course, many Americans are conflicted or have nuanced views that may vary depending on the particular time in pregnancy, or the particular circumstances of a pregnancy.

The issue before this Court, however, is not the policy or morality of abortion. The issue before this Court is what the Constitution says about abortion. The Constitution does not take sides on the issue of abortion. The text of the Constitution does not refer to or encompass abortion. To be sure, this Court has held that the Constitution protects unenumerated rights that are deeply rooted in this Nation's history and tradition, and implicit in the concept of ordered liberty. But a right to abortion is not deeply rooted in American history and tradition, as the Court today thoroughly explains.[1]

On the question of abortion, the Constitution is therefore neither pro-life nor pro-choice. The Constitution is neutral and leaves the issue for the people and their elected representatives to resolve through the democratic process in the

---

[1] The Court's opinion today also recounts the pre-constitutional common-law history in England. That English history supplies background information on the issue of abortion. As I see it, the dispositive point in analyzing American history and tradition for purposes of the Fourteenth Amendment inquiry is that abortion was largely prohibited in most American States as of 1868 when the Fourteenth Amendment was ratified, and that abortion remained largely prohibited in most American States until *Roe* was decided in 1973.

States or Congress—like the numerous other difficult questions of American social and economic policy that the Constitution does not address.

Because the Constitution is neutral on the issue of abortion, this Court also must be scrupulously neutral. The nine unelected Members of this Court do not possess the constitutional authority to override the democratic process and to decree either a pro-life or a pro-choice abortion policy for all 330 million people in the United States.

Instead of adhering to the Constitution's neutrality, the Court in *Roe* took sides on the issue and unilaterally decreed that abortion was legal throughout the United States up to the point of viability (about 24 weeks of pregnancy). The Court's decision today properly returns the Court to a position of neutrality and restores the people's authority to address the issue of abortion through the processes of democratic self-government established by the Constitution.

Some *amicus* briefs argue that the Court today should not only overrule *Roe* and return to a position of judicial neutrality on abortion, but should go further and hold that the Constitution *outlaws* abortion throughout the United States. No Justice of this Court has ever advanced that position. I respect those who advocate for that position, just as I respect those who argue that this Court should hold that the Constitution legalizes pre-viability abortion throughout the United States. But both positions are wrong as a constitutional matter, in my view. The Constitution neither outlaws abortion nor legalizes abortion.

To be clear, then, the Court's decision today *does not outlaw* abortion throughout the United States. On the contrary, the Court's decision properly leaves the question of abortion for the people and their elected representatives in the democratic process. Through that democratic process, the people and their representatives may decide to allow or limit abortion. As Justice Scalia stated, the "States may, if they wish, permit abortion on demand, but the Constitution does not *require* them to do so." *Planned Parenthood of Southeastern Pa.* v. *Casey*, 505 U. S. 833, 979 (1992) (opinion concurring in judgment in part and dissenting in part).

Today's decision therefore does not prevent the numerous States that readily allow abortion from continuing to readily allow abortion. That includes, if they choose, the *amici* States supporting the plaintiff in this Court: New York, California, Illinois, Maine, Massachusetts, Rhode Island, Vermont, Connecticut, New Jersey, Pennsylvania, Delaware, Maryland, Michigan, Wisconsin, Minnesota, New Mexico, Colorado, Nevada, Oregon, Washington, and Hawaii. By contrast, other States may maintain laws that more strictly limit abortion. After today's decision, all of the States may evaluate the competing interests and decide how to address this consequential issue.[2]

In arguing for a *constitutional* right to abortion that would override the people's choices in the democratic process, the plaintiff Jackson Women's Health Organization and its *amici* emphasize that the Constitution does not freeze the American people's rights as of 1791 or 1868. I fully agree. To begin, I agree that constitutional rights apply to situations that were unforeseen in 1791 or 1868—such as applying the First Amendment to the Internet or the Fourth Amendment to cars. Moreover, the Constitution authorizes the creation of new rights—state and federal, statutory and constitutional. But when it comes to creating new rights, the Constitution directs the people to the various processes of democratic self-government contemplated by the Constitution—state legislation, state constitutional amendments, federal legislation, and federal constitutional

---

[2] In his dissent in *Roe*, Justice Rehnquist indicated that an exception to a State's restriction on abortion would be constitutionally required when an abortion is necessary to save the life of the mother. See *Roe* v. *Wade*, 410 U. S. 113, 173 (1973). Abortion statutes traditionally and currently provide for an exception when an abortion is necessary to protect the life of the mother. Some statutes also provide other exceptions.

amendments. See generally Amdt. 9; Amdt. 10; Art. I, §8; Art. V; J. Sutton, 51 Imperfect Solutions: States and the Making of American Constitutional Law 7–21, 203–216 (2018); A. Amar, America's Constitution: A Biography 285–291, 315–347 (2005).

The Constitution does not grant the nine unelected Members of this Court the unilateral authority to rewrite the Constitution to create new rights and liberties based on our own moral or policy views. As Justice Rehnquist stated, this Court has not "been granted a roving commission, either by the Founding Fathers or by the framers of the Fourteenth Amendment, to strike down laws that are based upon notions of policy or morality suddenly found unacceptable by a majority of this Court." *Furman* v. *Georgia*, 408 U. S. 238, 467 (1972) (dissenting opinion); see *Washington* v. *Glucksberg*, 521 U. S. 702, 720–721 (1997); *Cruzan* v. *Director, Mo. Dept. of Health*, 497 U. S. 261, 292–293 (1990) (Scalia, J., concurring).

This Court therefore does not possess the authority either to declare a constitutional right to abortion *or* to declare a constitutional prohibition of abortion. See *Casey*, 505 U. S., at 953 (Rehnquist, C. J., concurring in judgment in part and dissenting in part); *id.,* at 980 (opinion of Scalia, J.); *Roe* v. *Wade*, 410 U. S. 113, 177 (1973) (Rehnquist, J., dissenting); *Doe* v. *Bolton*, 410 U. S. 179, 222 (1973) (White, J., dissenting).

In sum, the Constitution is neutral on the issue of abortion and allows the people and their elected representatives to address the issue through the democratic process. In my respectful view, the Court in *Roe* therefore erred by taking sides on the issue of abortion.

II

The more difficult question in this case is *stare decisis*—that is, whether to overrule the *Roe* decision.

The principle of *stare decisis* requires respect for the

Court's precedents and for the accumulated wisdom of the judges who have previously addressed the same issue. *Stare decisis* is rooted in Article III of the Constitution and is fundamental to the American judicial system and to the stability of American law.

Adherence to precedent is the norm, and *stare decisis* imposes a high bar before this Court may overrule a precedent. This Court's history shows, however, that *stare decisis* is not absolute, and indeed cannot be absolute. Otherwise, as the Court today explains, many long-since-overruled cases such as *Plessy* v. *Ferguson*, 163 U. S. 537 (1896); *Lochner* v. *New York*, 198 U. S. 45 (1905); *Minersville School Dist.* v. *Gobitis*, 310 U. S. 586 (1940); and *Bowers* v. *Hardwick*, 478 U. S. 186 (1986), would never have been overruled and would still be the law.

In his canonical *Burnet* opinion in 1932, Justice Brandeis stated that in "cases involving the Federal Constitution, where correction through legislative action is practically impossible, this Court has often overruled its earlier decisions." *Burnet* v. *Coronado Oil & Gas Co.*, 285 U. S. 393, 406–407 (1932) (dissenting opinion). That description of the Court's practice remains accurate today. Every current Member of this Court has voted to overrule precedent. And over the last 100 years beginning with Chief Justice Taft's appointment in 1921, every one of the 48 Justices appointed to this Court has voted to overrule precedent. Many of those Justices have voted to overrule a substantial number of very significant and longstanding precedents. See, *e.g.,* *Obergefell* v. *Hodges*, 576 U. S. 644 (2015) (overruling *Baker* v. *Nelson*); *Brown* v. *Board of Education*, 347 U. S. 483 (1954) (overruling *Plessy* v. *Ferguson*); *West Coast Hotel Co.* v. *Parrish*, 300 U. S. 379 (1937) (overruling *Adkins* v. *Children's Hospital of D. C.* and in effect *Lochner* v. *New York*).

But that history alone does not answer the critical question: When precisely should the Court overrule an erroneous constitutional precedent? The history of *stare decisis* in this Court establishes that a constitutional precedent may be overruled only when (i) the prior decision is not just wrong, but is egregiously wrong, (ii) the prior decision has caused significant negative jurisprudential or real-world consequences, and (iii) overruling the prior decision would not unduly upset legitimate reliance interests. See *Ramos* v. *Louisiana*, 590 U. S. ___, ___–___ (2020) (KAVANAUGH, J., concurring in part) (slip op., at 7–8).

Applying those factors, I agree with the Court today that *Roe* should be overruled. The Court in *Roe* erroneously assigned itself the authority to decide a critically important moral and policy issue that the Constitution does not grant this Court the authority to decide. As Justice Byron White succinctly explained, *Roe* was "an improvident and extravagant exercise of the power of judicial review" because "nothing in the language or history of the Constitution" supports a constitutional right to abortion. *Bolton*, 410 U. S., at 221–222 (dissenting opinion).

Of course, the fact that a precedent is wrong, even egregiously wrong, does not alone mean that the precedent should be overruled. But as the Court today explains, *Roe* has caused significant negative jurisprudential and real-world consequences. By taking sides on a difficult and contentious issue on which the Constitution is neutral, *Roe* overreached and exceeded this Court's constitutional authority; gravely distorted the Nation's understanding of this Court's proper constitutional role; and caused significant harm to what *Roe* itself recognized as the State's "important and legitimate interest" in protecting fetal life. 410 U. S., at 162. All of that explains why tens of millions of Americans—and the 26 States that explicitly ask the Court to overrule *Roe*—do not accept *Roe* even 49 years later. Under the Court's longstanding *stare decisis* principles, *Roe* should be overruled.[3]

But the *stare decisis* analysis here is somewhat more complicated because of *Casey.* In 1992, 19 years after *Roe, Casey* acknowledged the continuing dispute over *Roe.* The Court sought to find common ground that would resolve the abortion debate and end the national controversy. After careful and thoughtful consideration, the *Casey* plurality reaffirmed a right to abortion through viability (about 24 weeks), while also allowing somewhat more regulation of abortion than *Roe* had allowed.[4]

I have deep and unyielding respect for the Justices who wrote the *Casey* plurality opinion. And I respect the *Casey* plurality's good-faith effort to locate some middle ground or compromise that could resolve this controversy for America.

But as has become increasingly evident over time, *Casey's*

---

[3] I also agree with the Court's conclusion today with respect to reliance. Broad notions of societal reliance have been invoked in support of *Roe,* but the Court has not analyzed reliance in that way in the past. For example, American businesses and workers relied on *Lochner* v. *New York,* 198 U. S. 45 (1905), and *Adkins* v. *Children's Hospital of D. C.,* 261 U. S. 525 (1923), to construct a laissez-faire economy that was free of substantial regulation. In *West Coast Hotel Co.* v. *Parrish,* 300 U. S. 379 (1937), the Court nonetheless overruled *Adkins* and in effect *Lochner.* An entire region of the country relied on *Plessy* v. *Ferguson,* 163 U. S. 537 (1896), to enforce a system of racial segregation. In *Brown* v. *Board of Education,* 347 U. S. 483 (1954), the Court overruled *Plessy.* Much of American society was built around the traditional view of marriage that was upheld in *Baker* v. *Nelson,* 409 U. S. 810 (1972), and that was reflected in laws ranging from tax laws to estate laws to family laws. In *Obergefell* v. *Hodges,* 576 U. S. 644 (2015), the Court nonetheless overruled *Baker.*

[4] As the Court today notes, *Casey's* approach to *stare decisis* pointed in two directions. *Casey* reaffirmed *Roe's* viability line, but it expressly overruled the *Roe* trimester framework and also expressly overruled two landmark post-*Roe* abortion cases—*Akron* v. *Akron Center for Reproductive Health, Inc.,* 462 U. S. 416 (1983), and *Thornburgh* v. *American College of Obstetricians and Gynecologists,* 476 U. S. 747 (1986). See *Casey,* 505 U. S., at 870, 872–873, 878–879, 882. *Casey* itself thus directly contradicts any notion of absolute *stare decisis* in abortion cases.

well-intentioned effort did not resolve the abortion debate. The national division has not ended. In recent years, a significant number of States have enacted abortion restrictions that directly conflict with *Roe*. Those laws cannot be dismissed as political stunts or as outlier laws. Those numerous state laws collectively represent the sincere and deeply held views of tens of millions of Americans who continue to fervently believe that allowing abortions up to 24 weeks is far too radical and far too extreme, and does not sufficiently account for what *Roe* itself recognized as the State's "important and legitimate interest" in protecting fetal life. 410 U. S., at 162. In this case, moreover, a majority of the States—26 in all—ask the Court to overrule *Roe* and return the abortion issue to the States.

In short, *Casey*'s *stare decisis* analysis rested in part on a predictive judgment about the future development of state laws and of the people's views on the abortion issue. But that predictive judgment has not borne out. As the Court today explains, the experience over the last 30 years conflicts with *Casey*'s predictive judgment and therefore undermines *Casey*'s precedential force.[5]

In any event, although *Casey* is relevant to the *stare decisis* analysis, the question of whether to overrule *Roe* cannot be dictated by *Casey* alone. To illustrate that *stare decisis* point, consider an example. Suppose that in 1924 this Court had expressly reaffirmed *Plessy* v. *Ferguson* and upheld the States' authority to segregate people on the basis of race. Would the Court in *Brown* some 30 years later in

---

[5] To be clear, public opposition to a prior decision is not a basis for overruling (or reaffirming) that decision. Rather, the question of whether to overrule a precedent must be analyzed under this Court's traditional *stare decisis* factors. The only point here is that *Casey* adopted a special *stare decisis* principle with respect to *Roe* based on the idea of resolving the national controversy and ending the national division over abortion. The continued and significant opposition to *Roe*, as reflected in the laws and positions of numerous States, is relevant to assessing *Casey* on its own terms.

1954 have reaffirmed *Plessy* and upheld racially segregated schools simply because of that intervening 1924 precedent? Surely the answer is no.

In sum, I agree with the Court's application today of the principles of *stare decisis* and its conclusion that *Roe* should be overruled.

III

After today's decision, the nine Members of this Court will no longer decide the basic legality of pre-viability abortion for all 330 million Americans. That issue will be resolved by the people and their representatives in the democratic process in the States or Congress. But the parties' arguments have raised other related questions, and I address some of them here.

First is the question of how this decision will affect other precedents involving issues such as contraception and marriage—in particular, the decisions in *Griswold* v. *Connecticut*, 381 U. S. 479 (1965); *Eisenstadt* v. *Baird*, 405 U. S. 438 (1972); *Loving* v. *Virginia*, 388 U. S. 1 (1967); and *Obergefell* v. *Hodges*, 576 U. S. 644 (2015). I emphasize what the Court today states: Overruling *Roe* does *not* mean the overruling of those precedents, and does *not* threaten or cast doubt on those precedents.

Second, as I see it, some of the other abortion-related legal questions raised by today's decision are not especially difficult as a constitutional matter. For example, may a State bar a resident of that State from traveling to another State to obtain an abortion? In my view, the answer is no based on the constitutional right to interstate travel. May a State retroactively impose liability or punishment for an abortion that occurred before today's decision takes effect? In my view, the answer is no based on the Due Process Clause or the *Ex Post Facto* Clause. Cf. *Bouie* v. *City of Columbia*, 378 U. S. 347 (1964).

Other abortion-related legal questions may emerge in the

future. But this Court will no longer decide the fundamental question of whether abortion must be allowed throughout the United States through 6 weeks, or 12 weeks, or 15
weeks, or 24 weeks, or some other line. The Court will no
longer decide how to evaluate the interests of the pregnant
woman and the interests in protecting fetal life throughout
pregnancy. Instead, those difficult moral and policy questions will be decided, as the Constitution dictates, by the
people and their elected representatives through the constitutional processes of democratic self-government.

*   *   *

The *Roe* Court took sides on a consequential moral and
policy issue that this Court had no constitutional authority
to decide. By taking sides, the *Roe* Court distorted the Nation's understanding of this Court's proper role in the American constitutional system and thereby damaged the Court
as an institution. As Justice Scalia explained, *Roe* "destroyed the compromises of the past, rendered compromise
impossible for the future, and required the entire issue to
be resolved uniformly, at the national level." *Casey*, 505
U. S., at 995 (opinion concurring in judgment in part and
dissenting in part).

The Court's decision today properly returns the Court to
a position of judicial neutrality on the issue of abortion, and
properly restores the people's authority to resolve the issue
of abortion through the processes of democratic self-
government established by the Constitution.

To be sure, many Americans will disagree with the
Court's decision today. That would be true no matter how
the Court decided this case. Both sides on the abortion issue believe sincerely and passionately in the rightness of
their cause. Especially in those difficult and fraught circumstances, the Court must scrupulously adhere to the
Constitution's neutral position on the issue of abortion.

Since 1973, more than 20 Justices of this Court have now

grappled with the divisive issue of abortion. I greatly respect all of the Justices, past and present, who have done so. Amidst extraordinary controversy and challenges, all of them have addressed the abortion issue in good faith after careful deliberation, and based on their sincere understandings of the Constitution and of precedent. I have endeavored to do the same.

In my judgment, on the issue of abortion, the Constitution is neither pro-life nor pro-choice. The Constitution is neutral, and this Court likewise must be scrupulously neutral. The Court today properly heeds the constitutional principle of judicial neutrality and returns the issue of abortion to the people and their elected representatives in the democratic process.

SUPREME COURT OF THE UNITED STATES

No. 19–1392

THOMAS E. DOBBS, STATE HEALTH OFFICER OF THE MISSISSIPPI DEPARTMENT OF HEALTH, ET AL., PETITIONERS v. JACKSON WOMEN'S HEALTH ORGANIZATION, ET AL.

ON WRIT OF CERTIORARI TO THE UNITED STATES COURT OF APPEALS FOR THE FIFTH CIRCUIT

[June 24, 2022]

CHIEF JUSTICE ROBERTS, concurring in the judgment.

We granted certiorari to decide one question: "Whether all pre-viability prohibitions on elective abortions are unconstitutional." Pet. for Cert. i. That question is directly implicated here: Mississippi's Gestational Age Act, Miss. Code Ann. §41–41–191 (2018), generally prohibits abortion after the fifteenth week of pregnancy—several weeks before a fetus is regarded as "viable" outside the womb. In urging our review, Mississippi stated that its case was "an ideal vehicle" to "reconsider the bright-line viability rule," and that a judgment in its favor would "not require the Court to overturn" *Roe* v. *Wade*, 410 U. S. 113 (1973), and *Planned Parenthood of Southeastern Pa.* v. *Casey*, 505 U. S. 833 (1992). Pet. for Cert. 5.

Today, the Court nonetheless rules for Mississippi by doing just that. I would take a more measured course. I agree with the Court that the viability line established by *Roe* and *Casey* should be discarded under a straightforward *stare decisis* analysis. That line never made any sense. Our abortion precedents describe the right at issue as a woman's right to choose to terminate her pregnancy. That right should therefore extend far enough to ensure a reasonable opportunity to choose, but need not extend any further—

certainly not all the way to viability. Mississippi's law allows a woman three months to obtain an abortion, well beyond the point at which it is considered "late" to discover a pregnancy. See A. Ayoola, Late Recognition of Unintended Pregnancies, 32 Pub. Health Nursing 462 (2015) (pregnancy is discoverable and ordinarily discovered by six weeks of gestation). I see no sound basis for questioning the adequacy of that opportunity.

But that is all I would say, out of adherence to a simple yet fundamental principle of judicial restraint: If it is not necessary to decide more to dispose of a case, then it is necessary *not* to decide more. Perhaps we are not always perfect in following that command, and certainly there are cases that warrant an exception. But this is not one of them. Surely we should adhere closely to principles of judicial restraint here, where the broader path the Court chooses entails repudiating a constitutional right we have not only previously recognized, but also expressly reaffirmed applying the doctrine of *stare decisis.* The Court's opinion is thoughtful and thorough, but those virtues cannot compensate for the fact that its dramatic and consequential ruling is unnecessary to decide the case before us.

I

Let me begin with my agreement with the Court, on the only question we need decide here: whether to retain the rule from *Roe* and *Casey* that a woman's right to terminate her pregnancy extends up to the point that the fetus is regarded as "viable" outside the womb. I agree that this rule should be discarded.

First, this Court seriously erred in *Roe* in adopting viability as the earliest point at which a State may legislate to advance its substantial interests in the area of abortion. See *ante,* at 50–53. *Roe* set forth a rigid three-part framework anchored to viability, which more closely resembled a regulatory code than a body of constitutional law. That framework, moreover, came out of thin air. Neither the Texas statute challenged in *Roe* nor the Georgia statute at issue in its companion case, *Doe* v. *Bolton,* 410 U. S. 179 (1973), included *any* gestational age limit. No party or *amicus* asked the Court to adopt a bright line viability rule. And as for *Casey,* arguments for or against the viability rule played only a *de minimis* role in the parties' briefing and in the oral argument. See Tr. of Oral Arg. 17–18, 51 (fleeting discussion of the viability rule).

It is thus hardly surprising that neither *Roe* nor *Casey* made a persuasive or even colorable argument for why the time for terminating a pregnancy must extend to viability. The Court's jurisprudence on this issue is a textbook illustration of the perils of deciding a question neither presented nor briefed. As has been often noted, *Roe*'s defense of the line boiled down to the circular assertion that the State's interest is compelling only when an unborn child can live outside the womb, because that is when the unborn child can live outside the womb. See 410 U. S., at 163–164; see also J. Ely, The Wages of Crying Wolf: A Comment on *Roe* v. *Wade,* 82 Yale L. J. 920, 924 (1973) (*Roe*'s reasoning "mistake[s] a definition for a syllogism").

Twenty years later, the best defense of the viability line the *Casey* plurality could conjure up was workability. See 505 U. S., at 870. But see *ante,* at 53 (opinion of the Court) (discussing the difficulties in applying the viability standard). Although the plurality attempted to add more content by opining that "it might be said that a woman who fails to act before viability has consented to the State's intervention on behalf of the developing child," *Casey,* 505 U. S., at 870, that mere suggestion provides no basis for choosing viability as the critical tipping point. A similar implied consent argument could be made with respect to a law banning abortions after fifteen weeks, well beyond the point at which nearly all women are aware that they are pregnant, A. Ayoola, M. Nettleman, M. Stommel, & R. Canady, Time of Pregnancy Recognition and Prenatal Care Use: A Population-based Study in the United States 39 (2010) (Pregnancy Recognition). The dissent, which would retain the viability line, offers no justification for it either.

This Court's jurisprudence since *Casey,* moreover, has "eroded" the "underpinnings" of the viability line, such as they were. *United States* v. *Gaudin,* 515 U. S. 506, 521 (1995). The viability line is a relic of a time when we recognized only two state interests warranting regulation of abortion: maternal health and protection of "potential life." *Roe,* 410 U. S., at 162–163. That changed with *Gonzales* v. *Carhart,* 550 U. S. 124 (2007). There, we recognized a broader array of interests, such as drawing "a bright line that clearly distinguishes abortion and infanticide," maintaining societal ethics, and preserving the integrity of the medical profession. *Id.,* at 157–160. The viability line has nothing to do with advancing such permissible goals. Cf. *id.,* at 171 (Ginsburg, J., dissenting) (*Gonzales* "blur[red] the line, firmly drawn in *Casey,* between previability and postviability abortions"); see also R. Beck, *Gonzales, Casey, and the Viability Rule,* 103 Nw. U. L. Rev. 249, 276–279 (2009).

Consider, for example, statutes passed in a number of jurisdictions that forbid abortions after twenty weeks of pregnancy, premised on the theory that a fetus can feel pain at that stage of development. See, *e.g.,* Ala. Code §26–23B–2 (2018). Assuming that prevention of fetal pain is a legitimate state interest after *Gonzales,* there seems to be no reason why viability would be relevant to the permissibility of such laws. The same is true of laws designed to "protect[] the integrity and ethics of the medical profession" and restrict procedures likely to "coarsen society" to the "dignity of human life." *Gonzales,* 550 U. S., at 157. Mississippi's law, for instance, was premised in part on the legislature's finding that the "dilation and evacuation" procedure is a "barbaric practice, dangerous for the maternal patient, and

demeaning to the medical profession." Miss. Code Ann.
§41–41–191(2)(b)(i)(8). That procedure accounts for most
abortions performed after the first trimester—two weeks
before the period at issue in this case—and "involve[s] the
use of surgical instruments to crush and tear the unborn
child apart." *Ibid.*; see also *Gonzales*, 550 U. S., at 135.
Again, it would make little sense to focus on viability when
evaluating a law based on these permissible goals.

In short, the viability rule was created outside the ordinary course of litigation, is and always has been completely
unreasoned, and fails to take account of state interests
since recognized as legitimate. It is indeed "telling that
other countries almost uniformly eschew" a viability line.
Ante, at 53 (opinion of the Court). Only a handful of countries, among them China and North Korea, permit elective
abortions after twenty weeks; the rest have coalesced
around a 12–week line. See The World's Abortion Laws,
Center for Reproductive Rights (Feb. 23, 2021) (online
source archived at www.supremecourt.gov) (Canada,
China, Iceland, Guinea-Bissau, the Netherlands, North Korea, Singapore, and Vietnam permit elective abortions after
twenty weeks). The Court rightly rejects the arbitrary viability rule today.

II

None of this, however, requires that we also take the dramatic step of altogether eliminating the abortion right first
recognized in *Roe.* Mississippi itself previously argued as
much to this Court in this litigation.

When the State petitioned for our review, its basic re-
quest was straightforward: "clarify whether abortion prohibitions before viability are always unconstitutional." Pet.
for Cert. 14. The State made a number of strong arguments
that the answer is no, *id.,* at 15–26—arguments that, as
discussed, I find persuasive. And it went out of its way to
make clear that it was *not* asking the Court to repudiate

entirely the right to choose whether to terminate a pregnancy: "To be clear, the questions presented in this petition do not require the Court to overturn *Roe* or *Casey*." *Id.,* at 5. Mississippi tempered that statement with an oblique one-sentence footnote intimating that, if the Court could not reconcile *Roe* and *Casey* with current facts or other cases, it "should not retain erroneous precedent." Pet. for Cert. 5–6, n. 1. But the State never argued that we should grant review for that purpose.

After we granted certiorari, however, Mississippi changed course. In its principal brief, the State bluntly announced that the Court should overrule *Roe* and *Casey*. The Constitution does not protect a right to an abortion, it argued, and a State should be able to prohibit elective abortions if a rational basis supports doing so. See Brief for Petitioners 12–13.

The Court now rewards that gambit, noting three times that the parties presented "no half-measures" and argued that "we must either reaffirm or overrule *Roe* and *Casey*." *Ante,* at 5, 8, 72. Given those two options, the majority picks the latter.

This framing is not accurate. In its brief on the merits, Mississippi in fact argued at length that a decision simply rejecting the viability rule would result in a judgment in its favor. See Brief for Petitioners 5, 38–48. But even if the State had not argued as much, it would not matter. There is no rule that parties can confine this Court to disposing of their case on a particular ground—let alone when review was sought and granted on a different one. Our established practice is instead not to "formulate a rule of constitutional law broader than is required by the precise facts to which it is to be applied." *Washington State Grange* v. *Washington State Republican Party*, 552 U. S. 442, 450 (2008) (quoting *Ashwander* v. *TVA*, 297 U. S. 288, 347 (1936) (Brandeis, J., concurring)); see also *United States* v. *Raines*, 362 U. S. 17, 21 (1960).

Following that "fundamental principle of judicial restraint," *Washington State Grange*, 552 U. S., at 450, we should begin with the narrowest basis for disposition, proceeding to consider a broader one only if necessary to resolve the case at hand. See, *e.g., Office of Personnel Management* v. *Richmond*, 496 U. S. 414, 423 (1990). It is only where there is no valid narrower ground of decision that we should go on to address a broader issue, such as whether a constitutional decision should be overturned. See *Federal Election Comm'n* v. *Wisconsin Right to Life, Inc.*, 551 U. S. 449, 482 (2007) (declining to address the claim that a constitutional decision should be overruled when the appellant prevailed on its narrower constitutional argument).

Here, there is a clear path to deciding this case correctly without overruling *Roe* all the way down to the studs: recognize that the viability line must be discarded, as the majority rightly does, and leave for another day whether to reject any right to an abortion at all. See *Webster* v. *Reproductive Health Services*, 492 U. S. 490, 518, 521 (1989) (plurality opinion) (rejecting *Roe*'s viability line as "rigid" and "indeterminate," while also finding "no occasion to revisit the holding of *Roe*" that, under the Constitution, a State must provide an opportunity to choose to terminate a pregnancy).

Of course, such an approach would not be available if the rationale of *Roe* and *Casey* was inextricably entangled with and dependent upon the viability standard. It is not. Our precedents in this area ground the abortion right in a woman's "right to choose." See *Carey* v. *Population Services Int'l*, 431 U. S. 678, 688–689 (1977) ("underlying foundation of the holdings" in *Roe* and *Griswold* v. *Connecticut*, 381 U. S. 479 (1965), was the "right of decision in matters of childbearing"); *Maher* v. *Roe*, 432 U. S. 464, 473 (1977) (*Roe* and other cases "recognize a constitutionally protected interest in making certain kinds of important decisions free from governmental compulsion" (internal quotation marks omitted)); *id.*, at 473–474 (*Roe* "did not declare an unqualified constitutional right to an abortion," but instead protected "the woman from unduly burdensome interference with her freedom to decide whether to terminate her pregnancy" (internal quotation marks omitted)); *Webster*, 492 U. S., at 520 (plurality opinion) (*Roe* protects "the claims of a woman to decide for herself whether or not to abort a fetus she [is] carrying"); *Gonzales*, 550 U. S., at 146 (a State may not "prohibit any woman from making the ultimate decision to terminate her pregnancy"). If that is the basis for *Roe*, *Roe*'s viability line should be scrutinized from the same perspective. And there is nothing inherent in the right to choose that requires it to extend to viability or any other point, so long as a real choice is provided. See *Webster*, 492 U. S., at 519 (plurality opinion) (finding no reason "why the State's interest in protecting potential human life should come into existence only at the point of viability").

To be sure, in reaffirming the right to an abortion, *Casey* termed the viability rule *Roe*'s "central holding." 505 U. S., at 860. Other cases of ours have repeated that language. See, *e.g.*, *Gonzales*, 550 U. S., at 145–146. But simply declaring it does not make it so. The question in *Roe* was whether there was any right to abortion in the Constitution. See Brief for Appellants and Brief for Appellees, in *Roe* v. *Wade*, O. T. 1971, No. 70–18. How far the right extended was a concern that was separate and subsidiary, and—not surprisingly—entirely unbriefed.

The Court in *Roe* just chose to address both issues in one opinion: It first recognized a right to "choose to terminate [a] pregnancy" under the Constitution, see 410 U. S., at 129–159, and then, having done so, explained that a line should be drawn at viability such that a State could not proscribe abortion before that period, see *id.*, at 163. The viability line is a separate rule fleshing out the metes and bounds of *Roe*'s core holding. Applying principles of *stare decisis*, I would excise that additional rule—and only that rule—from our jurisprudence.

The majority lists a number of cases that have stressed the importance of the viability rule to our abortion precedents. See *ante,* at 73–74. I agree that—whether it was originally holding or dictum—the viability line is clearly part of our "past precedent," and the Court has applied it as such in several cases since *Roe. Ante,* at 73. My point is that *Roe* adopted two distinct rules of constitutional law: one, that a woman has the right to choose to terminate a pregnancy; two, that such right may be overridden by the State's legitimate interests when the fetus is viable outside the womb. The latter is obviously distinct from the former. I would abandon that timing rule, but see no need in this case to consider the basic right.

The Court contends that it is impossible to address *Roe*'s conclusion that the Constitution protects the woman's right to abortion, without also addressing *Roe*'s rule that the State's interests are not constitutionally adequate to justify a ban on abortion until viability. See *ibid.* But we have partially overruled precedents before, see, *e.g., United States* v. *Miller,* 471 U. S. 130, 142–144 (1985); *Daniels* v. *Williams,* 474 U. S. 327, 328–331 (1986); *Batson* v. *Kentucky,* 476 U. S. 79, 90–93 (1986), and certainly have never held that a distinct holding defining the contours of a constitutional right must be treated as part and parcel of the right itself.

Overruling the subsidiary rule is sufficient to resolve this case in Mississippi's favor. The law at issue allows abortions up through fifteen weeks, providing an adequate opportunity to exercise the right *Roe* protects. By the time a pregnant woman has reached that point, her pregnancy is well into the second trimester. Pregnancy tests are now inexpensive and accurate, and a woman ordinarily discovers she is pregnant by six weeks of gestation. See A. Branum & K. Ahrens, Trends in Timing of Pregnancy Awareness Among US Women, 21 Maternal & Child Health J. 715, 722

ROBERTS, C. J., concurring in judgment

(2017). Almost all know by the end of the first trimester. Pregnancy Recognition 39. Safe and effective abortifacients, moreover, are now readily available, particularly during those early stages. See I. Adibi et al., Abortion, 22 Geo. J. Gender & L. 279, 303 (2021). Given all this, it is no surprise that the vast majority of abortions happen in the first trimester. See Centers for Disease Control and Prevention, Abortion Surveillance—United States 1 (2020). Presumably most of the remainder would also take place earlier if later abortions were not a legal option. Ample evidence thus suggests that a 15-week ban provides sufficient time, absent rare circumstances, for a woman "to decide for herself" whether to terminate her pregnancy. *Webster*, 492 U. S., at 520 (plurality opinion).*

III

Whether a precedent should be overruled is a question "entirely within the discretion of the court." *Hertz* v. *Woodman*, 218 U. S. 205, 212 (1910); see also *Payne* v. *Tennessee*, 501 U. S. 808, 828 (1991) (*stare decisis* is a "principle of policy"). In my respectful view, the sound exercise of that discretion should have led the Court to resolve the case on the narrower grounds set forth above, rather than overruling *Roe* and *Casey* entirely. The Court says there is no "principled basis" for this approach, *ante,* at 73, but in fact it is firmly grounded in basic principles of *stare decisis* and judicial restraint.

---

*The majority contends that "nothing like [my approach] was recommended by either party." *Ante,* at 72. But as explained, Mississippi in fact pressed a similar argument in its filings before this Court. See Pet. for Cert. 15–26; Brief for Petitioners 5, 38–48 (urging the Court to reject the viability rule and reverse); Reply Brief 20–22 (same). The approach also finds support in prior opinions. See *Webster*, 492 U. S., at 518–521 (plurality opinion) (abandoning "key elements" of the *Roe* framework under *stare decisis* while declining to reconsider *Roe*'s holding that the Constitution protects the right to an abortion).

The Court's decision to overrule *Roe* and *Casey* is a serious jolt to the legal system—regardless of how you view those cases. A narrower decision rejecting the misguided viability line would be markedly less unsettling, and nothing more is needed to decide this case.

Our cases say that the effect of overruling a precedent on reliance interests is a factor to consider in deciding whether to take such a step, and respondents argue that generations of women have relied on the right to an abortion in organizing their relationships and planning their futures. Brief for Respondents 36–41; see also *Casey*, 505 U. S., at 856 (making the same point). The Court questions whether these concerns are pertinent under our precedents, see *ante,* at 64–65, but the issue would not even arise with a decision rejecting only the viability line: It cannot reasonably be argued that women have shaped their lives in part on the assumption that they would be able to abort up to viability, as opposed to fifteen weeks.

In support of its holding, the Court cites three seminal constitutional decisions that involved overruling prior precedents: *Brown* v. *Board of Education,* 347 U. S. 483 (1954), *West Virginia Bd. of Ed.* v. *Barnette,* 319 U. S. 624 (1943), and *West Coast Hotel Co.* v. *Parrish,* 300 U. S. 379 (1937). See *ante,* at 40–41. The opinion in *Brown* was unanimous and eleven pages long; this one is neither. *Barnette* was decided only three years after the decision it overruled, three Justices having had second thoughts. And *West Coast Hotel* was issued against a backdrop of unprecedented economic despair that focused attention on the fundamental flaws of existing precedent. It also was part of a sea change in this Court's interpretation of the Constitution, "signal[ing] the demise of an entire line of important precedents," *ante,* at 40—a feature the Court expressly disclaims in today's decision, see *ante,* at 32, 66. None of these leading cases, in short, provides a template for what the Court does today.

ROBERTS, C. J., concurring in judgment

The Court says we should consider whether to overrule *Roe* and *Casey* now, because if we delay we would be forced to consider the issue again in short order. See *ante*, at 76–77. There would be "turmoil" until we did so, according to the Court, because of existing state laws with "shorter deadlines or no deadline at all." *Ante*, at 76. But under the narrower approach proposed here, state laws outlawing abortion altogether would still violate binding precedent. And to the extent States have laws that set the cutoff date earlier than fifteen weeks, any litigation over that timeframe would proceed free of the distorting effect that the viability rule has had on our constitutional debate. The same could be true, for that matter, with respect to legislative consideration in the States. We would then be free to exercise our discretion in deciding whether and when to take up the issue, from a more informed perspective.

*   *   *

Both the Court's opinion and the dissent display a relentless freedom from doubt on the legal issue that I cannot share. I am not sure, for example, that a ban on terminating a pregnancy from the moment of conception must be treated the same under the Constitution as a ban after fifteen weeks. A thoughtful Member of this Court once counseled that the difficulty of a question "admonishes us to observe the wise limitations on our function and to confine ourselves to deciding only what is necessary to the disposition of the immediate case." *Whitehouse* v. *Illinois Central R. Co.*, 349 U. S. 366, 372–373 (1955) (Frankfurter, J., for the Court). I would decide the question we granted review to answer—whether the previously recognized abortion right bars all abortion restrictions prior to viability, such that a ban on abortions after fifteen weeks of pregnancy is necessarily unlawful. The answer to that question is no, and there is no need to go further to decide this case.

I therefore concur only in the judgment.